HIS FATHER'S SON

THE LIFE OF GENERAL
TED ROOSEVELT JR.

TIM BRADY

NEW AMERICAN LIBRARY
NEW YORK

NEW AMERICAN LIBRARY
Published by Berkley
An imprint of Penguin Random House LLC
375 Hudson Street, New York, New York 10014

Library of Congress Cataloging-in-Publication Data
Names: Brady, Tim, 1955– author.
Title: His father's son: the life of General Ted Roosevelt Jr./Tim Brady.
Description: First edition. | New York, New York: New American Library, 2017. |
Includes bibliographical references and index.
Identifiers: LCCN 2016030885 (print) | LCCN 2016031208 (ebook) |
ISBN 9781101988152 | ISBN 9781101988176 (ebook)
Subjects: LCSH: Roosevelt, Theodore, 1887–1944. | Generals—United States—Biography. |
Politicians—United States—Biography. | Children of presidents—United States—Biography. |
Roosevelt, Theodore, 1858–1919—Family. | World War, 1939–1945—Biography. | World War,
1914–1918—Biography. | Medal of Honor—Biography
Classification: LCC E757.3.B73 2017 (print) | LCC E757.3 (ebook) | DDC 973.91/1092 [B]—dc23
LC record available at https://lccn.loc.gov/2016030885

First Edition: January 2017

Printed in the United States of America
1   3   5   7   9   10   8   6   4   2

Jacket photo of the Normandy landing by Time Life Pictures/The Life Picture
Collection/Getty Images; photo of Theodore Roosevelt Jr. by US Army Signal Corps/
The National World War II Museum
Jacket design by Pete Garceau
Book design by Kristin del Rosario

TO THE BRADY CLAN

Contents

HIS FATHER'S SON

THE CROWDED HOUR

On the evening before the deciding battle of the Spanish American War—a conflict that would forever change his life and political fortunes—Theodore Roosevelt slept peacefully beneath a raincoat on the edge of the Cuban jungle, a few miles southeast of Santiago. He was content with his circumstances and excited by the prospects the next day would bring. His main concern, beyond the dangers of battle, was that he not miss out on the fighting. He hoped that he would be courageous in the melee to come, and that his courage would be noticed not only by the men he led, but also by those who would later tell the story. To be in the thick of a wild fight, holding tight to the reins of his horse, Little Texas, as the two reared against a smoke-filled sky, this was the dream of Lieutenant Colonel Roosevelt as he slept that night.

That he might find himself here, slumbering beneath a canopy of banyan trees on a Caribbean isle, was no accident of fate. Born the son of a wealthy New Yorker also named Theodore Roosevelt, the man beneath the slicker had been a sickly child who through sheer will and exercise had turned his puny, asthma-racked body into the rock-solid frame of an enthusiastic young boxer by the time he went off to college at Harvard. A dandified and effete undergrad with an interest in the natural sciences and New York politics, Theodore was elected to the statehouse in Albany, where as a precocious legislator he won the grudging respect of hard-bitten ward pols and upstate rubes alike.

On one devastating Valentine's Day in 1884, he suffered the loss of his beautiful young wife, Alice, and his mother within hours of one another. A daughter had been born to him only two days prior, but stricken with grief and incapable of caring for her, he headed to the Dakotas to serve an exile in the Badlands, where he came to love the rough personalities and wide-open spaces of the nation's West.

Still a deeply political animal full of outsized ambition, he returned to the East, married an old flame, started a new family, built a house at Oyster Bay on Long Island, commenced a new career, wrote history books, served as a civil service administrator in Washington, as a police commissioner in New York, and again in Washington as assistant secretary of the navy. In every position he pushed his own ideas, his own notions of reform and righteousness, and assumed that his manner of getting things done was superior to those of those who served above him. He stepped on toes, he irritated, he exacerbated, he bullied and provoked, but he also won deep admiration from those who saw him as a man who lived and worked above the muck of modern politics.

He was ethical and smart and fearless. Good-humored and interesting. He didn't care if he ruffled feathers in his own Republican Party on matters of civil service patronage. He didn't care that in his attempts at cleaning up the streets of New York City as a crusading police commissioner, going out every night into the violent and corrupt haunts of Manhattan's precincts looking for dirty cops and illicit behavior, and banning Sunday drinking in the city, he made himself a mortal enemy not just of Tammany Hall, but also of most every working stiff in the city who had just that one day to bend an elbow at the local quaffing house. He didn't care that as assistant secretary of the navy he had done everything in his power to help foment this war against Spain, even as he planned all along to resign his post, raise a regiment of boots-and-spats volunteers, and participate in the brawl himself, leaving the secretary of the navy in the lurch to clean up after him.

Even his large and beloved family, to whom he was an adoring father and faithful husband, was secondary to his ambition. His wife, Edith, gave birth to their fifth child, Theodore's sixth, in November 1897. Soon after, she became seriously ill with abdominal tumors, which laid her up for months as the Cuban crisis escalated in the winter and spring of 1898, yet her husband continued to make plans to go to war.[1]

Theodore's oldest son and namesake, ten-year-old Ted Jr., suffered for months with severe and debilitating headaches during the lead-up to war. After he had visited five different experts looking for a diagnosis and relief, the headaches disappeared only when the family doctor urged his parents to ship Ted off to an aunt's home in New York in the spring of 1898, to take a vacation from his beloved yet overbearing and risk-taking father.[2]

From his earliest years, Ted Roosevelt Jr. was judged to be more combative, more determined, more fearless than his brothers and sisters. He was also sensitive to the burdens of being his father's oldest son. Ted was very much like Theodore, and began to emulate him at an early age, assuming the future president's facial expressions and habits of speech at a precocious age. The famed Roosevelt exclamation "D-e-e-e-lighted!" was used by son as well as father. "Cunning" was a favorite adjective of both, used as a compliment for clever thinking and smart characters. As a small boy, Ted even liked to clomp around in his father's big shoes.[3]

For all his mimicking, Ted was not an obvious heir to his father's legacy. Undersized for his age and born with a wayward right eye that seemed to focus on the tip of his nose, Ted looked a bit like the runt of a squirming and rambunctious litter. Corrective glasses worn from about five years of age onward gave him a studious countenance, but even more pronounced in photographs was his perpetual look of intent seriousness. Even wearing the long-haired ringlets, short pants, and feminine straw hats in which he and most other toddler boys were posed in the 1890s, Ted couldn't seem to muster a childlike expression. He appears burdened, a boy with the weight of the world on his shoulders. The earliest professional photographs of him enhanced the characterization: he was twice pictured reading in the library of the family's home at Sagamore Hill on

Oyster Bay off Long Island Sound, holding a book open and studiously staring at some unknown passage, wearing the straw hat, the curls, and the intensity. He looks for all the world like a precocious Talmudic scholar.

But everyone in the family, including little Ted, had to take a backseat to Theodore's ambitions during the Cuban war. When in early April the secretary of war invited Roosevelt to serve as a commander of a volunteer regiment in the service, a long list of friends advised him not to take the position, not to risk life, limb, and promising career, not to leave that adored family. Even the president pleaded with him to stay in the Department of the Navy. But as he wrote to a friend several years later, as sick as Edith and Ted Jr. were, "I made up my mind that I would not allow even a death to stand in my way." Going to Cuba "was my one chance to do something for my country and for my family and my one chance to cut my little notch on the stick that stands as the measuring-rod in every family. I know now that I would have turned from my wife's deathbed to have answered that call."[4]

Theodore Roosevelt could never contain his flair for the dramatic, even to protect his children. They understood, more or less, the dangers that their father might be facing, in part because he was not reluctant to share them. In the Spanish American War, even after ten-year-old Ted's debilitating headaches, Theodore couldn't help himself. After finally going off to battle, Theodore sent a number of letters to his wife and the older boys in which he frankly assessed his odds of getting killed (one in three, he wrote Edith). He also asked her in a letter to present his sword and revolver to Ted and son Kermit should he not return. She passed this information on to the boys, who collapsed in tears at the prospect of their father's death.[5, 6]

Lying in the Cuban jungle about four miles outside of Santiago in the early morning of July 1, 1898, Theodore Roosevelt could feel the rightness of what he was doing. He was a man who believed in destiny, and he felt his resided right here beside Colonel Leonard Wood, the commander of the volunteer regiment the two men had cofounded two and a half months earlier.

The regiment itself was there as well, sleeping along the narrow jungle trail, grandly called El Camino Real, that led from the Caribbean Sea to San Juan Hill, their destination that day. These were the Rough Riders, the eclectic mix of Western cowboys and Eastern college types spread out now around Roosevelt and Wood. Thanks primarily to the colorful nature of the troops and Roosevelt's accessibility to the bevy of war correspondents who accompanied American forces in this immensely popular war, the nickname of the regiment was already common parlance to Americans north, south, east, and west.

The romance of the outfit, the mix of class and regions, the dream of a democratic fighting unit caught the imagination of the people, as did its commanders. Both epitomized the character of the Rough Riders: Roosevelt, having been raised in East Coast brownstones but tempered in the wide-open Dakotas; Wood, similarly raised in the East and educated in the Ivy League, but who as a young army officer serving in the Southwest won a medal of honor for his bravery in the hunt for Geronimo. Never mind that they were extremely ambitious and competitive friends, both eager to win glory and its rewards here in Cuba. To the general public they were twin dynamos leading the most colorful outfit in the service.

Rising before dawn, the pair ate a quiet breakfast of beans, bacon, and hardtack and doused their campfires with unfinished coffee. A hill at their campsite, El Poso, rose just beyond the edge of the jungle behind them, and as the sun broke the eastern horizon, a thunderous battery of field guns appeared on its side. Teams of great and muscular horses, urged by the lash, pulled the cannons up its heights, wending back and forth on the bare hillside to spot the guns above the Spanish to the west at San Juan Hill and to the north at a fort called El Caney. The expertise of the teamsters, the manes of the horses flowing back on the reins, the audible shouts of drivers and thundering hooves of twenty-four horses lugging half a dozen guns in the otherwise still morning made a stirring tableau that reminded the men of their own duties that day, and the fact that they were serving in a righteous war. The blood of the Rough Riders quickly rose.

A mix of American troops, volunteer and regular army, was arrayed along the trail for a couple of miles through the dense jungle before it opened in a sort of basin beneath the Spanish positions to the north and west. The regular army infantry under the command of General Henry Lawton was set to lead American forces into this day's battle at El Caney, while General Joe Wheeler's troops, including the Rough Riders, were to be positioned beneath San Juan Hill and another, smaller hill slightly to the east. Unnamed on American maps, it was soon given the nickname Kettle Hill because on top of it, in addition to a small ranch building, rested two large, black, sugar-boiling cauldrons visible from the valley below.

Wheeler, an old Confederate cavalryman who'd sat for a few terms in Congress between the Civil War and this one, was intended to serve as the commander of the Cavalry Division for the assault on San Juan. However, he'd succumbed several days earlier to a tropical fever, as many Americans had already in their brief time in Cuba. A sawed-off old fireplug with a white beard and little hair on top of his head, Wheeler was so enthusiastic for this fight that a few days earlier, at the tail end of the first action between the Spaniards and Americans at Las Guasimas, he'd gotten his wars mixed up. "We got the Yankees on the run!" he was heard to yell as the Spanish left the battlefield.

Too sick now to direct the battle at San Juan Hill, Wheeler gave command of the Cavalry Division to General Samuel Sumner, while leadership of the division's 2nd Brigade went to Wood. This chair-shifting led Roosevelt to be promoted to the direct command of the Rough Rider regiment, for which he was more than ready and eager. It meant he would be with the troops in the field while Wood oversaw command of the brigade from back of the front lines.

After breakfast, Roosevelt dressed for battle in the same muddy khaki pants that he'd slept in, then pulled on a pair of custom-made, mahogany-colored hiking shoes and his sweat-stained campaign hat, ventilated with small holes in its crown to release some of the unbearable Cuban heat from the top of his head. His only flair was a blue bandanna with white polka dots that he tied into the rear brim of his hat, so that he would be quickly recognized by the men following him.[7]

At 6:00 a.m. the first guns of the battle opened up from the Spaniards at El Caney, and the American batteries responded from the ridge behind

Roosevelt and the Rough Riders. Wood noted that the American artillery, firing over their heads, made a direct line toward the enemy, which meant the Spaniards' return fire, aimed at the American cannons, would be coming back in their direction in the form of whining shells. "Hardly had he spoken," Roosevelt noted later, "when there was a peculiar whistling, singing sound in the air, and immediately afterward the noise of something exploding over our heads. It was shrapnel from the Spanish batteries."[8]

Roosevelt and Wood jumped on their horses just as a second shell exploded, wounding four members of the Rough Rider regiment, not counting Theodore, who had a piece of shrapnel raise a welt on his wrist, or Wood, whose horse was killed from beneath him. Roosevelt formed up the Rough Riders and followed the rest of the 2nd Brigade down the jungle trail into the basin formed by a pair of rivers, which ran beneath San Juan and Kettle Hills to the west and north, respectively.

Both of these heights were topped by Spaniards, who began firing at the American troops as they moved into the river basin. Soon it was revealed that in addition to the infantry on top of the hills, the Spanish had scattered sharpshooters in the trees in the jungle both in front of and behind the American brigade. These snipers were particularly hard to find because of the denseness of the foliage and the fact that their Mauser rifles fired smokeless gunpowder that made it impossible to pick out the shooters among the leaves.

Progress on the trail was slow. The crowd of troops sent soldiers bumping along the way, with snipers in the trees taking potshots all the while as the Americans inched along. Despite their popularity with the press and the general public, Roosevelt's Rough Riders were not scheduled to lead American troops into battle that day. The fancy volunteer unit was not nearly so applauded by the regular troops of the American army, who resented the regiment's quick rise to fame and its reported rough-and-tumble fighting capabilities, accrued after all of three months of training down in "San Antone." The cowboys and Knickerbocker Blue Bloods, meant to be a cavalry unit, had been turned into infantry by the fact that there hadn't been room for most of their mounts in the hastily arranged shipping from Florida to Cuba at the start of the campaign. Horseless, they marched right along with the regulars down toward a ford on the Aguadores River, which had already been crossed by the 1st Brigade, which consisted of the 3rd, 6th, and 9th U.S. Cavalry. Already down at the ford were two more cavalry units, the 1st and the 10th.

Their orders were vague. The infantry was to wait for the troops of the 2nd Infantry Division, battling at El Caney to the north under General Lawton, to take that fort and then join with Sumner's force, including the Rough Riders, to head jointly for an assault on San Juan Hill, scheduled to begin at about noon that day. First among many problems with this plan was that Lawton and his infantry were not having the successes they were supposed to be having at El Caney. By the time the Rough Riders reached the ford at 10:00 a.m., Lawton's forces were nowhere to be found.

Roosevelt led his troops through the shallow crossing and stationed them on a sunken road which ran to the base of Kettle Hill, then swung around it to the north. Meanwhile, the Mauser fire from the Spanish hilltops and the sniper positions in the nearby brush and jungle grew in intensity. Adding to the misery of the American troops was the fact that a detachment from the U.S. Signal Corps chose this moment to launch an observation balloon intended to spot Spanish positions up on the hilltops.

Since no reconnaissance of those positions had been done in preparation for the battle, it was thought that the balloon could serve as an invaluable tool for pinpointing Spanish fire so that both American artillery and infantry could respond in kind. Instead, the position of the balloon, directly above the Rough Riders and other units of the 1st Brigade, served to plant a big arrow above the American positions for the Spaniards. Their fire immediately focused on the balloon and all that rested beneath it, bringing the brightly colored inflatable quickly to the ground, where it drew even more intense fire, "causing severe loss of life, as it indicated the exact position where the Tenth and the 2nd Cavalry and the infantry were crossing," Roosevelt recorded. "The Mauser bullets drove in sheets through the trees and tall jungle grass, making a peculiar whirring or rustling sound; some of the bullets seemed to pop in the air, so that we thought they were explosive; and, indeed, many of those which were coated with brass did explode, in the sense that the brass coat was ripped off, making this a plate of hard metal with a jagged edge, which inflicted a ghastly wound."[9]

Casualties began mounting among all units. The Rough Riders quickly lost a football star from Princeton named Horace Devereaux, and a West Point cadet, Ernest Haskell, a trumpeter from the regiment band. Roosevelt lost two orderlies in quick succession; and most devastatingly the Rough Riders lost one of their most famed and fearless officers, Captain William "Bucky" O'Neill, a lawman, populist politician, explorer of the Grand Canyon and mayor of Prescott, Arizona, who was standing in front of his men, smoking a cigarette, testing a personal theory that officers ought never to take cover in front of their men. When one of his men advised him that the moment was not right to test the theory, he laughed and boasted, "The Spanish bullet isn't made that will kill me." He was immediately proved wrong when a shot from a Mauser rifle entered his mouth and exited the back of his head.[10]

Still pinned down on the sunken road, still suffering grievously from snipers and the massed fire of the troops on the hilltops, and still waiting with little hope for Lawton's troops to arrive from their assault on El Caney to the north, Roosevelt determined that no matter the dangers of an assault up the hills in front of them, it would be better to charge upward than to duck here in the basin down by the river ford, taking fire from the Spaniards up on San Juan and Kettle Hills. He sent back a string of messengers to Wood and General Sumner, stationed at El Poso, asking for permission to move forward against the Spanish heights directly before him at Kettle Hill.

Unfortunately, Sumner and Wood were waiting for the same permission from their superior officer, the overall commanding general of American forces in Cuba, General William Shafter, an aging whale of a man who had been sick with gout and fever almost from the moment he set foot in Cuba. Shafter was in a tent well back of El Poso. He had designated a young aide, Lieutenant John Miley, as his representative on the battlefield. Sumner finally found Miley and through this convoluted chain of command received the lieutenant's permission to advance. Shortly thereafter, Sumner through more vague means got word to Roosevelt that he could move out.

"The instant I received the order," Roosevelt wrote later, "I sprang on my horse and then my 'crowded hour' began."[11]

He formed his troops in a column in skirmishing order, and though he had intended to lead them up Kettle Hill on foot, the heat was so oppressive that he feared he would quickly exhaust himself, running back and forth, urging his men forward, even as he climbed the hill. Roosevelt decided to mount Little Texas instead so that he could both manage the advance better and be seen by his troops. The fact that he could be seen quite well by Spanish sharpshooters as well didn't seem to faze him. He rode down the line of Rough Riders in the sunken road, urging them forward.

He came upon a soldier seeming to hide in a bush and shouted, "Are you afraid to stand up when I am on horseback?" The man suddenly pitched forward, shot through with a Mauser bullet. It was like a sign to Roosevelt that he'd made the right decision in riding Little Texas. Undeterred, he spurred his horse on.[12]

With the regiment now advancing across the open basin and up Kettle Hill, Roosevelt nudged Little Texas forward between the rows of his climbing men. Up ahead and to the left of the Rough Riders was stationed a portion of the 9th Regular Army regiment, a unit of African American soldiers. Even farther to the left, three more regiments—the 3rd, the 6th, and the 10th—fronted the far left side of Kettle Hill.

As Roosevelt urged his Rough Riders forward, they impinged upon the troops of the 1st and the 9th, who were not yet advancing. When Roosevelt shouted at the regulars that he had received orders to move forward, a captain from the 9th still hesitated and refused to budge. Roosevelt yelled, "Then let my men through, sir!" and again spurred Little Texas forward. "When we started to go through, however, it proved too much for the regulars," Roosevelt wrote later, "and they jumped up and came along, their officers and troops mingling with mine, all being delighted at the chance."[13]

The Spaniards were firing in volleys from the height of Kettle Hill. They would stand, aim downward at the Americans, and then duck to reload before rising to volley again. In the pauses, the Rough Riders would continue their charge until the Spanish rose again, at which time the U.S. troops dived for cover, tried to aim back, and fired. As he realized that the men were all finally starting up the hill, Roosevelt continued to urge them forward, riding back and forth, waving his campaign hat with its brightly colored blue and polka-dot kerchief flowing in the breeze.

Roosevelt could see the Spaniards running out of the ranch buildings next to the kettles at the top of the hill and sensed that he and the Rough Riders were carrying the battle, but he was forced to halt forty yards from the hill's summit by a wire fence that ran around the property. Theodore jumped off Little Texas, turning the animal loose and assuming that he'd never see his horse alive again. Then he made his way over the fence, continuing on foot toward the summit.

Another Roosevelt orderly, a man named Henry Bardshar, paused just ahead of him to aim and fire at two Spaniards just above them. They fell dead and Theodore and Bardshar continued toward the summit, arriving simultaneously with a mob of Rough Riders and black troops from the 9th Regiment at the top of Kettle Hill.

There was much more to come that day: almost immediately after American troops arrived on top of the hill, they were hit by Spanish artillery and infantry fire so that a number of Rough Riders wound up employing those sugar refining kettles at the summit as cover. Off to the west, San Juan Hill, the bigger and more strategically important obstacle on the way to Santiago, had yet to be taken; and Lawton's troops still had not arrived from El Caney. The infantry charging up San Juan Hill was stymied by Spaniards firing from a blockhouse built near its summit, so Roosevelt ordered his Rough Riders to rush to their assistance. After some initial reluctance, they joined his charge. Once again, Roosevelt and Bardshar found themselves facing two Spanish soldiers near the top of San Juan Hill, firing from a trench above them; the Spaniards fired and missed from point-blank range, then turned heel up the hill. Roosevelt raised his revolver, coincidentally a weapon salvaged from the battleship *Maine*. He fired at the retreating soldiers and missed with his first shot. A second bullet, however, hit its mark, and Theodore Roosevelt had killed a man, a fact that he was proud to tell in his account of the charge.

By this time, the story of the battle was being written in the minds of the correspondents trailing the action, and its heroes were "Teddy" Roosevelt and the Rough Riders.

Richard Harding Davis, the most famed reporter in the war, would describe Roosevelt charging up Kettle Hill with his blue polka-dot kerchief floating behind his head like a guidon.[14] "No one who saw Roosevelt take that ride expected he would finish it alive," wrote Davis. "As the only mounted man, he was the most conspicuous object in the range of the rifle pits, then only 200 yards ahead. Mounted high on horseback and charging the rifle pits at a gallop and quite alone, he made you feel like you would like to cheer."[15]

Another famed writer serving in Cuba as a war correspondent, Stephen Crane, called the charge up the hill nothing less than "the best moment of anyone's life."[16]

Following the lead of Davis, Crane, and other war correspondents, some who had witnessed the action and some who hadn't, newspapers across the country picked up the story and added lively details to the original reporting, confusing facts as they inflated the glory of what had transpired. Teddy Roosevelt was pictured on its summit galloping alone and triumphantly astride Little Texas. Neglected was any mention of the African American troops who arrived at the top simultaneous to "Teddy" and the Rough Riders.

No matter for Roosevelt. The story of Roosevelt and the Rough Riders' charge quickly became legend. He was the man of the hour, the bespectacled hero of the conflict that John Hay would soon label "that splendid little war." Theodore Roosevelt was barely down the hill in Cuba when he was being touted back in New York as a prime Republican candidate for the governor's office in the fall elections that year.

In mid-September, Theodore Roosevelt would accept the nomination of the GOP; in November, he would be elected governor of New York. He would jump from that office to the vice presidency, two years later. And from the vice presidency, he would succeed William McKinley to become the twenty-sixth president of the United States and progenitor of one of the most famous political families in American history. For the rest of his days he would recall his "crowded hour" as the moment that launched his life and career. So would his children.

The Spanish American War ended just a few weeks later. The famed Rough Riders stayed in Cuba for a few weeks longer before the threat of yellow fever sent them home to quarantine at a camp on Long Island a hundred miles from Sagamore Hill.

When their mother recovered from her illness and Ted Jr.'s headaches went away, the whole family gathered in the late summer of 1898 at Sagamore Hill to follow the progress of Theodore and the Rough Riders in Cuba. They read the stirring and heroic dispatches of Richard Harding Davis and Stephen Crane in the New York papers. They followed the progress of the army as it took Santiago, remained camped in Cuba, and then was quarantined at a camp in Montauk, on the eastern tip of Long Island. They knew their father was now one of the most famous men in America and likely would be the next governor of the state.

Finally, in September, the quarantine at the Rough Riders' camp was lifted and Edith and the older children in the family were given the go-ahead to visit Theodore. A bright blue sky shined over the dunes and beaches at Montauk, and a great fuss was made over the colonel's children. Alice, the oldest girl and Theodore's only child by his first wife, Alice, was fifteen years old and all flirtatiousness and adoring eyes toward the dashing contingent of Rough Riders who congregated around her father.

Edith's happiness at having her husband home at last was somewhat tempered by news that he was going to accept the nomination of the Republican Party to lead their ticket in state elections that fall. Once again, she was going to lose Theodore to public service and ambition.

The two oldest boys, Kermit and Ted Jr., spent the day following their father through the camp, eating at his mess, shaking hands with the volunteer soldiers and their officers who'd served heroically under the colonel and now, to the boys, had nothing to say about him except that he was the most extraordinary man any of them had ever met and that the boys had mighty big shoes to fill. So faithful to and considerate of those who served with him was their father that even his horse, Little Texas, who had unexpectedly survived that fateful day in Cuba, was coming home with him. He would soon be shipped to the stable at Sagamore Hill and live a long life as a happy horse with the Roosevelt family.[17]

Ted and Kermit got to spend the night in their father's tent, with Kermit sleeping on his air mattress[18] as Ted occupied his father's cot. From his vantage, Ted could see boots and belts shuffle into and out of his father's company; hear quieted voices talking of military matters with grown-up seriousness, or of jocular matters in the friendly tones of comrades in the wake of a war survived. A romantically inclined and adoring boy such as Ted could hardly witness his father in a more admirable light. Theodore Roosevelt was the center of attention, bathed in the esteem of these strong and brave men.

Any sense of crisis, any sense of impending doom, lingering doubts, headaches that he might have felt at his father's going off to war, were now gone. All he could see was a hero.

Surely the ten-year-old Ted Roosevelt dreamed of being a Rough Rider that night, just like his father. How could he not?

ONE

ALL IN THE FAMILY

Family dinner was called on a gong suspended from a pair of elephant tusks. This was set in front of the fireplace in the great hall that served as the entrance to Sagamore Hill. An old brown sofa nearby was draped with a buffalo hide skinned and tanned by Theodore in the days when he lived out on his North Dakota ranch. Hanging above it was a print done by Native Americans depicting the massacre of General George Armstrong Custer and the 7th Cavalry. Bright splashes of red blood poured from the lifeless bodies of the soldiers scattered around the scene.

All around the hall and the rooms that spoked from it—a sitting room for Mrs. Roosevelt; a library with shelves, desks, and tables teeming with books; the family dining room; and a space they called the North Room— were arrayed more books, an assortment of game trophies, and a mixture of rugs and animal skins for the floor, including a polar bear hide presented to President Roosevelt by Robert Peary upon his return from an Arctic expedition.

Every item had a story, either family-sourced or living history or both. The flag in the North Room was the one Ted's father had taken with him up San Juan Hill in Cuba back in 1898. On either side of it were buffalo heads that Theodore had shot out in the Badlands as the species dwindled to next to nothing. Ted's father was in the habit of hanging his Spanish American campaign hat on the horn of one of these wall mounts.

It wasn't all about Theodore. There was a footstool owned by Ted's great-great-grandfather; wall hangings and furniture were designated by landmarks on the family calendar—this picture was hung "the year Quentin was born"; that settee came soon after the colonel had returned from his trip to Africa with Kermit.

Still, the remarkable life of Theodore Roosevelt was the most omnipresent source for the treasures that rested in scattered spots around the house. Here was a rug, a present of the shah of Persia; there were elephant tusks gifted to Roosevelt by the emperor of Abyssinia. A cabinet housed a suit of armor from the emperor of Japan.[1]

In a reminiscence written many years after his childhood, Ted called Sagamore "a bastard Queen Anne" in its design. But as a place it was never about its form. "The house has the air of having been lived in which is the requisite of every home. It never has and never will be entirely in repair. There are always boards missing in the lattice underneath the piazza and there is many a place where a lick of paint would not come amiss." It was a house that got *used*. A fantastic home to be raised in, a home straight out of some strange Victorian tale that promised pirates and cowboys, flying children, and adventure in faraway lands. There was a hint of mustiness in the house from all of the animals, remnant and extant, who, in the first case, hung mounted on the walls or rested in taxidermied poses on bookshelves and tables, and in the second case wandered through the living quarters like they were part of the natural landscape, sometimes accompanied by children and sometimes not.[2]

Born in 1887, Theodore Roosevelt Jr. was given the junior in his name despite the fact that he was actually the third Theodore Roosevelt. Ted, as he was called by the family, was the second oldest of his father's six children. He was born after Alice (1884), the daughter of Theodore's first wife, Alice Hathaway Lee Roosevelt, who died two days after giving birth to their daughter. The other Roosevelt children in order were Kermit (1889), Ethel (1891), Archie (1894), and young Quentin (1897). The boys tended to pair off by ages: Ted and Kermit were the oldest, often compared, and tight childhood companions. Likewise, Archie and Quentin, the younger boys, were measured one against the other. Ethel, the middle child and the only girl after Alice, grew up closer to Ted and Kermit than to the younger boys.

Ted's moral education began early. It is difficult to overemphasize how deeply ingrained in Ted's life were the ethics of manly honor and being a Christian soldier. "My father believed very strongly in the necessity of each boy being able and willing not only to look out after himself but to look out for those near and dear to him," Ted would write. "This gospel was preached to us from the time we were very, very small. . . . Father told me one day always to be willing to fight anyone who insulted me."[3]

Both mother and father "believed in robust righteousness . . . *Pilgrim's Progress* and *The Battle Hymn of the Republic* we knew when we were very young. When father was dressing for dinner he used to teach us poetry. I can remember memorizing all the most stirring parts of Longfellow's *Saga of King Olaf, Sheridan's Ride,* and the *Sinking of the Cumberland.*"[4]

His father taught Ted Jr. "the gallant incidents of history" on walks to work with Theodore when the future president was serving in the first McKinley administration. He would pause to sketch out Civil War battle positions, the epic struggles of Union and Confederate troops, in the dust of the Washington city streets for his son before proceeding on to his workday.

Ted was immersed in his father's erudition from the moment he was born. "His knowledge stretched from babies to post-Alexandrian kingdoms," Ted would write many years later. "It made little difference into what channels the conversation turned. Sooner or later Father was able to produce information which often startled students of the theme under discussion. He knew the species of Hannibal's elephants through the shape of the ears as shown through the Carthaginian coins of the period. He could recite 'The Song of Roland' in the original French. He knew the latest laws of reorganization of the State government in Illinois. He could tell you in detail the history of the heavyweight boxing champions. It was never safe to contradict him on any statement, no matter how recent you might feel your information was."[5]

Ted was swept away by the romance of his father's stories. In time, he would himself memorize scores of poems and amaze his own soldiers with his ability to recite poetry from the large compendium stored in his own mind. On his own, Ted and his siblings read books by the armfuls. He had a particular interest in epic poetry and French history. At Groton, he wrote poems that suggested their impact and the heroic and tragic day-dreams that inhabited his mind: "Would God I might die my sword in my hand; My gilded spur on my heel/with my crested helmet on my head/ and my body closed in steel/Would God when the morning broke/I might by friends be found/Stiff in my war worn harness/Ringed by dead foes all around."[6]

For all the romantic and moral instruction inculcating the family, there was a leavening force as well. It was virtually impossible to be a child of Theodore Roosevelt and not have a heightened spirit and active sense of play. If their father was home and working, there came a moment in every day when he would close down his office and head outdoors with commands for the children to gather. When he wasn't directing them in what Theodore liked to call "a scramble"—which was really a set of phys-ical tests, like an obstacle course, or a fast-paced hike over rugged terrain, always done as a staggered race to compensate for the youngest among them—he was ordering them to the horses for a ride, or the rowboats for a paddle across the bay, or to the fishing poles to drop a line, or to the woods for a game of hide-and-seek or a nature hike or a campfire or a race down Cooper's Bluff, the steep drop-off that fronted Oyster Bay.

Alternate forms of scrambles were called "beelines" or "point-to-point." In these variations, everyone followed precisely behind "Father," whether that was over hills, down steep inclines or cliffs, across rivers, or through muddy swamps. There was no shirking the route, no going around obsta-cles.[7] Trips through the stables at Oyster Bay, including down manure chutes and mucky barnyards, were typical in the chase. Each barrier was met and passed exactly as it was found on the path. Ted almost always led the pack behind his father.

Younger brother Ted teased Alice so consistently about not being part of the second family of Roosevelts, the one mothered by his mother, Edith, that they often bickered. Theodore was so bereft at the loss of his first wife that he refused ever again to talk of her and could barely stand hearing the sound of her name. As a consequence, Alice was called "Sister" by her half siblings. She spent the first couple of years of her life being raised by Theodore's sister Anna (called Bamie or Bye by the family), and would periodically afterward be sent to live with Bama throughout her adolescence. She grew up willful and independent, and didn't get along with her stepmother. As dearly as she loved and worshipped her father, she bickered with him, too, deeply resenting what she saw as his preference for Edith's children. Sister Alice and Ted wouldn't grow tight until both had outgrown Ted's little-brother meanness.

Ted was close with Kermit, but Kermit was a different type of character: dreamier, more literary, more sensitive, and less athletic than his older brother. Kermit was less subject to the pressures that Ted felt, and Edith felt that Ted actually shielded Kermit from some of the burdens shouldered by her oldest son. One of Ted's chief functions in the family, she noted, was to act as a sort of heat shield protecting the other children from their father's sometimes overbearing ambitions for them, which meant Kermit "was able to grow up pacific, remote, not inclined to define himself by physical prowess."[8, 9]

Edith's ancestry stretched all the way back to the *Mayflower*, and strong in her makeup was the sense of democratic sacrifice and egalitarianism that was drilled into the children as deeply as their moral education. No one put on airs around her, or if they did, she did not suffer their presence for long.

For all Theodore's dominance and need to be front and center in family life, Edith was the Roosevelt family's judge and lawmaker. The children toed the line when faced with her disapproval, but she did little to check their many pursuits and enthusiasms. Mrs. Roosevelt believed in "children owing their parents obedience" but also in keeping them children as long as possible.[10]

The various creatures that roamed over Sagamore Hill included a badger named Josiah; a bear called Jonathan Edwards, after the old Puritan minister (from whom Edith was a direct descendant); a mountain lion;

a flying squirrel; a long string of guinea pigs (each of the children had their own, which they usually slept with and carried in bloused shirts); mice; snakes; dogs; and a full stable of horses, which ranged in size from the colonel's warhorse to Shetland ponies. Behind Sagamore Hill was a pet cemetery marked by a boulder with the lettering "Faithful Friends." All activity was done at an unencumbered decibel level and with a level of self-confidence and certitude in whatever activity was being pursued that always made it the right thing to do.[11]

Other Roosevelt families inhabited properties adjoining Sagamore Hill on Oyster Bay. A photo from 1897 shows a line of sixteen Roosevelt first cousins in descending order of height from the right of the photo to the left, with Alice second tallest and Archie bringing up the rear (Quentin was not yet born). Cousins were all around at Oyster Bay, including occasional visits from first cousin Eleanor, the orphaned daughter of TR's brother Elliot, who had died a forlorn alcoholic, estranged from Theodore; she often felt picked on by the other Roosevelts and inadequate in the face of their boisterous clannishness. A tall fifth cousin named Franklin Roosevelt, from the Hudson River branch of the family, also visited, and like most who came to Sagamore Hill, relished the opportunity to romp with other Roosevelts led by Theodore. Ted, who was five years younger than Franklin, nonetheless saw in the distant relative a rival and took pains to try to beat him in the various contests—like the race down Cooper's Bluff—that marked these gatherings.[12]

Ted often played with children of Cove Neck, the town built on Oyster Bay, just below Sagamore Hill, which rose some 160 feet above the shoreline. Most of these were the kids of people who worked for the landholders in the town, including the Roosevelts. When Ted was a boy, his father described him as "exceedingly active and normally grimy." He was distinguished from the other boys in town, however, by an early devotion to the poetry of Rudyard Kipling; by the fact that he lived in the big house up on the hill; and by his quick willingness to put up his dukes, which became a focus of subsequent talks with his father. He was a boy with a chip on his shoulder. Undersized and ready to take umbrage at offenses real or exaggerated.[13]

When Ted and his siblings weren't engaged in physical play, they were studying, collecting, or classifying all manner of wildlife. Ted collected birds' eggs and along with brother Kermit practiced taxidermy. One time Ted stuck a dead mouse in the icebox, thereby disgusting his family, who were not mollified by his explanation that he was saving it for later dissection. The home was already stuffed with enough beasts from their father's collection to make a small natural history museum.

When Ted was given his first rifle, a .22, he happened to unwrap it while Theodore was upstairs taking a bath. Ted could hardly contain his enthusiasm and rushed up to show the gun to his father. Theodore's enthusiasm matched his son's; in fact, the colonel was so excited that he felt compelled to illustrate the proper use of the rifle while still immersed in the tub, firing once into the ceiling, and then making Ted promise not to tell his mother what had happened.

Ted's initial hunting trips were taken around the salt marshes of Oyster Bay, shooting duck and shorebirds. Bigger hunts were soon a rite of passage. Ted got his first deer on a trip to the Adirondacks when he was twelve years old. His first moose, shot in Maine, would come three years after that, and his first big adventure out west to his father's old stomping grounds in the Dakotas when he was still in prep school.

Despite living on a bay just off Long Island Sound, the Sagamore Hill Roosevelts were not sailors—unlike the more effete Roosevelts of Hyde Park. Instead they loved the plebeian exercise offered by rowing, and would often set out in a fleet of rowboats for picnics at various points around the bay.

While home base was the house on Long Island, there were a couple of stints in Washington, D.C., in Ted's first dozen years. Theodore Roosevelt took a job in the Harrison administration's Civil Service Commission in 1889, returned to New York to serve as the commissioner of the New York Police Department in 1895, then went back to Washington to serve with McKinley.

The family moved back and forth several times in a dizzying eleven-year span. With their father's professional fortunes attuned to political administrations, the kids learned to follow politics. During William McKinley's first race for the presidency, against William Jennings Bryan, when Theodore was still serving as police commissioner in New York but interested in a role in a would-be McKinley White House, Ted kept abreast of the campaign issues. He was caught by his mother offering a lecture on the front porch at Sagamore Hill to the staff on the fallacy of free silver.[14]

The first Theodore Roosevelt, Ted's grandfather, had established within the family a tradition and ethic of civic duty. In fact, he had devoted most of his life to working for the betterment of the public. Deeply admired by his son for just these traits, he had, however, one gaping flaw in his record of service. The first Theodore Roosevelt had paid for a substitute to serve in his stead during the Civil War. The facts of the situation were complex: his wife, Theodore's mother, Mittie, had come from a dyed-in-the-wool Southern family. She had three brothers who served in the Confederate cause, and she herself, by her son's own admission, was an unreconstructed Southerner. Mittie had insisted that her husband not serve in the Union Army during the war. Instead, Roosevelt did all he could for the Union cause, including helping to found the Union League Club to promote the North during the war, and helping to establish an allotment system for Union soldiers, which was a sort of payroll deduction plan that allowed military men to set aside a portion of their wages to support their families back home.

For all this, the fact that Theodore Sr. did not serve in the army cast a lengthy shadow over his son's life. Though Theodore never wrote of it nor offered any sort of explanation of how it impacted him, his own life, as well as the lives of his children, was guided in profound ways by a need to serve his nation in the military. In Ted's case, it would become the deepest-felt obligation he would ever know.

The whole family understood that at the root of the breakneck speed of Theodore Roosevelt's rise in the world of New York and national politics was his courageous actions in Cuba. The colonel had not only been ready when his nation called, he had urged war, and having urged war, he refused to let others fight battles that he had set in motion. Roosevelt pulled together his ideal of a democratic fighting force and led them into combat—and to glory.

Father was also quick to remind son that his legacy would carry on to Ted. Before the Rough Riders returned to the United States, soon after the famed battle at San Juan, his father had written to Ted that in years to come he would see many of the men whom Theodore had just fought with in Cuba "at my home." And in fact all through the remainder of the colonel's life he kept in contact with scores of Rough Riders, who were always welcome either at the White House or at Sagamore Hill.[15]

Ted's life, too, was subsequently studded with visits and connections from his father's days in Cuba as he became the surrogate commander of the remnants of the Rough Riders. Twenty-five years down the road, however, after Ted had himself witnessed a far more catastrophic war, the romance of his father's regiment seemed quaint.

"Thank you for forwarding me the letter from the ex-Rough Rider," he wrote to his cousin Eleanor in early September 1924, just as Ted was preparing to run for governor of New York (and Eleanor was planning to take the lead in opposing him). "I have inherited a goodly galaxy of veterans who write to me on everything from getting them out of jail to stopping their wives from divorcing them! Not only do my own people from the war regard me as their actual guide, philosopher and friend but the Rough Riders have also descended on me. A little while ago I received a letter explaining to me that one of the Rough Riders who had lived in the Philippines had just died and left six . . . Philippino [sic] children and what was I going to do about it.

"Best wishes to you and Franklin and the rest of the family. Theodore Roosevelt, Jr."[16]

TWO

FIRST BOY

In the summer of 1900, President William McKinley tapped Theodore Roosevelt as his running mate with some reservations (some said a great many reservations) at the GOP national convention in Philadelphia. Theodore was hardly a favorite of the president's chief adviser, Senator Mark Hanna, and others of their generation, such as Secretary of State John Hay. They trusted neither his reform instincts nor his independence, and they didn't believe in his willingness to play second fiddle to the president. Yet Teddy Roosevelt, war hero and symbol of youth, brought undeniable enthusiasm and vote-getting appeal to the Republican ticket. And the question of where he could do more harm to the administration—continuing to serve as governor of New York, the office he'd won in the wake of his exploits in Cuba, or as vice president—was bandied about by cynics in the party in the weeks leading up to the Republican gathering; in the final estimation, McKinley's advisers judged that Theodore could be handled more easily in Washington than in Albany.

The fact that the sluggish McKinley chose to run his reelection race from the comfort of his front porch in Canton, Ohio, rather than taking to the rails to win votes also added to Roosevelt's appeal on the party ballot. With his boundless energy and fist-pounding enthusiasm, TR was a fit and vigorous campaigner and quickly proved his value on the stump for the president, cutting through a wide swath of the Midwest and mountain states, the home territory of McKinley's opponent, who once again was populist William Jennings Bryan. It was tough duty. Not only were the distances great, but also the feelings of the voters were unfriendly when not downright hostile. In Colorado, threats of violence were made against the former Rough Rider, with one headline suggesting that WYO-MING IS STIRRED UP, another that ROOSEVELT ROUSES BUTTE.[1]

Meanwhile, Ted arrived at Groton School in the fall of 1900, the first time he had lived apart from his family. Though he'd spent the previous year at an academy in Albany, and before that some time studying at the public school in Cove Neck, it was also the first time he'd been subjected to serious study. Much to his own embarrassment, Ted found himself lagging behind his classmates. The majority of his fellow students had been in prep school for a couple of years already, and Ted had catching up to do. This was in addition to the usual sense of displacement, tortures of trying to fit in, and general homesickness, all of which made for a miserable fall, which was alleviated only somewhat when he joined the football team and choir and began making friends.

Ted's reputation as a kid quick to raise his fists, first noted with playmates in Cove Neck, continued at Groton and was exacerbated by his being new and the son of such a famed father. Aside from his heroics on San Juan Hill, Theodore was well-known as the former governor of New York who had just accepted the nomination of the Republican Party to be William McKinley's vice-presidential running mate that summer.

To his son, Theodore's meteoric rise was more of a burden to bear than a source of pride. His early letters to his father from school show no interest in his father's life on the campaign trail. They typically began with reports on his boxing and wrestling matches, usually describing a string of victories until the point when he met a bigger opponent and offered a game but ultimately losing effort. He wanted to make sure his father knew that he was always ready to stand up for himself.

TR liked that in his boy, encouraging Ted's willingness to stand up for himself as long as it was carried out in the manner of a virtuous soldier.

In November, just after he and McKinley won the election, Theodore received a letter from a friend, a *Harper's Weekly* writer and frequent correspondent named Edward Martin. Martin had a son who was a classmate of Ted's at Groton, and he advised the vice president elect that reports from school had Ted already "lick[ing] every boy in his form." The intimation was that Ted's temper was not fully checked.

Theodore's defense of his eldest son was remarkable for the depths to which it went in explaining Ted's character and, by extension, his own. "Now about small Ted's fighting," he wrote, "I believe you will find that he is not quarrelsome and above all is not a bully." All of his fights, Theodore explained, had taken place "in amicable wrestling and boxing bouts that in your boy's words [Ted] has 'licked all the boys in his form.'" Theodore admitted that "In a measure, I am responsible for some of his fighting proclivities for instilling in [all of his boys] the theory that they ought not to shirk any quarrel forced upon them.

"Now do you want to know the real underlying feeling which has made me fight myself and Ted want to fight? Well, I summed it up to Ted once or twice when I told him, apropos of lessons of virtue that he could be just as virtuous as he wished *if only he was prepared to fight*. Fundamentally this has been my own theory. I am not naturally at all a fighter, so far as any person is capable of analyzing his own impulses and desire, mine incline me to amiable domesticity and the avoidance of effort and struggle and any kind of roughness and to the practice of home virtues. Now I believe that these are good traits not bad ones. But I believe if unsupported by something more virile, they may tend to evil rather than good. The man who merely possesses these traits, and in addition is timid and shirks effort, attracts and deserves a good deal of contempt."[2]

Edith was left to deal with Ted's more sensitive proclivities: his homesickness, his difficulties making friends, and his lag in studies. She spent the fall torn between solicitousness for her son Ted, settling into his new existence at Groton, and concern for her exhausted husband, who was adjusting to the idea that he would soon be the vice president of the United States. The campaign ended back in home territory in New York, where a triumphant appearance at Madison Square Garden and a well-attended GOP parade that featured TR driving up Broadway in a downpour to the cheers of the drenched throngs presaged the outcome of the election in a week's time. McKinley and his new, heroic vice president won the election in a cakewalk.[3]

The Roosevelts opted to stay at Sagamore Hill through the winter in preparation for the move in the spring back to Washington, where Theodore would assume his duties as vice president. The whole family was in the Senate gallery on March 4, 1901, when TR entered the chamber to make his inaugural address as president of the Senate. Included in the assembly were his sisters, Anna and Corrine; Alice, who at seventeen was about to make her debut on the Washington social scene; the younger boys, Quentin and Archie, whose lapels were festooned with McKinley/ Roosevelt campaign buttons; the middle sister, Ethel; and the two older boys, Kermit and Ted, who displayed a unique style of mismatched dress, including a coat, vest, and pants culled from three different suits. When his mother asked about the getup, Ted explained that when she had told him to bring his best clothes down from Groton, he had done just that, packing his best pants, his best vest, and his best coat, never mind that they had come from three different outfits.[4]

All of the children leaned far over the railings in the Senate gallery to watch their father, sporting a red carnation in his lapel, give what Edith characterized as a "dignified" speech. Emphasizing the responsibility of the duties he and the president were about to assume, Theodore suggested that the youthful energy and power of the United States were of vital importance not just to the future of the nation, but to generations to come all around the world. "As we do well or ill," Teddy told his audience, "so shall mankind in the future be raised or cast down."[5]

It was the sort of bold statement for which Theodore Roosevelt would be known in the years to come. Spoken as the newly elected vice president, however, its resonance didn't carry much beyond his own cheering family and the U.S. Senate chambers.

A little more than six months later, in the wake of an assassination, the speeches of President Theodore Roosevelt would carry a far piece more.

On September 6, 1901, a former steelworker who'd lost his job in the economic Panic of 1893 stepped forward as William McKinley was shaking hands at a reception in the Buffalo, New York, Pan American Exposition's Temple of Music, and fired two shots from a concealed .32-caliber revolver at the president. Leon Czolgosz had grown despondent, isolated, and deeply political in the years since losing his job. He read socialist and anarchist political tracts and decided after long consideration, and with the example of a number of European anarchists at the time, that it was his duty to kill the man whom he had grown to consider his chief oppressor.

McKinley did not immediately die. In fact, he was well enough to tell the men who had surrounded and were thoroughly pounding Czolgosz to please forgo any more beating. Then he was helped to a chair, where it was determined that one of the two bullets had deflected off a button on his jacket, merely grazing him. The other, however, had lodged in his abdomen, and McKinley was rushed to the exposition's hospital, which unfortunately lacked good lighting and basic surgical equipment.

For the next few days, McKinley seemed to be doing well. He took broth, toast, and coffee in the days following his operation to remove the bullet, and his vice president, who along with the rest of the cabinet and Senator Mark Hanna had rushed to Buffalo in the wake of the shooting, was confident enough in McKinley's recovery to head off on a family vacation in upstate New York. Just two days later, McKinley took a turn for the worse, and specialists called to examine him discovered that gangrene was growing on the walls of his stomach. The president soon began to drift into and out of consciousness, and on September 13, Roosevelt was summoned from his retreat on Mount Marcy, high in the Adirondacks. William McKinley died the next day, and Theodore Roosevelt became the twenty-sixth president of the United States of America.

Just days later, Ted began his second year at Groton. While the rest of the family settled into life at the White House with a range of emotions, from Edith's trepidation at what this change might bring for her family, to Alice's barely contained excitement at being the most visible and newsworthy debutante in the land (only marginally stifled by the fact that her "coming out" was prompted by the assassination of a president), Ted tried to show a supreme indifference to what was happening to his father and the rest of the family. He was barely fourteen years old now and still wore the corrective glasses that had yet to completely straighten his eye; still was slight of frame and now shorter than his younger brother Kermit; still had the gaze of a serious-minded boy. He was trying to show more maturity. When a classmate dubbed him "the first boy" after his father had assumed the presidency, Ted stifled any offense that he might have felt: "I wish my father would soon be done with holding office," he responded simply. "I am sick and tired of the whole thing."[6] It was only later that he challenged the boy to a fight and proceeded to wallop the transgressor.

Yet for all his ongoing pugnaciousness, Ted generally got along better at school that fall, even showing what would become a lifelong proclivity for making and keeping friends. That said, he was also earning a bit of a bad-boy reputation among Groton administrators, or at least that of a boy capable of leading others astray. According to reports from the school administration, a fad that Ted had inspired caused an outbreak of visits to the infirmary. Following "the first boy's" lead, others at Groton had quit wearing caps during outdoor play. After Ted led a group of classmates on a bareheaded race through the woods—an adventure that sounded much like one of his father's "scrambles"—several boys came down with colds. Ted soon followed suit, and his illness quickly morphed into a very dangerous case of pneumonia.[7]

On February 7, 1902, less than six months after his father became president, Ted lay on the verge of death. One lung had filled with fluid, and his fever had ranged upward of 103 degrees. He lay in a sweat in the school infirmary, his breathing labored. His mother was urged to come from Washington as quickly as possible. Edith took the 4:30 p.m. train to Groton and was at Ted's bedside by 10:00 a.m. the next day.

Her appearance cheered Ted, and his symptoms stabilized. But concern for the teenage boy quickly stretched across the nation and around the world. New York and Boston reporters arrived on the scene, and the Associated Press dispatched stories to newspapers in the far corners of the country to reach the morning and evening news editions. Ted's health was covered overseas as well. Reports on the boy's physical well-being and progress were updated on a nearly hourly basis.

The seriousness of an illness such as pneumonia was well understood in this preantibiotic age; and the large and raucous family of the new president had become the source of countless stories and intense public interest since Theodore Roosevelt had come to occupy the White House that past fall. Washington had not seen such a youthful president and family since the days of Abraham and Mary Todd Lincoln. Though no print report mentioned the fact, it wasn't hard for the public imagination to recall that Abraham Lincoln had lost a child to illness while in the White House, to the president's everlasting sorrow.

Groton's sprawling greens and redbrick sanctuaries were closed for two weeks to prevent further outbreaks, and the students were sent home. A *New York Times* reporter corralled a group of Groton boys coming into New York at Grand Central Station, and they told him that Ted's illness had been precipitated by the fact that he'd won the race with such ease that waiting bareheaded for the others to finish was the real reason that he'd come down with a cold. Along with Ted, two boys remained in the Groton infirmary, while a third had sadly died of the condition in late January.

In Washington, Theodore communicated via cable with Edith through-out the day. He was in the midst of delicate negotiations regarding a Senate bill that would provide funding to purchase rights to the Panama Canal. In addition, he had just had Booker T. Washington to the White House for dinner, the first time an African American had ever dined with the president at his home, and Roosevelt was taking flak for that decision. Nonetheless, TR decided to head to Groton on the morning of the ninth to check on his son. He arrived that evening to find Ted resting comfort-ably at the school hospital, his mother at his side.

The president spent the night at the home of one of the school instruc-tors, an old friend, while Edith rested on a cot in Ted's room. Overnight the infection spread from one to both lungs, Ted's fever rose again, and his respiration grew weak. The attending physician reported that his pulse remained strong and that the boy's spirits were hiked by the presence of both parents. But the general decline of Ted's health prompted Theodore and Edith to call Alexander Lambert, the same family doctor who had diagnosed the remedy for Ted's headaches during the Spanish American War, to come north to offer his assistance.

The president canceled a state visit from Prince Henry of Prussia scheduled for the end of February and proceeded to sit for most of the day in Ted's room along with Edith. In the afternoon, Theodore took a brisk fifteen-minute walk around the grounds.

A hard night followed, and then a day of fluctuations as the illness reached a critical point. Pleurisy developed in the right lung in the night, and Ted's temperature spiked in the early afternoon and remained high into the evening. But by eleven o'clock, his fever had dropped and his condition had steadied. His left lung cleared considerably, and his respiration and pulse had shown little variation. A good night followed, and by early evening on the twelfth, Ted and his two companions in the infirmary were all doing so much better that the president made plans to get back to the business of the nation.

Letters and telegrams started to pour into White House offices: old family friends, relatives, common citizens, and heads of state and foreign leaders, including Abdul Hamid, the sultan of Turkey, Prince Henry of Prussia, and King Edward VII and Lord North of Great Britain, sent notes expressing their concern. So did hundreds of acquaintances and associates of Ted's father.

Theodore returned to work and his son soon regained enough strength that he was able to travel to Washington with his mother in a week's time, and he would remain there for the rest of the semester, recovering from his illness.[8]

The deep and intense public concern over Ted stunned the family. That the president always made great copy was to be expected (and mostly welcomed by Theodore), but the overwhelming interest in the rest of the family, as exemplified by this concern for Ted, was unprecedented. Edith and the children were accustomed to a relatively private life at their home on Sagamore Hill, but in the fishbowl of Washington, D.C., they became subject to intense scrutiny.

Alice, the sassy ingenue, was a natural for the press to glom on to. So, too, it turned out, were the wild-haired boys romping around the White House, oblivious to its decorum with all their animals and antics. After the stodgy presidency and tragic death of William McKinley, Roosevelt and his family were seen in Washington and across the nation as a breath of fresh air, a brilliant new force to help ring in the new century.

Mrs. Roosevelt had her moments in the spotlight as well. She was featured in a lengthy profile for *Ladies' Home Journal* written by TR's friend the journalist and social reformer Jacob Riis, who had been Roosevelt's boon companion back in his days as New York police commissioner. Riis characterized Edith as a perfect mate to her high-energy, high-maintenance husband. She was viewed as the doyenne of a remarkably democratic family and household where "Perfect equality based upon perfect trust between children and parents [was] the distinguishing trait of the family." The Roosevelts knew "Nothing of aristocratic pretense, nothing of class or privilege, still less of snobbery." Edith's duties were not easy, according to Riis, but somehow she managed to provide companionship to her husband "while neglecting none of [her children]." To top things off, she was a fine horsewoman who accompanied her husband on long afternoon rides at Oyster Bay and in Washington.[9]

When Riis came to the White House that spring of 1902 to profile the first lady and her children, he noted that Ted, recovering in Washington after his recent illness, was "as like his father as two pins in his absolute fearlessness and occasional disregard for conventionalities." Fearless he certainly was: among the menagerie of animals now quartered at the White House, Ted kept a favorite close—a macaw that perched on the boy's shoulder as he piloted around the home. Its beak was so sharp, Riis wrote, that it suggested "the shears of an armored plate clipper down at the Navy Yard." He wrote that the bird was the one creature in the White House that the president feared. Ted had no qualms, however, about letting the big bird sit near his ear, and even would put his finger between the bills of that razor-sharp beak.[10]

Riis characterized Ted as marshaling the younger boys in a sort of absentminded yet effective fashion, wandering the White House with the macaw perched threateningly on his shoulder, settling disputes between Kermit and Archie with "judgment . . . worthy of Solomon."[11]

Alice, the eldest of the children, was already the talk of Washington. She was now eighteen years old and remarkably independent-minded, pushing boundaries with her father and stepmother. Riis declared "Miss Alice . . . her father's daughter." Not so astute was his judgment that "She is a sweet, unassuming, dutiful girl," but he was more accurate when he wrote that she "enjoys life and does not care if everybody knows it. Rather, she would have them all join in for their share of the fun."

After his health was restored in Washington, Ted took a trip out west to learn the ways of life in the Dakotas under the tutelage of Seth Bulloch, a former Deadwood sheriff and old friend of his father's. He made a second trip with his cousin George Emlen Roosevelt the following summer, during which he and George and some of Bulloch's hired men did cattle work on Bulloch's ranch, camped in the Black Hills, and hunted and fished in the rocky hills and mountain streams of the territory. In a thank-you note to Bulloch and his wife for their hospitality, Theodore wrote that the boys "had the time of their lives" and especially appreciated the opportunity to do some shooting. Bulloch wrote TR with high praise for his son, saying Ted was "hard as nails," that there was "good leather" in him, and that Ted might "make a good citizen in time if he were allowed to complete his education out west."[12]

Back for what would be his final term at Groton in the fall of 1903, Ted turned his ambition toward the school's football team. Despite being told by the rector at Groton, in midseason, that he was too small to play against the heavier boys on the school's varsity team, Ted wrote a pleading letter to Theodore, asking for his permission to remain with the squad. "I have played in three games against the first eleven already," he argued, "and have not been hurt in the least."[13]

Ted was able to convince his father to write the rector granting his blessing for Ted to play. The president gave the nod under the theory that the dangers of Ted's potential resentment at not being allowed to play were greater than the dangers of playing itself. "I think the chance of damaging yourself in body is outweighed by the possibility of bitterness of spirit if you could not play."[14]

Theodore added lengthy thoughts on football and sports in general: "I am delighted to have you play football," he wrote. "I believe in rough manly sports. But I do not believe in them if they degenerate into the soul of one's existence." He reminded Ted of Pliny's letter to Trajan "in which he speaks of its being advisable to keep the Greeks absorbed in athletics because it keeps their minds distracted from serious pursuits." He also told Ted of his belief that the British officers in the recent Boer War "had their efficiency gravely reduced" because of an "inordinate and ridiculous love of sports."[15]

As Theodore was negotiating with Ted about playing football, he was once again in the midst of Panama Canal business, this time encouraging a revolutionary movement in the region. The state of Panama was governed at the time as part of Colombia. But Colombia had grown tired of negotiating with the United States and was suspicious of U.S. intent for the proposed canal. To circumvent this obstacle, Roosevelt collaborated with business interests in Panama to help foment a revolution that would liberate it from its parent country. If Colombia was no longer interested in negotiating with the United States, the new nation of Panama certainly would be. A bloodless coup took place on November 3, 1903, as the cruiser U.S.S. *Nashville* appeared off the coast of Panama to suggest American support for the cause. Several days later, Roosevelt penned the world's first diplomatic recognition of the new nation.

Meanwhile, after getting the go-ahead to continue his football career, Ted broke his nose in a game at Groton. He either severely strained or broke his ankle during the same contest. His father expressed gratitude that the season was coming to a close, but couldn't contain his enthusiasm for Ted's play. His concern over Ted's physical well-being was contradicted when in the same sentence that he advised his son to do everything possible to fully mend the ankle, he also suggested that in subsequent play Ted should "get the best ankle support possible" because "You don't want to find that next fall Webb [his rival for the position] bested you for end because your ankle gives out and his doesn't."[16]

Theodore was proud of his son's athletic prowess. Under the guise of seeking expertise in the physical development of his children, he wrote a letter in 1903 to Pierre de Coubertin, the founder of the modern Olympic Games, in which he took the opportunity to brag about his son: "The eldest, Ted, is fifteen . . . a regular bull terrier and though I don't believe he is quarrelsome among his friends he is everlasting having sanguinary battles with outsiders. In most branches of sport he has already completely passed me by. He can outwalk and outrun me with ease, and could perhaps outswim me—although I think not yet; I am inclined to think him a better rider than I am, and owing to his weight he can certainly take my horse over jumps that I would not care to put them at unless there was a necessity. On account of my weight I can still probably best him at boxing and wrestling, but in another year he will have passed me in these. I do not shoot at all the shotgun while he has already become a good wing shot. I am still best with the rifle. He plays football well. In the game last year he broke his collar bone, but finished the game all right."[17]

The comparison of Ted's skills with his own suggests an ongoing competitiveness between father and son that marked their relationship as Ted grew more physically able. They began sparring with one another, wrestling and boxing; their scrambles became endurance struggles between father and son, which were still usually won by Theodore. While Kermit soon became their father's favorite correspondent, often exchanging back-and-forth assessments of Ted's character, Ted and Theodore continued their physical bouts.

That fall Ted began to consider his higher education and thought that he might be cut out for a military academy rather than for Harvard. His scholarly standing at Groton had improved since his delayed beginning, but he had never been one of the school's outstanding students. His father dutifully sent Ted the entrance exams for West Point and Annapolis, but in what he called "a business letter" Theodore made his feelings about the military life well understood. "I feel on the one hand that I want to give you my best advice," he wrote, "and yet . . . I don't want to constrain you against your wishes. If you have definitely made up your mind that you have an over mastering desire to be in the Navy or the Army, and that such a career is the one in which you will take a really heart-felt interest—far more so than any other—and that your greatest chance for happiness and usefulness will lie in doing this one work to which you're especially drawn—why, under such circumstances, I have but little to say."

On the other hand: "In the Army and the Navy the chance for a man to show great ability and rise above his fellows does not occur on the average more than once in a generation. When I was down at Santiago it was melancholy for me to see how fossilized and lacking in ambition, and generally useless, were most of the men of my age and over who had served their lives in the Army ... I have actually known lieutenants in both the Army and the Navy who were grandfathers—men who had seen their children married before they themselves attained the grade of captain."

On and on went the letter, painting an indelible picture to Ted: *I don't want to stand in your way, son, but this would be a grave mistake.* It was obvious Theodore had great things in mind for his oldest son's future, and as much as Ted might be enamored with ideas of the military life, it was not the direction his father envisioned.

"I want you to think over all these matters very seriously," he closed. "It would be a great misfortune for you to start into the Army or Navy as a career, and find that you have mistaken your desires."[18]

Harvard it would be. To both appease Ted, who had grown tired of Groton, and prepare him for the rigors of the Harvard entrance exam, it was decided to keep him out of prep school in the fall of 1904. Instead, he would be tutored at the White House by a young teacher named Matt Hale, who was also expected to keep Ted occupied and out of trouble. The biggest concern of Ted's mother and father was that the Washington social scene would turn his head in a fashion similar to what it was currently doing to Alice. As a consequence, Ted went off with Matt Hale to wild and distant Maine in September, where Ted shot and killed his first bull moose.

Through the remainder of the fall, Ted studied, taught Sunday school, played tennis, boxed, and went on scrambles with his father. On election night in early November, he tracked vote tallies in the White House alongside his father as they both learned of TR's landslide victory over the Democratic candidate, New York judge Alton B. Parker.

Ted broke his nose once again, this time sparring with Hale at the White House. Dr. Lambert warned that if Ted broke his nose one more time, he would risk permanent damage to his septum.[19] Ted was unfazed. He continued his physical regimen through the winter and spring, including tennis and more of his father's "scrambles," which took place in Washington's Rock Creek Park, and included anyone willing—or intimidated enough by the president—to join in the exercise.

In March 1905, the Roosevelts gathered in Washington to witness Theodore's inauguration. Among those who were at the festivities were cousin Eleanor and her fiancé, Franklin, the tall fifth cousin from the Hudson River Roosevelts. Franklin was a recent graduate of Harvard, and though a Democrat, he was already making plans to emulate his cousin Theodore's political career, beginning in the New York State legislature.

A couple of weeks later, Theodore's family traveled to New York City to attend the wedding of Franklin and Eleanor. Edith had offered Eleanor the use of the White House for the ceremony, but Eleanor declined; the two Roosevelt women had always been a little uncomfortable with one another, with Eleanor believing that her aunt had fostered a strain between her and her cousin Alice, when in fact the two had been close as children. The strain would deepen in decades to come. Eleanor was pleased, however, that her uncle Theodore was to give her away in Manhattan. Always uncertain of her standing with the Roosevelts of Oyster Bay, she set the wedding date for St. Patrick's Day, March 17, 1905, knowing the president would be in the city anyway for the annual parade. Alice was still close enough to her cousin to serve as Eleanor's bridesmaid.[20]

THREE

LEFT END

By the time Ted was ready to head off to Harvard in the fall of 1905, the Roosevelts, with the exception of Alice, had grown thoroughly tired of reporters. Unfortunately, the "Kodak creatures," as the president was now labeling the press, were out in full force for Ted's arrival in Cambridge. The swarm began to buzz in late September, when Ted's mother accompanied him from the Roosevelt home at Oyster Bay to No. 15 Claverly Hall on the Harvard campus. Reporters followed them all the way from the train station to his "commodious" dorm room in Claverly. There they witnessed Ted's mother apply her "deft" touch and "woman's taste" to make young Roosevelt's room bright and cheerful. Beyond that there was not much to report—not that that stopped the press. It "was a very quiet [day]," wrote one newsman for the *New York Times,* "but more activity would come the next [day] when he registered." Not much more.[1]

In his first few weeks on campus, reporters trailed Ted to lectures and lunches amid the cozy nestle of red brick and white-trimmed buildings. Strolling across the greens, or taking in Harvard Square, Ted was watched as he chatted with new friends and visited the library. Of greatest interest was his football practice, which prompted stories on his size (five feet, eight inches tall when stretched); his prior football-playing experience at

Groton; his recent growth (one month in training and he was already ten pounds heavier than he'd been when he arrived); and the fact that even with those pounds, pushing him to 145, he was still the lightest man on the team. "Among these men," read one obviously exaggerated report, "Roosevelt, Jr. is a mere pygmy."[2]

Reporters covered his first appearance with the freshman squad, an intrasquad scrimmage in which Ted emerged from a pile with a bloody slit over the eyebrow and a cauliflower ear.[3] They reported on Ted's hustle in a game later that month against Worcester Academy in which he made a touchdown-saving tackle, but was injured in the process, and forced to leave the game.[4] They reported in embarrassing fashion, gossiping and trying to curry favor at the same time, that when he made the freshman first team for the Yale game, he did so "on merit without pull or influence against rivals who loomed over him physically like so many Goliaths."[5]

Ted didn't need any boosterism from the press: he had a realistic assessment of his abilities in football. As much as he loved the game, he understood that he was not going to be a star. Before he found out that he'd made the starting squad, he had written his father to say that though he was still on the first team, "I really don't think I will stay there long . . . I have not been hurt much," he added, "but I will be lucky if I'm not."[6]

Ted had no interest in being the object of a hounding press. He was barely eighteen years old, a college freshman, and sensitive about fitting in, sensitive about his size and appearance, sensitive about being the son of the president. Unfortunately for him, his sister Alice was currently holding court on a diplomatic tour of the Far East headed by Roosevelt's secretary of war, William Howard Taft, and including a contingent of broad-bellied, cigar-puffing congressmen, among them at least one serious suitor, Congressman Nicholas Longworth of Cincinnati, Ohio. Theodore and Edith had decided to allow Alice to go, thinking it might keep her out of the papers at home for a while. Thus the principal focus of the press's interest in the Roosevelt children that fall fell on Ted. They gathered around him in Cambridge, trailing him like a gaggle of courtiers scratching notes on the sullen young prince's disposition.

From the White House, the president offered what solace he could to his son. Suspecting that Ted was being intimidated about playing football by the constant presence of reporters, he advised that "you can never afford to let them drive you away from anything you intend to do, whether it is football or anything else." He offered Ted a strategy for dealing with the press: "The thing to do is to go on just as you have been evidently doing, attract as little attention as possible, do not make a fuss about the newspaper men, camera creatures, and idiots generally, letting it be seen that you do not like them, but not letting them betray you into any excessive irritation."[7]

The problem, however, was compounded by football itself. Not only was "the first boy" participating in a wildly popular sport that placed him in the public eye; in 1905 the game itself was in the midst of its most controversial year since its inception. The inherent violence of football had become cause for great concern throughout the country. Almost every college game that fall was being viewed with a little more scrutiny than it had in the past. Further, Ted's father was playing a role in the larger, ongoing controversy.

The Ivy League had served as cradle to the sport, and thirty years into its existence, it still was home to the best coaches, best players, and most enthusiastic fans in the country. Within the league, no rivalry was more intense than Harvard and Yale's. Though Yale had come to dominate the series since the early '90s, that only seemed to magnify the interest and enthusiasm of Harvard alum such as President Roosevelt.

Excesses in the game, however, had prompted increasing criticisms: football was said to be too violent; unsavory elements, including gamblers and paid "ringers," had begun to attach themselves to the sport; the amount of money that was flowing into and around football programs through game attendance and concession sales at ever-larger football stadiums was troubling. The salaries of the nation's best football coaches were exceeding the income of the colleges' highest-paid faculty.[8] Most important, critics, many of them the nation's leading scholars and academics, were wondering if this was what college athletics should be about.

One of the main reasons for the level of brutality was the style of play, which saw bodies concentrated en masse in the center of the field. The offense had three downs to make five yards for a first down; if stopped short, it gave up the ball and ten yards to the opposing team. Forward passing was illegal, which encouraged teams to pound into the line with brute force. The notorious "flying wedge," in which the whole offensive team would form a V shape well back of the line of scrimmage and barrel toward the defense at full throttle, had been outlawed by 1905, but other strategies, such as linking arms for a massed charge through the center of the line, were still part of the game.

Only a few players wore helmets (Ted was not among them); they were leather and clamped tight to the head with no padding and no air cushioning blows to the cerebellum. Makeshift pads for thighs, knees, and shoulders were made of thick felt and worn outside of jerseys. There were just two referees per game, one chosen by each of the teams playing, and much was missed in the tight scrums, where fouls went unseen and unpunished.

So serious had these matters become early in October—even as his son was trying out for the freshman team in Cambridge—that President Roosevelt called to the White House the football coaches of Yale, Harvard, and Princeton, as well as Walter Camp, adviser to the Yale program and considered the "father" of college football. Having just brokered a peace treaty that fall between Russia and Japan, ending the Russo-Japanese War (negotiation for which he would win the Nobel Prize for Peace in the coming year), the president was obviously in a peacemaking mood. He asked the coaches and administrators to Washington, in his own words, "to inaugurate a movement having for its object absolutely clean sport and the eradication of professionalism, money making, and brutality from college games."[9]

The issues at hand were of special importance to the president: not only was he himself a big fan and follower of college football, particularly at his alma mater, but also he had long since established himself as the nation's chief proponent of vigorous and manly virtues. He relished sports and outdoor activity like no other president before or since. In fact, in a speech on the subject the prior June, he had said, "I believe in outdoor games and I do not mind in the least that they are rough games or that those who take part in them are occasionally injured."[10]

That was a bit of an understatement. "I have no sympathy whatever with the overwrought sentimentality that would keep a young man in cotton wool," Roosevelt went on to say, "and I have a hearty contempt for him who counts a broken arm or collarbone as of serious consequence when balanced against the chance of showing that he possesses hardihood, physical address and courage."[11]

While it was later suggested that Roosevelt was interested in banning college football if the sport couldn't reform itself, he was, in fact, primarily interested in cleaning up any unwarranted brutality that might exist. The ethic at play here was about the intentional violence that was often prevalent in the games. This is what the president could not abide: "When these injuries are inflicted by others, either wantonly or of set design, we are confronted by the question, not of damage to one man's body but of damage to the other man's character."[12]

It was the same morality that Roosevelt was careful to teach to his own six children, particularly Ted, who was about to offer a public example of the sort of virtuous and tough-spirited play that his father, the president, so admired.

November 17 saw the only time in the 1905 season that the Harvard freshmen would play an Ivy League opponent. For the frosh boys, the game against Yale marked the beginning, the middle, and the end of the "real" season, and would be followed on Monday by a team celebration called Beer Night. A couple of days earlier, Harvard's entire freshman class had gathered at the Union for a rally to pump up the boys. Varsity head coach Bill Reid, who had been one of those gathered down at the White House a month earlier, spoke briefly, urging the freshmen to get out and support the team for Saturday's game.[13]

Though Harvard-Yale varsity football games were always an event, the freshmen teams wouldn't normally draw this much attention, let alone reporters from Boston, New York, and Washington papers. But there they were, lining the sidelines, waiting to watch Theodore Roosevelt Jr. line up at defensive end for the Harvard freshmen eleven.

The game was played on the well-worn freshman field in the shadow of a new thirty-thousand-seat varsity stadium. A large contingent of students had heeded Reid's call and stood along the sidelines with the usual "Kodak creatures." The weather was fall-like, chilly and overcast, but not rainy. The field was gridded in a checkerboard fashion, as was the custom and rule at the time. Lines ran both parallel to the end zones and perpendicular to them. Teams were not allowed to "split" ends outside the five-yard limits that the perpendicular lines marked.

As the teams took the field it was apparent that Yale's squad was bigger and faster, and it soon became obvious that they were more athletic as well. Ted was bareheaded as he and his teammates went through their warm-up drills, and his broad Roosevelt grin was nowhere in evidence as he measured the size of the Elis. They, too, were measuring his size, no doubt with more confidence.

As if to toy with him, the Yale boys focused their offense to the right side of Harvard's line, opposite Ted's left end. They ran at him only once, and he stopped the runner for no gain. As the game progressed, however, Yale attacked more and more on Ted's position, hoping to expose his lack of size with bone-crushing hits. Yale's heavier linemen and blocking backs kept pounding at Harvard's left end with speed and precision. The felt pads on his shoulders and elbows banged hard against ribs and knees, offering little protection. Despite his size, Ted took on interference and made tackles against the fullback and the quarterback, and caught one runner with a long diving stop that likely prevented a touchdown.[14]

In the second half, Yale hit Ted again and again. According to reports, he was at the bottom of almost every pile. "He tackled low and hard, and although light [of weight], he got into every play."[15]

But getting into every play meant taking elbows and knees to the head; shoulders to the rib cage; the weight of muscular two-hundred-pound college students grinding nose and cheekbones into the worn turf of the freshman field.

Covering a punt, he was hit by Yale blockers and was laid out for a full minute, feeling the spinning world of a semiconcussed head. Ted refused to quit, and as a result was fast winning over skeptics in the crowd who felt he had been chosen to start on the freshmen eleven because of his father.[16]

Yale scored a couple of touchdowns and a four-point field goal (the value of the score in that day) and was generally dominating play. The Elis had a solid 16–0 lead toward the end of the game, when a last Yale run toward Ted's side of the field knocked him loopy once again. As the *Washington Post* reported, "Finally a play came around his end that proved too much for the 145-pound boy. When the whistle blew and the men were pulled off the heap, there underneath everyone else, lay young Roosevelt, cut, bruised, and bleeding, unable to stir. This time he did not protest, but allowed himself to be carried to the locker building where he was patched up under the doctor's care." He left the field propped up between two teammates, his arms draped over their shoulders and his nose splayed across his face. Blood dripped down his chin. The crowd cheered long and loud for "young Roosevelt."

The Yale players showed respect for Ted after the game, particularly the Yale end who lined up opposite the president's son. Despite being several pounds heavier, he said Ted played him "to a standstill." Yale's coach provided the postmortem on his performance. "Too bad he's so light. He's the pluckiest man on the team, and if he had a little more beef he'd make things just a little more interesting."[17]

Ted's father wrote the next day to tell his son how proud he was, and also how glad he was that Ted weighed too little to be on the varsity team next year. On campus, so loud and sustained was the applause for Ted's gritty performance that speculation was rife that he'd ride a wave of new-found popularity to high office in the Harvard freshman class, perhaps even president.

A few days after the game, Ted wrote a note to reassure his mother regarding the newspaper reports he knew she had seen. "Saturday's game was a hard one," he said, "as I knew it was bound to be. I was not seriously hurt at all, just shaken up and bruised. The only thing that happened was that I broke my nose. . . . The setting of my nose caused me scarcely any pain at all."[18]

It also, Ted was pleased to note, happened to straighten the septum, which had been as crooked as a country road through earlier breaks. In Ted's mind, any pain and suffering caused by the game was nothing compared to the gains he'd made. He was now a college football player, a genuine Big Man on Campus of his own accord, and had gained a straight nose in the process, all while abiding by Roosevelt family principles. He had earned his spurs on the football field before all those reporters, all those doubters, all those naysayers who might have suspected that a cross-eyed little guy, the pampered son of the president, wasn't worthy.

FOUR

COMMENCEMENT

Nick Longworth was thirty-four years old and already saddled with the reputation of a hard-drinking Lothario when Alice, fourteen years younger and not deeply averse to any of his flaws, set her sights on him on the diplomatic tour of the Far East. Prematurely bald and in many ways an unlikely Romeo, Longworth was also a Harvard man, a member of the Porcellian Club—which included Theodore Roosevelt on its elite roster—and, most important in Alice's estimation, a protégé of William Howard Taft and thus a rising star in Republican circles. Her interest in Washington politics was already deep and abiding, and would last for the length of her long life, thus making Longworth a solid catch.

Taft became something of a chaperon for Longworth and Alice on the trip to the Far East, but Alice's expressiveness was not easily curtailed. On the cross-country train to San Francisco, even before the tour set sail for Japan, she made the papers by shooting fireworks off the back platform and taking potshots with a rifle at passing telegraph poles. When their ship, the *Manchuria,* landed in Hawaii for a layover, she and Nick lingered scandalously on Waikiki Beach so long that they missed their boat back to the ship. Back on board, Alice caused a scandal by jumping fully clothed into a pool on the ship's upper deck and luring one traveling congressmen to jump in after her. When Taft and the rest of the tour had finished its mission and set sail back to the States from Hong Kong, Alice and Longworth instead departed for China to visit the dowager empress in the Royal Palace near Peking.

By the time they wound their way home through Seoul and Japan, the pair had become unofficially engaged. By the end of November, after he'd asked the president for his daughter's hand, there was nothing unofficial about the relationship. TR thought that the older Longworth might help settle Alice down, a sentiment shared by Edith, who felt she sensed a growing maturity in her stepdaughter. At least she would not be primarily their problem now. The wedding was set for February 17, 1906.[1]

As his sister prepared for marriage, Ted was priming for eye surgery. He'd gone to the doctor for a checkup just after the New Year, and in early March the doctor advised Ted's parents that his wayward right eye was not getting better and ought to be corrected. Surgery would be necessary. "He says," wrote Theodore to his son at Harvard, "that the operation is painless and safe and could be done without interfering much with your studies."

This last consideration came with a heightened meaning: Ted had been placed on academic probation at Harvard after his first semester. Citing distractions from the newspaper crowd and normal adjustments to college life, Ted had proclaimed to his parents his innocence from simple neglect of his studies. But in fact, the press had caught Ted in a number of incriminating moments away from the books during the semester: at a James Corbett heavyweight boxing match in Boston ("I'd walk 100 miles to see a good set-to," he told a reporter afterward);[2] hunting for elk and wild boar in the mountains of New Hampshire with Harvard friends ("Roosevelt is a corker when it comes to shooting," said one of his companions to the newspapers);[3] and showing off his skills with a bullwhip at a sportsmen's show in Buffalo, New York, driving a team of bison across the arena to the delight of the audience.[4]

Writing to Kermit, who had recently entered Groton, the president bemoaned Ted's "Pendennis"-like characteristics—Pendennis being a character from a William Makepeace Thackeray novel who goes off to college, gets into a series of troubles, and must turn time and again to a rich uncle to bail him out.[5]

In fact, Ted was not innocent. Feeling his oats, making new friends at Harvard, developing a personality beyond the one nurtured and shaped by his father and mother, Ted was turning out to be a bit of a slacker.

The eye surgery was penance for his wayward ways. Either the doctor or the president had been a little misleading when they advised Ted that the surgery would be painless. In its wake, his father turned a little more sympathetic. "The doctor operated yesterday," Theodore wrote in another letter to Kermit, "and said Ted stood the knife as mighty few people can stand it. But it was a painful operation and painful afterwards, and [Ted] had to be kept for some hours in a dark room with a constant succession of cold water cloths put on his eye."[6] Ted's eye "looked gruesome" in the aftermath.[7]

There was another purpose to Theodore's letter: Kermit had earlier asked his father if he could graduate early from Groton, as brother Ted had. But Ted's freshman year at Harvard had hardly set a shining example for his younger brother. Part of the problem was Ted's simple lack of maturity, according to his father. "I do not think Ted has done particularly well this year at Harvard, in spite of getting on the freshman football team. He has not studied as I had hoped that he would study, and stands far behind George and even behind Monroe [two Roosevelt cousins]. He is off probation, but the Dean does not regard him as amounting to much."[8]

This hard assessment was not modified by Ted's next semester. In October, just weeks after the start of school, Ted went to the theater in Boston and was hustling across the Common to jump aboard a streetcar back to Cambridge. He felt someone chasing him as he ran and turned and stopped. He gave his pursuer what he later described as a shove, but it turned out the man Ted pushed was actually a plainclothes police officer patrolling the area because there had been a recent string of robberies there. The cop thought Ted might have been the thief in question.

Ted was hauled into the police station, grilled, and threatened with arrest. He was released after he was identified as the president's son. The arresting officer, however, subsequently claimed that Ted's little "shove" had actually consisted of some well-aimed punches. The policeman said that Ted, the college boxer, had broken his nose and a rib in the melee.

The chastened eldest son of the president headed down to Washington after the dust settled in Boston and waited for the fallout from his family. His punishment was mostly self-inflicted and came in the form of quiet reflection in his parents' company. Describing for Kermit what had happened, his father wrote, "Ted appeared early Friday morning; and that little bird was very, very glad indeed to get back to the nest. . . . During the three days [in Washington] he has never left the White House grounds and has spent the entire time in the company either of mother, Ethel or myself. . . . There never was any bunny person more delighted to come home and more keenly alive to his good luck in having such a sanctuary now that the world had gone hard with him."[9]

The dean at Harvard was forgiving of Ted. It turned out that the arresting officer, an Irish cop named Moran, was no political friend of Theodore Roosevelt or Republicans in general, and was trying to make "political capital" of the incident. According to the dean, Ted was innocent of the charges against him, including breaking the man's nose. "Still, although everyone now feels indignant on Ted's account, I suppose it cannot help having some little damaging effect on him, because the notoriety is unpleasant, and after a while people entirely forget the rights and wrongs of such a case and simply remember that there has been some disagreeable scrape in which the man was implicated."[10]

It was becoming obvious that Ted's college career was not going to be stellar. Though there were social and athletic triumphs—despite his predilection for bluntness of manner, he was a popular man on campus and got accepted into the Porcellian Club as his father had been, and he once again made the football team the following fall—Ted remained an academic disappointment. It was hard to know where, if in any direction, his scholar-ship was leading him.

By the following summer, he and his family agreed that it would probably be a good idea for Ted to graduate in three years, by the spring of 1908, rather than drag things out for another couple of terms. In August, Ted visited an old Rough Rider friend of his father's, John Greenway, in northern Minnesota. Greenway ran a mining company in that state's Iron Range, and Ted was interested in landing a postgraduate job under Greenway. He came back east with tentative plans to return to Harvard that fall (he was interested in playing one more year of football), but to close his college career the following spring. He would then head out to Minnesota to work in the mining industry.[11]

As it turned out, injuries kept Ted from playing much football in 1907, and by the time his last semester rolled around, beginning that winter, Ted's mind was wandering so far from school that he wound up once again on academic probation. Ted cut such a slew of classes that the dean wrote to his father, saying, "You may know where your son Ted is. We do not." In fact, Ted skipped a total of thirty-eight lectures that semester.[12]

His father's response was blistering: "There is not leeway for the small-est shortcoming on your part," he wrote his eldest boy. "Under no circum-stances and for no reason short of sickness which makes you unable to leave your room, should you cut class or a theme or fail to study hard right along. . . . I need not say to you to pay no heed whatever to athletics, to the social life, or to anything else that will in the slightest degree interfere with your studies. It is no use being popular in the class if you are going to be dropped out of class."[13]

Theodore let stream his exasperation further to Kermit. "Alas for Pendennis Ted . . . Now he is on probation again and for conduct so utterly silly that it is very hard to keep my patience with him. . . . I am really at a loss to understand how Ted could have been so silly." After comparing ten-year-old Quentin to his eldest son and to Archie, the least intellectu-ally gifted of his children, TR wrote that "I am not only irritated but I also become apprehensive as to how Ted will do in after life. All I can hope is that when he leaves college he will put away boyish things and turn in seriously, to work as he worked, and to show the character that he showed, during the year before he went to college."[14]

Theodore Roosevelt had long before made a promise not to seek a second full term as president, but as 1908 approached, many questioned whether he had made an error in judgment. While most elements of the Republican Party leadership, especially those corporate interests in the Eastern financial corridors of power who had felt the brunt of his Progressive reforms over the years, were more than happy to see him step aside, Roosevelt remained enormously popular with the general electorate, and the tug of that support was intoxicating.

He was finding, too, that his status as a lame duck president was emboldening his political opponents to stall reform efforts in both the legislative and judicial branches of government, which similarly stoked the president's righteousness. TR had thrown his support behind his secretary of war, William Howard Taft, as his successor, but already doubts that Taft would be a stalwart torch carrier for Roosevelt's legacy were beginning to invade Theodore's consciousness.

All of these doubts needed dampening, and the president decided to do so by planning a postpresidential journey. Kermit was graduating from Groton in the spring and Theodore decided that he and his second son should go on a grand hunting tour of East Africa. Keeping the details of the trip on the lowdown from Edith for the first part of the year—she would not be pleased to know that her husband, having just spent nearly eight years in the White House, was now considering a nine-month tour shooting big game on the continent of Africa—Theodore and Kermit plotted their adventure, swapping maps of their proposed hunting grounds and letters suggesting the best rifles to pack for their journey.[15]

As Theodore made preparations for life after the presidency, Ted finally buckled down and finished his studies at Harvard. He showed that if he applied himself, he could do the work, making excellent marks in his last term. Not only was he taken off probation, but he actually made the dean's list, pleasing both mother and father.

To further prove his maturation, Ted found his first job that summer on his own. It had been rumored that he would take a "high post with the Steel Trust"—the job with John Greenway's mining company, presumably—but that was not going to happen. Opting not to move to Minnesota, Ted instead took a post with the Hartford Carpet Company, a business owned by a fellow member of the Harvard Porcellian Club named Robert Perkins. In September, Ted moved to Thompsonville, Connecticut, and began learning the business from the ground up.

Ted's arrival in Connecticut quickly became news. The president's son taking a menial position in a carpet factory in a one-industry town "to face an almost barren social existence" was worrying to the *New York Times* in September 1908.[16] Beyond the fact that "Theater attractions [in Thompsonville] are limited to 'Uncle Tom's Cabin' and other productions as ordinary," there were questions about how long a Roosevelt would be willing to play the role of a working stiff. With the young man's full acquiescence, Perkins placed Ted in no special post in the company and paid him a workman's wage. "While the pictures of him in overalls work-ing overtime to master the business are doubtless not prophetic," Ted would be starting out in a low post.

His father, on the other hand, was all for a humbling turn for Ted. Theodore visited the company that month and pronounced himself "greatly impressed." He had always made clear to his sons that his income, through family means, book writing, and political offices, would never be enough to extend into the next generation; each of his boys would need to earn their own way in the world. Ted had set out to do just that.

It would be a stretch to say that Ted was cut out for the carpet busi-ness, but he certainly developed a way of working that would serve him well in the future. He entered into his job determined to keep his head down, be a regular guy, and learn the business he'd chosen to pursue from his new boss, Bob Perkins.

Ted was at least two inches shorter than younger brother Kermit, slightly built, with a sinewy and tough frame, as his father had had as a young man. Ted's wayward eye was improved somewhat by his surgery a couple of years earlier, but it still was not fully centered, and he still wore glasses. Ted's gaze in formal portraits continued to be serious, but he focused directly on the camera with a forthright expression.

Though Ted tried to remain anonymous to his fellow workers in Connecticut, any subterfuge was busted even before his father visited in his first month on the job. The fact that the press, which found novelty in the idea of a president's son working as a mill hand in New England, continued to write stories about him also made Ted stand out. As was the case almost everywhere he went, however, Ted became popular with his coworkers and actually acquired talents in the business. He developed a reputation as a skilled wool sorter—one of the chief talents at a carpet company. Through feel, smell, and actually tasting the raw wool, Ted was able to offer sound judgment on its quality—a decided gift in the world of carpets.[17]

While his long-range goals were somewhat uncertain, it is probably safe to say, as one historian does, that "Ted of all the boys . . . understood his role most clearly: to help his father in politics."[18] In the meantime, Ted was committed to learning something of the world of business from the ground up. Perhaps he was not pursuing a sparkling career, but sparkling was not turning out to be his character.

FIVE

LOVE AND MARRIAGE

"It was on the platform of the railroad station at New Haven, Connecticut, in October 1908 that I first saw Ted Roosevelt," wrote his future wife, Eleanor, many years after the fact. "I was not eager to meet the President's eldest son, whose name seemed always in the papers, as I thought he would be conceited and bumptious," she continued, sounding a bit like a Jane Austen imitator, "but there was no avoiding it because we were both going to a weekend party at Mrs. Arthur M. Dodge's at Simsbury."[1]

Rather than bumptious and conceited, young Ted turned out to be, in her eyes, a gallant young man, a good listener, and someone with a "remarkable faculty of making one feel one's best."[2] She was seated next to Ted at dinner that night, and by the end of the evening, he was bold enough to ask her to ride with him the next day in a chase that was part of the weekend entertainment. She agreed and went to bed that night "pleased with the world."

Eleanor Alexander was a slight young woman, with wavy chestnut-colored hair. She had pixyish features, and liquid eyes touched with a bit of melancholy that belied a surprisingly spunky personality. She and her mother had spent the summer out west at Yellowstone National Park, where they had done much horseback riding, and Eleanor was proud of her equestrian skills. In Yellowstone, she had grown used to Western-style riding and was made uneasy the next day, at Mrs. Dodge's stable, when she was given an Eastern-trained polo pony and a tiny English racing saddle. When she and Ted set out riding toward a field where the chase was to begin, Eleanor immediately began to slip and slide off the saddle. He helped her remount and adjust as best she could, but Eleanor's long hair came undone in the process and her mortification was immense. She stuffed her locks back beneath her hat as Ted held her bridle and reassured her. Eleanor was too unsettled to finish the ride, she told him, but worried about how all of this would be explained to her hostess and the other guests. She didn't have to worry about explaining anything to anyone, Ted told her. "Never make unnecessary explanations," he said with a Rooseveltian finality.[3]

As successful as their first meeting was, Ted and Eleanor didn't see one another until December, when they met again at the White House. Eleanor had been invited to Washington for a coming-out party for Ted's sister Ethel. Sparks lit once again, and Ted and Eleanor danced often that night. At the end of the evening, he asked Eleanor which train she was taking back to New York the next day, promising that he would be on it as well. A mix-up prevented the immediate continuation of their romance—he missed the train—but they were both smitten.

With his father and brother Kermit heading off to Africa on their extended hunting trip, Ted had no male presence looking over his shoulder and no brother to whom he would be compared. He seemed to thrive on the freedom, courting Eleanor with the same sort of dogged determination with which he was learning the carpet business. After working all week he traveled to New York on Saturday afternoons, spending the evening and the next day taking Eleanor out on walks to quiet areas of the city—up Riverside Drive, out around Grant's Tomb, back through the park—before returning to Connecticut to start his workweek again bright and early on Monday. It took persistence. Eleanor's mother, blue-blooded and moneyed, had the prejudice of the Wall Street crowd against the Roosevelt family. Being the son of Theodore Roosevelt brought no points in his favor.

Then again, feelings were mutual on the Roosevelt side; not only did TR, when first learning of the romance, confess in a letter to his sister that he deeply disliked Eleanor's father, but Eleanor's New York society background suggested to the Roosevelts the sort of pampered upbringing that they despised.

On her part, Eleanor sensed the feeling. Her first visit to Sagamore Hill did nothing to assuage her nervousness at meeting the formidable Roosevelt clan (even without Theodore and Kermit). No one was at the train station to greet her when she arrived at Oyster Bay. Of course there was nothing intentionally slighting about the lack of attention to her arrival; it was just that this sort of formality was unimportant to the Roosevelts. The ten minutes it took for the daunting wife of the ex-president to finally arrive in a little surrey to pick her up made Eleanor no more comfortable, nor did the fact that Edith was dressed like a housewife in the middle of a busy day while Eleanor was in a recent Fifth Avenue summer style. That Ted's mother proceeded to make a point of commenting about the stylish white kid gloves that Eleanor was wearing didn't help either—they weren't exactly country wear or Roosevelt style, Edith suggested. Nonetheless, Eleanor weathered the storm. In fact, somewhat like Edith herself, she turned out to be tougher emotionally than she appeared.

Her childhood had been difficult. Eleanor was raised by warring parents of high society who divorced when she was three years old, only to remarry when she was five, and divorce again when she was twelve. Her father, Henry Addison Alexander, was an attorney of Scottish descent (the family would summer in Scotland for many years) whose own primly Protestant family took the side of Eleanor's mother in the divorces. Her mother, Grace Green, had multiple ties to old New England that stretched back to the *Mayflower* (in fact, 120 by her mother's precise count), though the family money came by way of a dry goods business established by family "pioneers in the west" (Columbus, Ohio), as Eleanor put it in her autobiography.[4]

Eleanor was raised as an only child by her mother, her grandmother, and a variety of aunts and cousins. She lived in family homes in New York, California, Scotland, Rome, and Paris. Her mother, like Edith, was an intimidating presence whose guidance of Eleanor mixed the strictures of Victorian society mores and a cosmopolitan upbringing surrounded by artistic friends and relatives in New York and the capitals of Europe. Eleanor's relatively isolated upbringing made her a shy, sometimes uncertain girl, but one with grit and determination.

After her parents' second divorce, Eleanor and her mother returned to New York, where Eleanor attended Miss Spence's School for Girls, on the Upper East Side in Manhattan, on part of what is now Hunter College. She graduated in 1907 and met Ted the following year.

Their engagement was announced in February 1910 and predictably elicited a flood of newspaper copy and attention. Ted was used to it; Eleanor and her mother were not. Ted's future mother-in-law was appalled, and thought all of the notoriety was in the worst taste possible. She held Ted and the Roosevelt family responsible for the press circus.

Ted had written early to his father about the engagement, but he was still traveling. Though the African portion of the journey was over, the president had built several European sojourns into his schedule for the trip home and was in the midst of these when word of the engagement reached him. Ted's letter was full of excitement and anticipation. He wrote that Eleanor was much like his mother and sister Ethel but that she was nervous about meeting him. "It has been quite a nightmare for her," Ted wrote, "the thought of seeing you in case you did not like her. This has been largely removed by dear mother who assured her that you would. She also told Eleanor how to manage me and details of my character in which I resembled you. I asked Eleanor what they were and she said she might tell me in ten years after we were married."

He asked his father, if he hadn't done so already, to please write her a reassuring letter (which TR would soon do). A postscript to Ted's letter to his father suggests both Ted's feelings and his inability to fully express them. He was one nervous young man: "It is very difficult to write anything which really tells what one feels . . . I trust mother to let you know."[5]

Stories on the courtship and engagement had been in the news for weeks prior to the wedding day, with features and photographs speculating on what sort of dress Eleanor might wear and the fact that Ted was "no doubt . . . experiencing the most interesting chapter of his life."[6] The Roosevelt family might have been out of the White House for the past year, but to the newspapers, they remained the first family and Ted, the first son. As the story of his and Eleanor's romance dotted the society pages in the spring of 1910, he continued to return to the factory in Connecticut each Monday, where he would "don overalls and jumper"[7] and get busy sorting wool. In fact, he'd already left the floor and moved into sales, a first step up in the company. It was also announced that Ted had accepted a post as the Western manager of the carpet company in San Francisco, which is where he and his new bride would head soon after their wedding. More adventures were to come for Ted and Eleanor.

Ted and his best man, Kermit, stood at the front of the Fifth Avenue Presbyterian Church in Manhattan at four o'clock on June 20, 1910, awaiting his bride. Fifteen hundred invitations had been sent out, filling the church from pew to pew. Even more gawkers, well-wishers and Roosevelt supporters lined the sidewalks, standing six or seven deep for several blocks, cordoned off by mounted police to keep the crowds from halting traffic to the church.

Eleanor remembered the day as exceedingly hot, with guests awaiting her arrival fanning themselves in church pews. Neither bride nor groom was particularly religious (nor would they ever be), but they chose, despite getting married in the Fifth Avenue Presbyterian Church, to have the service conducted in Episcopalian traditions by a Methodist preacher who was a friend of Ted's. (The Presbyters would take a measure of revenge for this slight to their own church services and pastor. Eleanor found out many years later that the church failed to record their marriage in its annals.)[8]

Among those gathered on Fifth Avenue was a large contingent of ex–Rough Riders dressed in the khaki-colored uniforms of their service. Invitations had been extended to these men at the last moment from their former commander, Colonel Roosevelt. Upon TR's return from his hunting trip in Africa just two days earlier, he was greeted at the docks in New

York by this same contingent of his former mates. The colonel had naturally let it be known that they were welcome to come to the wedding of his eldest son. Now here they were. Twenty minutes before the service, some forty chosen Rough Riders marched in and sat as a unit within the church, the only guests allowed in the chapel without cards.

Other male guests at the service, the *New York Times* noted, were for the most part dressed in black coats and silk hats, except for a group of young men wearing straw boaters who turned out to be old friends of Ted's from Harvard's Hasty Pudding Club.

While Ted and Kermit waited at the altar, Theodore and Edith, along with sister Alice and her husband, Congressman Nicholas Longworth, were shown to their seats. Ethel, Archie, and Quentin all preceded the bride down the aisle as well.

Finally, Eleanor arrived at a side entrance to the church, stepping into the sanctuary to the strains of the "Bridal Chorus" from *Lohengrin*, wearing a gown of white satin draped in white tulle. Her bouquet was a mix of lilies of the valley and orange blossoms. A handful of bridesmaids, and her mother, who was to give the bride away, accompanied her. The service itself lasted only twenty minutes, before the couple exited the church at Fifth Avenue and climbed into a waiting car. They drove just around the corner to the reception at the home of Eleanor's uncle, across the street from the Plaza Hotel.

The reception was sparkling, though Eleanor later remembered that the Rough Riders ate most of the wedding cake.[9] Among the dignitaries at the reception was a host of Theodore's old Washington friends, including Henry Stimson, Senator Chauncey Depew, and Gifford Pinchot, who had served as TR's chief of the U.S. Forest Service. Toward the end of the festivities, while Eleanor disappeared with her bridesmaids to change into a "going away frock," Ted gathered with Porcellian friends in an upstairs library. There, the black steward of the Cambridge-based club, a man named Lewis, who was the third generation of his family to hold that position, concocted "his famous punch" for club members, with which they toasted Ted and his new bride.[10]

Kermit tied an old white shoe to the wedding getaway car, while an usher tied a box of rice with a hole cut in it, to leave a trail of grain behind the couple as they sped away. Ted had arranged with traffic cops outside the reception to prevent reporters from following their car as they left Manhattan, and he and Eleanor were successful in their getaway. The lovebirds were planning to honeymoon in California as a means to both see the ocean and investigate their new home in San Francisco. They spent the first few nights of marriage registering as Mr. and Mrs. Rogers in a Philadelphia hotel, then in a Chicago hotel. It was at the Blackstone in Chicago, however, that the press discovered the ruse and proceeded to follow them all the way to the St. Francis Hotel in San Francisco. There, Ted agreed to meet with one reporter if he would share the contents of the interview with the rest. It was done, and Ted sat with a single journalist who passed on the news, such as it was, to the others. Years later, recalling this moment in her marriage prompted Eleanor to write, "The disadvantage of being a great man's son far outweigh the advantages."[11]

Ted and Eleanor spent two happy newlywed years in California, living in a little house overlooking the Golden Gate strait. The home was framed by pink geranium-filled window boxes and gardens lush with roses, dahlias, and spring-flowering bulbs. They were quick to begin a family—their daughter, Grace, was born there in 1911—and Ted learned enough about business to gain the confidence to move beyond carpet manufacturing.

Ted also began to inch his way into the political world. In California, he became more politically independent, leaning strongly toward the Progressive causes of his father and away from the Republican Party of William Howard Taft. Even before Theodore had returned from Africa, Ted had written his father with criticisms of Taft's presidency, emphasizing the president's lack of "character." "No one attributes anything wrong to him but all say that he is a weak man and incapable of filling so large a position to anything but disadvantage. It seems to me that they are probably right. His policy has been one long vacillation."[12] Later, before his father inched into the 1912 presidential race, Ted wrote to Theodore that he would be inclined to vote for Woodrow Wilson in a race between Taft and the New Jersey governor, about as near to heresy as a son could get in the lifelong Republican Roosevelt family. In 1910, Ted was an early supporter of the reformer and progressive candidate for California governor, Hiram Johnson, who would win the office in November.

Ted wrote to his father about his upcoming professional plans as well. Despite his comfort in San Francisco, Ted thought he would stay on the West Coast for just two more years, and was already entertaining an offer from a friend in New York "so that I could have two strings to my bow." He appreciated his Connecticut friend and mentor Bob Perkins—"all the way through [he] has really made me . . . by doing something far harder than advising, namely not advising, and keeping his finger out of the pie and letting me learn things by myself." It was clear, however, that the carpet business was a stepping-stone to something else.[13]

Ted did well ingratiating himself to the community of businesspeople in San Francisco. When he was accused by an anonymous reporter for an Oakland paper at a 1912 event of "seeking at a social party by direct and ill-mannered inquiry to discover the presidential preferences of those present," the *San Francisco Chronicle* editorial staff took exception: "By all who knew Roosevelt, this story stands discredited on its face. It is not possible that this young man, who through two years' residence here has won general respect by his amiability, his graciousness, and his unvarying modesty should all of a sudden descend to the character of a rudely insistent political inquisitor."[14]

In most everything he did, Ted's efforts were intense and consuming. So it was in San Francisco, where he put in long hours in the carpet manufacturing business despite the fact that he had no intention of making a career of it. Eleanor traced the intensity of effort to Theodore, to whom Ted always "must prove worthy." Financial gain meant little. "His business career was nothing but the means to an end," she wrote. "His desire was to get it over and done with as fast as possible. Personal ambition meant little."[15]

In early 1912, Ted accepted a position at a New York financial firm. The guests at a going-away party thrown for him at the Pacific Union Club on Nob Hill was a who's who of San Francisco politics and business, both Democrats and Republicans. Young Roosevelt was saluted "for himself as much as for his illustrious father." For his part, Ted hinted that he might have a political future in California. "I am leaving tomorrow for New York but I am not going to say goodbye to you. If I ever get the chance, and I am going to try to make the chance, I am coming back. It has been a great privilege to work with you for the interest of the city and the country."[16]

In Manhattan, Ted and Eleanor found a house on East Seventy-fourth Street—"not half as attractive" as their home in San Francisco, according to Eleanor, "but Ted always loved any house we had and thought it was beautiful." He worked selling bonds for a firm called Bertron Griscom & Company and at the same time made his first foray into national politics by helping his father at the Republican National Convention of 1912 in Chicago, and then helping to form the new Bull Moose Party afterward.

The campaign turned out to be disastrous in a number of ways. TR's efforts at reclaiming the presidency as a third-party candidate proved too steep a hill to climb. In the process, he alienated many old friends in the Republican Party, including the Republican he ran against, William Howard Taft. TR essentially handed the presidency to Democrat Woodrow Wilson.

Not only that, but while TR was on the campaign trail in Milwaukee, on October 14, 1912, a would-be assassin named John Schrank fired a pistol at point-blank range into Roosevelt's chest. The shot was deflected by Theodore's glasses case as well as by the folded and lengthy address that he was about to give, both of which he carried in his breast pocket. This padding saved his life but didn't prevent the bullet from penetrating his chest. In a show of remarkable fortitude, TR didn't cancel his speech, but instead wound up orating for an hour and a half with the lead buried just shy of his lungs.

He finally consented to emergency care after his talk, and then traveled from Milwaukee to a hospital in Chicago. He was joined there the next day by Edith, Ethel, Alice, Ted, and the faithful Dr. Lambert. His wound ultimately laid him up for two weeks in the vital closing days of the campaign, but his defeat was all but certain. By the time Theodore was well enough to make the long train ride home to New York and convalesce at Sagamore Hill, the election was over but for the counting of votes. In the first week of November, returns indicated that Woodrow Wilson would be the new president.[17]

Theodore subsequently busied himself with writing projects over the winter, and pretended to be content as a man of leisure in Oyster Bay. Nick Longworth had lost his congressional seat in the November election, and he and Alice felt the gloom as well. Alice, in particular, was out of sorts because she was exiled back to Cincinnati, Nick's hometown, where she was forced to exist in the provinces, well outside of the Washington social scene.

In the spring, Ethel married a lanky Manhattan doctor named Richard Derby. They honeymooned in Europe, where Edith soon joined them. Meanwhile, back at Oyster Bay, her husband began to formulate plans for a new grand adventure. Just as he had after his last bout with gray skies, back when he first gave up the presidency to Taft, Theodore was thinking of traveling. Again he would call on Kermit as his companion, but this time they would head to South America. There flowed a great, unexplored river that twisted right through the heart of Brazil north to the Amazon. Never mind that Theodore was now in his midfifties, that he'd just been shot in the chest, that his grandchildren were beginning to fill the family home, and that his wife was looking forward to his company. Theodore Roosevelt was not a man to settle down. The jungles of the Amazon beckoned.

Eleanor finally got her first extensive dose of life at Oyster Bay that summer. Theodore announced one day that they were all going on a picnic. About a dozen Roosevelts, including cousins, were gathered by ten on a morning already scorched with heat. After walking a half mile through woods thick with mosquitoes to the beach "as fast as we could put one foot before the other," they hit the sand, where five rowboats rested. Eleanor thought she would be offered a comfortable chair set up in the stern of one of the boats, but she was wrong. After a scramble for seating, she found the only space available to her was in the bottom of a boat helmed by her father-in-law and a cousin. She was squeezed in with a basket of clams and a jug of water.

The five boats rowed out into the sound, checking for premier picnic spots as they sweated at the oars. After a time, Eleanor began to eagerly suggest locations—any location—but all were turned down as being not good enough. After two hours, "we landed on a beach precisely like the one we had started from except that it was farther from home."

Despite the heat, seaweed and stones were gathered, a searing fire was lit, and the clams were steamed and readied for eating. Eleanor had never eaten clams baked in such a manner, and she burned her mouth on her inaugural bite and subsequently found the mollusk sand-filled and rubbery. She looked for an opportunity to dispose of it and tried to shove it discreetly under the log on which she was sitting, but she was caught and teased for it by her father-in-law.

When the picnic was finally done, the whole crew climbed back in their rowboats and set off, once again, for Oyster Bay. Unfortunately, a headwind and a leaky boat doubled the time it took them to return. As evening came and they finally reached shore, all of the Roosevelts, according to Eleanor, declared this "one of the best picnics we ever had."[18]

Of all the Roosevelt brothers, Kermit remained the one most intimately connected to their father—or at least the one who appealed most to TR's literary, artistic, and intellectual bents. Their correspondence was voluminous and deep. But Ted was asserting himself as the leader of the next generation, a fact that TR recognized in a letter to Kermit: "Not only do I feel that you can count on him . . . I feel he will be a competent advisor for Archie and Quentin when they are launched into the world."[19]

Archie, the latest Roosevelt to attend Groton, had grown depressed there; it was a condition that would periodically visit him for the rest of his life. In typical family style, it was thought that the best medicine was a stint in the great outdoors. So he was sent out to the Arizona high desert for a term, where he became more independent and self-reliant. "He is sometimes short on intellect," TR wrote Ted, "[but] he is long on character, which is a might [*sic*] sight more important."[20] Unfortunately Archie, who had always seemed to take moral suasion a little bit more seriously than the others, was turning into a bit of a prig. He was unpopular at Harvard, in part because he had ratted on a pair of fellow students who had brought a "loose" woman into campus lodgings.[21] He didn't get invited to join the Porcellian Club despite efforts on his behalf from Porcellian Ted.

Quentin, the fair-haired baby of the family, was off to Groton. Those closest to the Roosevelts felt he might prove to be the real star of the next generation: he was intelligent and witty, and had a gift for writing. He was also mechanical and liked to monkey around with motorcycles.

Kermit had returned from his African hunting trip to finish his studies in engineering at Harvard. He was already showing a deep propensity for travel and adventure. He took a trip to New Brunswick in 1911 to stalk moose, then a solo trip across the Sonoran Desert in Mexico, which he wrote about for *Scribner's*. In early 1913, he made plans to move to South America to work for an engineering firm—the move that first prompted his father's interest in the expedition up the River of Doubt.

Theodore wrote a revealing letter detailing family dynamics to Kermit in 1913, just after his move to Brazil. Edith was still in Europe when Ted, Eleanor, and Alice arrived to keep TR company. The visit reminded Theodore of old times when "you were all small." His guests "chattered immensely and had an immense number of plans and none of the plans ever came to anything. Ted and Eleanor and Alice had a feeling as if in the absence of mother that they could impose all their least desirable friends on pagan old father. Accordingly, they planned various delightfully wicked feasts of friends whom they thought mother would not like to have, and enjoyed themselves as much as if the feasts had come off, although as a matter of fact, nothing ever happened except for two very small stodgily virtuous dinners."

When Archie and Quentin joined the gathering later in the week, Archie, the puritan of the clan, "felt there were too many people in the house and started to assume control. . . . Alice, Eleanor and Ted at once formed a furious league against him, and after twenty-four hours we reached a working compromise and definitely enthroned Eleanor as sole mistress. She runs the household admirably, and is too darling for anything. I tell you, Ted's a lucky fellow. I hope you will be as lucky when you marry—remember you can marry whenever you want to, for that is the kind of expense for which mother and I will be only too delighted to give up anything."[22]

When Edith got wind of the gathering at Sagamore, she rushed home from Europe to take charge of her own household and put a leash on any more frivolity. Any residual anger at the partying quickly dissipated at Oyster Bay, however, as Edith acknowledged that there were greater problems to worry about. Her husband's plans to travel through the wilds of South America had now advanced to the point of inevitability. In October, she sailed with Theodore to Brazil, where Edith handed him off to the care of Kermit and the Almighty for their fateful trip up the River of Doubt. He returned the following May a changed man, one who had weathered the most serious health concerns of his life, both physical and mental. Struck by jungle fevers, barely surviving the journey to the extent that at one desperate point he seriously considered taking his own life so as not to slow the other suffering members of the expedition, Roosevelt pulled into New York Harbor grateful to be alive.

Ted was dockside to greet him. He offered an arm at the gangway to his obviously weakened father, who swatted it aside. "I am all right," he said. "I can take care of myself."[23]

Maybe for the time being, but the spirit of Theodore Roosevelt, challenged and battered in South America, would soon be tested in ways it had never been tested before.

SIX

PLATTSBURGH

At about lunchtime on May 7, 1915, a bright and beautiful day, passengers on the ocean liner *Lusitania*, the pride of the Cunard Line, were just sitting down to their meals when a torpedo slammed into the ship's hull. The cruiser was sailing east just off the coast of Ireland through the Irish Channel toward Liverpool, where it intended to deliver more than 1,200 passengers and a crew of seven hundred before the day was through. Lurking directly in its path was the German submarine *U-20*, hoping to intersect the course of just such a giant steamer as the *Lusitania*.

Three hundred fifty pounds of explosives erupted at impact against the hull of the liner, sending "a geyser of seawater, planking, rope, and shards of steel . . . upward to twice the height of the ship."[1] The ship continued forward as the geyser and its debris, bubbling for a moment on jets of water, finally rained down on helpless passengers and crew bobbing in the sea. As a hole "the size of a small house" appeared in the ship's starboard side, water began flooding into boiler rooms belowdecks, trapping engineers, firemen, and boiler tenders in the horrible maelstrom. Soon the ship was listing toward the weight of the seawater pouring in to starboard, and its fate was sealed. It traveled for two more miles, about fifteen minutes of a ghostly cruise, before its bow nosed down, its stern rose briefly from the water, and it sank to the deep.

Only six of the ship's twenty-two lifeboats were safely detached before the liner went down. Of the 1,900-some passengers and crew aboard the cruise, 764 were picked up by rescue craft speeding from the Irish coast. Among the dead were 123 Americans. News of the disaster quickly reached telegraph wires. Word of the treachery of the German U-boat was spread all over the world, and predictable outrage followed.[2]

Up in Syracuse, New York, Theodore, in the midst of a libel suit at the courthouse there, took a midnight call from an AP reporter, who gave the ex-president the full facts of the *Lusitania*'s sinking as they were known, and asked Roosevelt if he'd care to make a statement. TR had been apprised of the bare circumstances of the tragedy a few hours earlier, and was prepared for the call. Germany had committed a barbaric act of outright murder, he said. "It is warfare against innocent[s] traveling on the ocean, and to our fellow countrywomen, who are among the sufferers." The United States had to respond. It was "inconceivable" that the country could "refrain from taking action in this matter, for we owe it not only to humanity but to our own national self-respect."[3]

Roosevelt's bellicosity, hardly surprising since he'd been espousing a prowar line for months, had a good deal of support in the first few days after the sinking of the *Lusitania*. In New York, a huge crowd gathered in Times Square in a loud demonstration supporting war. Newspapers across the country editorialized in favor of some strong reaction against Germany, though significantly just a handful declared for an outright need for war.

Among Ted's peers in New York there was a strong sentiment in favor of a military response. He, along with many Wall Streeters, signed a petition to that effect and sent it to President Wilson. A gathering of Harvard grads that Ted attended and contributed to was held the day after the ocean liner sank. The attendees discussed creating a training camp for young men like themselves to prepare for service in the war. Ted and Eleanor had actually booked a future passage on the ship, and their concerns consequently had a personal sensibility. This unjust attack would have to be the tipping point for the Wilson administration to get involved in the war, they felt. Continued demonstrations on the streets of New York and elsewhere in the country urged Wilson toward action. Ted wrote brother Kermit, who was working as an engineer in South America, that in the wake of the sinking of the *Lusitania*, "I believe war is thoroughly possible."[4]

But the fact was that there was a stark division among the American people between those who saw this German aggression as the final straw in a long list of transgressions against U.S. sovereignty and those who wanted to avoid war in Europe even at the cost of the 123 American lives lost in the *Lusitania* tragedy. As a nation, the United States had a long tradition and commitment to staying in its own hemisphere and watching out for its own interests. European wars must be settled in Europe, went this argument; the problems plaguing "the Old World" would not be solved by the loss of even more American lives sent to fight in the terrible war currently being waged in France. The majority of the populace was no more inclined to jump full-bodied into that conflict than the administration, which continued to steer clear of the conflagration. Its response to the torpedo that sank the great ocean liner was a stern finger-shake at the kaiser and his aggressive U-boat campaign.

Not so Theodore Roosevelt. While he had shown some restraint in the first few months following the outbreak of war in Europe in 1914, Roosevelt was, in the words of one historian, "a warhawk by temperament and principle." He was soon urging the Wilson administration to prepare at the very least for the inevitable moment when the United States would be drawn into the conflict. Now, with the sinking of the *Lusitania*, his critique of Wilson's hesitance became harshly personal. TR began a relentless haranguing of the president, and anyone else who would listen, about the need to get involved in the European war.[5] When it became apparent that the Wilson administration was not going to steer the country into the fight, Roosevelt, with his son Ted's avid approval, began to argue for and formulate what has been labeled "The Gospel of Preparedness" in response.

Taking elements from military reforms suggested by his friend and former superior officer with the Rough Riders, Leonard Wood, the preparedness that Theodore espoused called first and foremost for universal national service. Wood and Roosevelt saw the military as a means to both bulk up the American army for war in Europe and to have it serve as a democratizing tool for the flood of immigrants coming into the nation. Many of these newcomers would inevitably wind up in service. What better means to educate them on the demands and privileges of their new nation than to have their introduction to the United States begin with service? This would also help to alleviate the roiling class conflicts that were at the heart of so much of the world's upheaval in the first years of the twentieth century.

Universal service would also incorporate society's upper crust. As with their experience forming the Rough Riders some seventeen years earlier, Wood and Roosevelt envisioned a service led by an invigorated elite of the sort TR was raising in his own family—physically fit and morally righteous. The young man of the Ivy League, the world of Wall Street, the educated classes across the country would be drawn into service to become better citizens, aware of the demands of their privilege and dedicated to their nation. Theirs would be an education primarily in the military arts.

Wilson and the many Americans who doubted the necessity of sending Americans to Europe to fight distant battles came to represent the antithesis of the Gospel of Preparedness. Their cautions, their championing of American isolation and restraint, their traditional American reservations about large armies and large governmental institutions fighting in wars on grounds outside the United States collided head on with Roosevelt's moral certitudes and "bully" assertions.

In the back of many American minds rested the deep trauma and scars of the Civil War. The dear sacrifices asked of and given by millions of Americans in that nineteenth-century war would not be given again cheaply in the lifetimes of their twentieth-century descendants.

Almost certainly, this very connection was the psychological root of the Roosevelt family obsession with military service. Theodore Roosevelt Sr.'s shirking of duty during the Civil War was a matter never discussed among the Roosevelt men, except perhaps as an allusion in an oft-quoted comment from Theodore to Ted: "I would much rather explain why I

went to the war than why I did not."[6] The fact that the Roosevelt men—
Theodore, Ted, Archie, and to a lesser extent, Kermit—held shirking,
especially among the rich, in utter disregard and contempt was inextri-
cably linked to the family's Original Sin.

Working in business in New York, Ted discovered that the name Roosevelt
was no great help on Wall Street; few titans of the business world could
countenance his father's progressive politics. Yet Ted's Ivy League connections and his God-given people skills made him a natural in the world
of finance. In 1914, Ted moved into a partnership at the Manhattan office
of a Philadelphia-based brokerage house, Montgomery, Clothier, and
Tyler, and quickly grew successful. Pumping most of his salary back into
the business and then borrowing funds from the firm to live on, Ted's
family saved money through their own frugality. The psychological effect
of living on borrowed money kept their spending to a minimum. According to Eleanor, Ted "practiced all sorts of economies . . . wearing his ready-
made suits til they shone, his shoes until they developed holes, smoking
the cheapest tobacco, taking few if any holidays." They didn't even own
a family car.[7]

Ted's business acumen led him into a world of money that the Roosevelt family had never been a part of, and some in the family turned up
their noses at the notion that he and Eleanor were now rubbing elbows
with Wall Street financiers and plutocrats. Ted's successes with finances,
however, would put him and his family on solid footing for decades to
come, a fact he was proud of. He and Eleanor had earned and saved enough
money to live on investment income and public service money for many
years, an advantage that allowed him to focus on other matters.[8] After the
informal gathering of the Harvard Club, in the wake of the *Lusitania* sinking, Ted and his well-heeled Wall Street friends held a follow-up meeting
to continue discussing an officers' training camp. Invited to address the
group of lawyers, bankers, and brokers was General Leonard Wood, who
had already organized some training camps for college students on the
East Coast. Now he suggested that similar training among postgraduates,

with an eye toward developing a coterie of reserve officers, would prove beneficial to the regular army.

A location for the training session was found near the Canadian border in New York, at an already established camp in Plattsburgh, and a month-long assembly was scheduled for August. Several thousand invitations were sent to college graduates through alumni associations throughout the country, and hundreds showed up for the first training session, in 1915.

From the very beginning of his instruction at Plattsburgh, Ted was a dedicated student of military training and tactics. Yet he had long shown an inclination toward military service. While a young man living at the White House, an army balloon ride convinced him to consider a future in aeronautics, and he signed up for membership in the D.C. Aero Club. Later, in Connecticut, he joined the local National Guard, and within three months was appointed by the state governor to the post of military aide at the Guard rank of major, resigning only after his move to San Francisco.

At Plattsburgh, a *New York Times* photographer caught several shots of Ted in intense drill, including one photo of him illustrating the proper use of a bayonet to a fellow camper. "We took it all very seriously," he would later write. "At one end of the company street you would see two prominent middle-aged business men trying to do the manual of arms properly, rain dripping off them, their faces set like day of judgment, crowned with grizzled hair. At the other would be Arthur Woods, the Police Commissioner of New York, boning the infantry drill regulations. George Wharton Pepper [a law professor and future U.S. senator from Pennsylvania] was promoted to sergeant, and was as proud of it as of any of his achievements in civil life. Bishop Perry of Rhode Island was named as color sergeant."[9]

The next summer, both Ted and Archie, just out of Harvard, went off to Plattsburgh, despite the fact that the first gathering had been criticized by, among others, Richard Harding Davis, his father's old champion from Spanish American War days, who thought the 1915 Plattsburgh camp had smacked too much of Ivy League mates playing at soldiering. Ted inadvertently added to this perception by lauding in a letter to Kermit the number of Harvard boys as compared to Yalies who had signed up for the camp, as if it were game day once again at Cambridge.[10]

With General Wood leading the training, Theodore Roosevelt giving his wholehearted blessing, and two of TR's sons not only participating at Plattsburgh, but also active in the organization of other camps, it was easy to see a correlation between these sessions and Roosevelt's creation of the Rough Riders a generation earlier. Eventually these camps would be modeled in other locales across the country and would provide the American Expeditionary Force (AEF) with several thousand officers (an estimated twenty thousand by some counts) in the early days of the war, when officer talent was at a premium.

In January 1917, Germany's foreign secretary, Arthur Zimmermann, cabled the Mexican government with an offer of support should Mexico try to reclaim the territory it had lost to the United States in the nineteenth century. It was a desperate attempt to nudge America's southern neighbor into the hostilities, thereby keeping the United States from becoming a threat to Germany. British intelligence intercepted the wire and passed it on to American officials. Soon after the notorious Zimmermann telegram was publicly revealed, the nation's momentum for war became overwhelming. A declaration of war finally came in the first week of April.

The day it happened, TR visited his cousin Franklin, who was serving in Theodore's old office in Washington as assistant secretary of the navy. First he encouraged Franklin to resign his post and volunteer for service, as the colonel himself had done back in 1898. Rebuffed in that request, TR asked for Franklin's help in getting an audience with the president to plug his idea of forming his own regiment. Through his boss, the secretary of the navy, FDR was able to arrange that meeting, but it did no good for Theodore, who in fact was given a subtle poke by Wilson's chief adviser as he was leaving the meeting. After his visit with the president came to a close, TR was escorted out by Colonel House. Discouraged, Roosevelt said to House, "I don't believe he will let me go to France. I don't understand. After all, I'm only asking to be allowed to die." To this

House is supposed to have said, drolly, "Oh? Did you make that point quite clear to the President?"[11]

With Theodore's hopes of serving in Europe dashed, he focused on situating his four sons in the service. By the spring of 1917, Ted and Archie were pretty well ensconced through the Plattsburgh camps. Kermit, who had just welcomed his first son with his wife, Belle, returned to the States from South America in preparation for heading overseas with his brothers. Efforts were made to find him a place in the 1917 camp at Plattsburgh, but he stayed there only briefly before joining British forces serving in Meso-potamia.[12]

Quentin was a senior at Harvard and contemplating his future. He had begun dating Flora Whitney, a great-granddaughter of Cornelius Vanderbilt and Henry Payne Whitney, two prime members of New York and Newport, Rhode Island, blueblood society. She was artistic, a budding sculptor—in fact, she would eventually come to run the Whitney Art Gallery in New York City. Quentin was literary and possessed a wicked sense of humor. The two fell in love in the year before America's entry into the war.

This sort of relationship was antithetical to the Roosevelt family's political and puritanical thinking. The Whitneys were too moneyed and frivolous for the Roosevelts' taste. Of course, the romance was perhaps even more antithetical to the wishes of the Whitney family.[13] Quentin had a bit of a rebellious streak, however, and wasn't certain he wanted to join the family in lockstep behind his father. Nor was he certain about heading off to war. Yet it would be impossible, given his father's sentiments about serving the country, to avoid service. He pondered joining his brother Archie in the infantry, but his weak eyes disqualified him.

Dutifully, Quentin phoned his father from Harvard and announced he was enlisting in the nascent air corps, where his mechanical abilities would stand him in good stead. He joined the air service and was sent off to train at an airfield in Mineola on Long Island. By the time of America's entry into the war, Ted and Eleanor were raising three children: Grace, Ted III, and newcomer Cornelius (the boys, only sixteen months apart, were called "the old baby" and "the new baby"). Despite his growing suc-cesses and his young family, Ted, now just shy of thirty years old, was the most enthusiastic of all the Roosevelt sons for heading to Europe, with the possible exception of brother Archie. With his father's example of being the most vocal and enthusiastic war supporter in the nation, its chief proponent of service, and a man with a personal history of heroic and voluntary war duty, it would have been extremely difficult for any of the Roosevelt men to avoid service in World War I, but Ted's enthusiasm was his own and deep and genuine.

His diligence and enthusiasm at Plattsburgh won him a commission as a major in the reserve officers corps, signed by President Wilson in February. After the declaration of war, Ted and Archie went off once again to Plattsburgh in preparation for heading to Europe. A month after arriving, rumors began circulating that a small expeditionary force was about to be shipped to France, and Ted called his father to see if TR could pull strings to get him and Archie sent along. They even offered to go as enlisted men, but General Pershing, who heard the request from the former president, determined that the Roosevelt boys would sail with his headquarters command with no reduction in rank. Ted and his brother Archie shipped from New York for Bordeaux on June 18, 1917, with a varied group of Red Cross workers and Frenchmen returning from the States to their homeland.

Just how much of Ted Roosevelt's enthusiasm for this war was colored by the example of witnessing, as an adoring ten-year-old, his father's triumphant action in the Spanish American War, and all of the subsequent fame and glory that came Theodore's way afterward, is speculation. That this war was a far different beast from that "splendid little" conflict in Cuba was common and accepted knowledge among the men shipping to Europe that June. Just how different would not be known until they arrived in its midst. The horrors of the Great War would challenge perceptions of fighting for millions around the globe for all time, not least of all for Theodore Roosevelt and all his children.

SEVEN

OVER THERE

From Bordeaux, Ted and Archie entrained to Paris, all the way entertaining questions from eager French passengers who wondered when the real body of American troops would be arriving. The French were impressed that the sons of the famed ex-president, known far and wide as an advocate for American entry into the war, were coming in the first wave of troops. But on the Fourth of July, in a parade designed to signify the arrival of an American force in Europe, only a single battalion marched through the treelined boulevards of Paris, where they presented the U.S. flag to descendants of Lafayette's troops at the Court of les Invalides. Despite all the pomp and circumstance, many Parisiennes could be forgiven for wondering where the rest of the doughboys were.

The U.S. Army's own chief of staff, General John Joseph Pershing, was himself less than enthused by what he saw; not only were their numbers skimpy, but also the deportment of the troops was hardly spit and polish. This was a force that was by no means prepared to join the French and British in the trenches anytime soon, and Pershing knew it. The first order of business for the freshly arrived troops was to be trained for battle, which meant that beyond the regular army officers and enlisted soldiers, some of the newly minted officer trainees from camps such as Plattsburgh would need to assume command roles from the start.

In mid-July, Major Theodore Roosevelt Jr. was given charge of the 1st Battalion of the 26th Infantry Regiment of the 1st Division, a nice feather in his cap. The commander of the regiment was short-staffed, Ted explained in a letter to his father, and his name came up to fill the post.[1] Ted wondered—as did the several officers in the regiment whom he leap-frogged to get the post—if any sort of favoritism had been employed to boost his standing. He mentioned these concerns to his father, but tried to dismiss any hint of his own uneasiness by writing with bluff, "it's all in a day's work and will make things interesting."

Interesting to say the least. Ted had vaulted beyond a couple of majors from the regular army to be chosen commander of the battalion, and resentments toward him were keen. According to the man who served as his adjutant for much of the war, Charles Ridgeley, everyone from Colonel Hamilton Smith, the regimental commander, "to the captains commanding companies in the First Battalion, all of whom had been sergeants in the regular army," treated him with faint respect. They quickly dubbed his unit "the White House Battalion" because it was assumed that his father had engineered his posting.[2]

For the time being, Ted had other concerns: Eleanor had decided to leave the children in the care of her mother and sail to France to serve in some capacity with the Allies. Ted hemmed and hawed over the idea, liking the notion that she would be there with him in Europe but concerned over her safety and the care of the children. Now despite his instructions to her not to come until he advised her that overseas travel was safe, Eleanor had sailed from New York of her own accord. She had learned of a plan to limit wives from traveling to France and quickly booked passage before it went into effect. As he settled into a training routine with his troops, she occupied a townhome with a garden on the Avenue du Bois de Boulogne, near the Seine and within sight of the Eiffel Tower. An aunt of hers owned the place adjacent, and she encouraged Eleanor to occupy the townhome as a sort of salon for all Roosevelts serving overseas (there would be many before the war was over). After establishing herself at her wartime residence, Eleanor sought out the YMCA to volunteer her services and was soon placed in charge of all women volunteers in the Paris office.

Ted wrote her, "Now that you are over here, I don't want you to leave until the war is over." He told her that he was "up against a very hard job," and was worried that he might not get to see her at all. He was determined to get his battalion into fighting shape as quickly and efficiently as possible so that he and it would be the first unit sent to the front lines.

Meanwhile, his father wrote to Archie to offer updates on the family and express his pride in what Ted and Archie were doing in France. He complained about the slow pace of the troop buildup in Europe, and again he pined for the opportunity to be there leading troops himself. "Not that I could do much with the training; but I would have at least one hundred thousand volunteers, of just the type of those in my regiment [in Cuba] in France now if I had been allowed to act six months ago."[3]

Ted and the 26th were quickly shuttled out of Paris and wound up billeted in a small French town named Demange-aux-Eaux to the east, near Nancy. There Roosevelt and the American doughboys acclimated to French provincial culture, which was more impoverished and rural than many anticipated. None of the homes had running water, so baths were taken in a stream that ran through the heart of the village. The infantrymen slept for the most part in haylofts in the family barns among the animals and farm implements. Ted had to often deal with outraged French families who accused his troops of stewing any number of the ubiquitous rabbits, which were a consistent part of the Gallic farms.

To help amuse and occupy his men, Ted wired Eleanor back in Paris and asked her, through her YMCA connections, to gather "12 BARRELS SOFT DRINKS TEN POUNDS TOBACCO PHONOGRAPH AND RECORDS COMPLETE BASEBALL OUTFIT TWELVE PAIRS BOXING GLOVES TWELVE SOCCER BALLS SIX BASKETBALLS EIGHT FIFES EIGHT DRUMS AND STICK GOOD SADDLE HORSES SADDLE AND BRIDLE."[4] He paid for the supplies out of his own pocket.

Training consisted of practice with hand grenades, rifle grenades, automatic rifles, rifles, bayonets, and trench digging. The American troops trained with a French battalion that was also billeted in Demange-aux-Eaux. The social and cultural differences caused some tensions. As veterans of the war, the French felt the Americans could learn much simply by watching them train. Asking a Roosevelt to sit back and observe, however, was a fool's errand. Most of the Americans felt the same way, but of course few of them knew much about throwing a grenade, firing a rifle or a mortar, or surviving a bombardment. To add to the oddity of the mix, the French troops were there as a break from action at the front. Training the Americans was light duty by comparison, and they were not terribly interested in overworking themselves. Roosevelt and the 26th, on the other hand, understood that they needed a lot of work to get combat ready and were eager to learn.

In August Ted traveled to the front for the first time. Touring with a group of field officers, he visited a locale near Nancy, near where Charles the Bold fought Louis XI in the fifteenth century, and much more recently, where the kaiser watched as his troops first streamed into France three years earlier. Here Ted saw his first trenches, and went on his first patrol into no-man's-land. The area between the trenches was broader and more cluttered with wire than he'd expected, but the nighttime patrol that he accompanied was undertaken with no casualties, and Ted returned safely to the Allied lines.[5]

Pershing had long anticipated that the 1st Division—first to be formed; first to be sent to France—would also be first sent into the front lines. As a consequence, the regiments and battalions of the 1st—the 26th Infantry among them—"received a very large proportion of the attention of General Pershing and his staff." Pershing was displeased with the progress of its training and was considering sacking its commander in early October. In the midst of these headquarters discussions, Pershing decided to inspect 1st Division troops and asked his chief aide, a young captain named George Marshall, who would go on to much higher rank and far greater fame in the Second World War, to arrange an exercise of offensive trench warfare to be conducted by one of the 1st Division battalions.[6]

Marshall, already a rising star in command headquarters and a figure of intellectual rigor and moral rectitude, had befriended Ted Roosevelt in the months since their arrival in France. Each respected the other's abilities, and Marshall decided to contact Roosevelt to see if his 1st Battalion might be willing to perform the exercise for Pershing. Ted was excited to do just that and expert at instilling enthusiasm in his own troops. "[Roosevelt] knew how to stir up morale all right," Marshall would recall later, "and he did it very well this time. So when General Pershing got out [to the site of the exercise], he had his chief of staff, and he had several new staff officers who later occupied very important positions [at headquarters]. This was their first visit to anything of this kind and their first exhibition of anything like this trench affair."[7]

The exercises commenced with "a lot of shooting . . . a lot of dashing around from trench to trench, and a lot of grenade throwing and general hullabaloo." When it was over, Pershing commanded the officers to assemble. He asked one of Roosevelt's men to critique the battalion's performance. According to Roosevelt, "a game little fellow named Wortley from Los Angeles who was afterward killed" stepped forward and told Pershing "that he thought everything went off well and he didn't think he had had anything to criticize." It was not the answer Pershing was looking for. He proceeded to give the whole battalion holy hell and was afterward heading off in a sour disposition when Marshall, at no small risk to his own reputation, stepped forward to defend the performance of the 26th. The problem was that the French had been schooling American troops in trench warfare, he reminded his commander, whereas it was Pershing's intention to break free of the bloodsucking trenches and have his American troops participate in open warfare.

The conflict between training for a war in the trenches, as America's allies wanted the U.S. forces to do, and training for open warfare, as Pershing wanted his forces to do, was an ongoing debate that would never be totally resolved through the length of the war. It was also a contention far beyond the pay grade of Ted Roosevelt or anyone else in the 26th Battalion. Thanks in part to Marshall's defense of him, Ted escaped any recriminations from the day's exercises and continued to shine as a commander.

The Roosevelt brothers remained among the most visible soldiers on the front. Ted was not just any old major. Heywood Broun, a well-known reporter for the *New York Tribune*, featured Ted's role in a story filed in late December. "Major Theodore Roosevelt, Jr. is one of the picturesque figures of the American army in France," Broun wrote. "He had something of a row to hoe, for his appointment to command a battalion which had a couple of captains much his senior created a great deal of comment. People said that Pershing was a friend of his father's and many such things, and there also came into being the remark of a regular army man 'I think there ought to be a rule that no reserve officer shall be appointed to command a battalion without the consent of his parents or guardian.'"[8]

According to Broun, however, "young Roosevelt has lived all that down." His actions continued to be enthusiastic and exemplary. The journalist cast Ted's visit to the front lines a couple of months earlier in more heroic terms than Ted did. Broun wrote that the attack came about in response to a German raid against American lines, in which prisoners were taken. Ted became the first officer in the war to lead American troops out of the trenches with a raiding party to sneak into the German trenches. Despite the fact that it wasn't his battalion that was raided, Ted was able to convince the French general commanding his unit, and Pershing, that he and his men should lead the responding party. Roosevelt selected 150 men from his unit and headed out into no-man's-land to recapture the soldiers taken prisoner. The raiding party waited patiently through a dark night, looking for an opportunity to ambush the Germans as they left their trenches, but to no avail; the German troops stayed at home through the night.

Just before the end of 1917, TR received a letter from Ted's brigade commander, General Duncan, saying that Ted was the best major in Duncan's unit. Ted's aide Charles Ridgeley and much of the battalion were beginning to think so, too. "He brought his battalion to a high degree of efficiency in the face of not only skepticism but downright opposition. I think I'm within the facts in saying that we never went into an action when he commanded the Battalion when we were not given the honor position."[9]

Meanwhile, Archie was champing at the bit to get into some fighting at the front, Quentin was sick with pneumonia and had been placed in charge of a squadron of fliers quarantined with the mumps, and Kermit was in Italy suffering from malaria.[10] In response to a letter in which Archie chided the French for their lack of sanitation, Theodore praised the courage of the Gallic allies and took an opportunity to once more slam the Wilson administration for its lack of preparation for war and the fact that it had "acted with such vacillation and confusion" that ten months in "we are still merely lookers on at the game."[11]

For all their dedication to the cause, the Roosevelt boys, like their father, could be caustic in their criticisms of military and executive command. Ted complained mightily about having to send his battalion out on maneuvers, calling it "a waste of valuable time that might be employed . . . to better advantage." These forays were designed to make sure that green units would stick together when they were finally sent into the line, but according to Roosevelt, they were primarily carried out to reassure the command. "The necessity for them, of course, was based on the fact that, great as was the ignorance of our junior officers, it was comparatively far less than the ignorance of our higher command and staff. These maneuvers were bitter work for the soldiers who would be out all day, insufficiently clad and insufficiently fed."[12]

Meanwhile Archie, still with Ted in the 26th, complained so vociferously to his father about the galling lack of supplies, including shoes, warm clothing, cannons, and automatic rifles, that Theodore warned him in a letter that as much as he agreed with Archie, his son should not complain too loudly for fear of "making things harder for yourself."[13] Archie, as it turned out, declined his father's suggestion and actually wrote an article outlining his complaints, which he then sent to Theodore to ask for help in finding a publisher. Its arrival coincided with the birth of Archie's first child, in Boston.

Theodore wrote back congratulating his son on his fatherhood, but declining to help with the article on the same grounds that he'd advised Archie to temper his earlier criticisms. He shouldn't make things harder than they already were. In another letter to son Kermit, he expressed a stronger frustration with Archie's temperament: "Both Archie and Quentin . . . write with exuberant and bitter frankness! The former, in spite of having just been promoted two ranks to captain, for efficiency and courage at the front, regards his superiors with iron disapproval and his surroundings with loathing."[14] Ted, on the other hand, "is always absorbed in what he is doing, and if he minds his experiences, as he sometimes must, he is very guarded about saying so."

Quentin's complaints had to do, primarily, with the fact that he couldn't get up in the air. American planes had yet to arrive in France; meanwhile, French and British pilots were loath to let the young and inexperienced American pilots practice with their aircraft. As a consequence, Quentin was grounded and doing guard duty at an aviation camp outside of Paris. All of this became an issue within the ultracompetitive Roosevelt family when Archie, in a letter to his young brother, endorsed by Ted, accused Quentin of not doing enough to get involved in the fighting. In his own defense, Quentin wrote his father, "I know both Ted and Arch feel that I am the embusce [sic—an embusqué is someone who shirks military duty] member of the family, and the trouble is they're right. The only thing is, that I am certainly not responsible for it. I am going ahead with my advanced flying down here as fast I can, and trying by every means possible, to go up in a French or British squadron. However, they have not one single man up yet. . . . What Arch and Ted don't see is that I really have done everything in my power to get out."[15]

In December, American allies began to press Pershing and Wilson to speed the timetable to get U.S. troops on the front line. The first American soldiers had arrived in France six months earlier, and though they had been training near the front since October, and the first handfuls of American troops had lost their lives in the war, they had yet to be placed on or to hold a sector of the trenches. At the same time, still dissatisfied with the speed of training in the 1st Division, Pershing decided to swap commanders. General Robert Lee Bullard replaced General William Sibert, giving Ted Roosevelt and the rest of the 1st Division new and more vigorous leadership.

In late January, the 1st Division was finally sent to the front line in a sector near Saint-Mihiel on the far eastern edge of the Western Front. It was considered a relatively quiet stretch of the more than two-hundred-mile-long Allied line, but that did not mean there would be a respite from the endless training for the 1st. In fact, because newly drafted soldiers were being rotated into the division, arriving green as grass, and including many new immigrants to the United States from Poland, Russia, and other Slavic nations, if anything more work was necessary to get them up to speed. "On the whole they were a fine lot," Roosevelt wrote, "but their knowledge of military matters was nil. A large percentage had never shot any firearms, and still a larger percentage had never shot the service rifle."[16]

While battalions were rotated into and out of the line in ten-day increments, those not getting their first taste of life in the trenches continued to engage in open warfare maneuvers of the sort that Roosevelt had complained of earlier, only now their marches and exercises were being conducted in a miserably cold winter. Troops had to tromp through snowy woods, in mud and icy streams. They suffered with the paucity of boots and warm clothing that Archie had written about. The men likened themselves to French and Indian War veterans—Leatherstockings, they called themselves—slopping through the snows of France.

It wasn't until the second week of March that Roosevelt's 26th Battalion rotated forward and spent their first nights in the trenches. For a sector judged to be quiet, there seemed to be quite a bit of activity and misery enough for all. The boys in Roosevelt's unit were subject to almost immediate artillery fire from the Germans. If they peeked their heads over the parapets, they became targets of sniping fire from the enemy across the hundred-yard stretch of no-man's-land. They also got their first lengthy taste of conditions in the trenches. They occupied a line that had been first dug three years earlier, when the sector was far more active and the trench was wall-to-wall troops. Now you could walk through knee-deep mud and scattered barbed wire for long stretches without meeting another soldier. A single company held a full kilometer of line, according to Roosevelt.[17]

Aside from the frequent artillery strafings, the Germans opposite the 26th staged a couple of raids. They also subjected the battalion to their first gas attacks. The difficulty in the case of the latter wasn't so much in detecting when the gas canisters were coming—there was a thumping sound that suggested a dud had been fired from the big guns; the hollow report would immediately prompt flares to be shot in the air or Klaxon horns to be sounded. Nor was the worst problem getting gas masks on in time—with the knowledge of what was coming, getting the masks on was doable; the bigger problem was the lingering effect of being trapped in a cloud of gas and its residue. Any contact with mustard gas caused mucus in the eyes and occasional blindness; rashes and blisters as bad as second- and third-degree burns to exposed skin; gagging, choking, and clogged breathing passages. Bloody noses that wouldn't stop bleeding and coughing that didn't cease were offshoots as well. Tongue sores, diarrhea, and vomiting might also occur. And the gooey residue left when the gas settled out of the air remained toxic, causing the same sorts of symptoms to those touched by the mustard for days to come.[18]

It was dangerous duty, but duty that offered little chance for retributive action. The members of the 1st were expected to take it with no orders to give it back.

Archie Roosevelt was soon one of the victims of these circumstances. On March 11, the Germans began strafing the lines with some light artillery fire that quickly turned heavy. Assuming an attack was about to commence, Captain Archie began to redispose his unit in preparation for the assault when he was hit in the left arm and left leg by shrapnel. He was left with serious wounds that quickly grew worse when the two men given the assignment of evacuating him were forced by cave-ins in the trenches to carry Archie over the top for part of the journey, exposing him to more fire back behind the lines, and lengthening his evacuation by a couple of hours. Ted, who was nearby when Archie was wounded, sent a telegram to Sagamore Hill as quickly as he could, describing Archie's injuries—a badly broken arm and shrapnel in the left leg. But his report was beaten by news from the journalists who were already stationed at Oyster Bay to report on the former president's own health.

Theodore had been admitted to the hospital in the first week of February, suffering from what he thought was simple indigestion. It turned out his body was, in fact, riddled with infection from abscesses in his right leg and ears, remnants of his near-fatal trip down the River of Doubt in South America four years earlier. The bile had worked its way into Theodore's intestinal tract, causing him intense stomach problems to go along with the pains in his ears and right leg. He was a very sick man.

Concern for Roosevelt was expressed across the country, and daily reports from the hospital were mentioned in the wire services and New York newspapers. An operation on his ears removed the abscesses and seemed to alleviate the intestinal problem, and the former president had been released to Sagamore Hill, where the reporters set up shop, got news of Archie's wound off the wire from France, and came marching up to the Roosevelt front door on the morning of March 13 to deliver it directly.

Theodore was no longer the same vigorous man he'd been, having never fully recovered from the hardships of his explorations in South America. It was plain that he had lost weight and energy and was starting to feel and look his age. But for a man as dynamic as Theodore Roosevelt, slowing down was no easy task. Even through his illnesses that February, March, and into April, TR continued to work and outline plans for a 1920 presidential race, which to most close observers was looking more and more unlikely. Still, he had already sent out feelers and garnered considerable support within the party for that race.

At Sagamore Hill, the first telegram off the wire had called Archie's wounds "slight." Ted's telegram, coming on its heels, also downplayed the seriousness of the injuries. Theodore and Ethel passed this information on to Archie's wife, Grace, who was tending to her newborn son, barely a month old. Theodore Roosevelt, dangerously ill himself, was reassured by Ted's telegram, but as could be imagined, Grace was less sanguine.

Late in March, TR was uplifted by news that Archie was to receive the Croix de Guerre for his heroism. He was also gratified to get a letter from Ted full of bully spirit as it described the action that had wounded Archie. Archie was now in a Paris hospital, Ted wrote, and would soon be cared for by Eleanor, who made plans to turn her Paris home into a ward.[19]

For all the encouraging words, however, the fact was that Archie's injuries would prove to be far more lasting and debilitating than Ted, or anyone else, understood. Archie's arm had been seriously shattered by the shrapnel, and had been essentially hanging by a sinewy thread of tendon when he was carried from the trenches. Many months of care and painful rehabilitation were in his future. Back at the front, the 1st Battalion continued its rotations into and out of the trenches in the Toul sector for the next month, doing a good deal of nighttime reconnaissance work. The 1st was hit by a number of raids, which typically began with early-morning strafing and then were followed by heavier shelling, as in the case of the artillery that wounded Archie. There was never any certainty about whether a German attack was coming.

Not surprisingly, some members of the 1st were itching to get out of the trenches and do some raiding on their own. One dark night Roosevelt sent a contingent of five crawling out under the barbed wire through no-man's-land, and they quickly lighted on a German listening post. They jumped two Germans in the foxhole, and after a struggle in which one of the Germans was bayoneted, the patrol subdued the other and dragged him back to American lines, where he became the first prisoner of war taken by the proud 1st Battalion.

More action, much more action, was to quickly come.

EIGHT

CANTIGNY

When the new Bolshevik regime took power in Russia in December 1917, they wasted little time in pulling their troops out of the war and began the process of suing Germany for peace. The fighting on the Eastern Front would soon be over, and scores of German divisions were sent to the front lines in western Europe to shore up combat-weary German troops in France. It was a surprise to no one when this influx of infantry prompted what the German command hoped would be a war-winning offensive at the end of March.

By this time, Ted considered his troops "veterans" and welcomed the rumors of a pending German drive; it would finally mean his men and the rest of the American fighting force would be thrown into the path of the Germans.

When the offensive came, it hit with intimidating power about two hundred miles northwest of the 1st Division, along a fifty-mile front running across the Somme River valley. The Germans had immediate and unprecedented successes against the British army. The Western Front, which had been basically static for many months, after incremental surges and retreats by both sides over the preceding three years, was now being pushed in the wrong direction and at an alarming pace for the Allies. Four miles and twenty thousand British prisoners were gained by the Germans in the first day of the offensive; after three days, the advance had gone twelve miles and the Germans had come close enough to Paris to have a quartet of Krupp guns lob shells into the city. In some places the advance had stretched to forty miles. There was deep concern among the Allies that the war might soon be over and Germany victorious. And all that Great Britain and the French had to counter the newly reinforced German army with were the untried, untested forces of General Pershing.[1]

In early April, the only American division capable enough to go into the line to help stem the tide was the 1st—twenty-eight thousand soldiers who, though they had been in Europe now for almost a full year, still had never faced the full onslaught of a German offensive. That was about to change.

In Major Roosevelt's battalion in the 26th, they learned snippets of what was happening two hundred miles away in the heat of battle. There were tales of desperate heroism in the British sector, where an English captain formed a fighting unit out of a hodgepodge of retreating forces to stem the German offensive; they heard of a thirty-six-hour period when contact between the French left and the British right was completely lost until a French cavalry division was trucked forward from the rear and into the breach. Finally, they heard that they were being moved out and sent, at last, into the heart of battle on the Western Front.

Military trains arrived—the famed forty *et* eight boxcars, sized to carry either forty soldiers or eight horses—and the 26th loaded up. They headed off to the west and shipped to a little town called Chaumont, from where they marched for four days north to the Montdidier sector of the front.

They traveled through the loveliest countryside Ted had yet seen in France. "Spring was on the land, the trees were budding, wild flowers covered the ground," he wrote. But they also met a stream of French refugees, prompted by the German offensive, fleeing south opposite the 1st Battalion. "Heavy home-made wagons trundled past," Roosevelt remembered, "drawn by every kind of animal, and piled high with hay and farm produce, furniture, and odds and ends of household belongings. Tramping beside them or riding on them were women and children, most of them dazed and with a haunted look in their faces."[2]

The sense of drama built as the 1st Division arrived near its destination.

On April 16, General Pershing came to a château in Chaumont and gathered before him all the officers of the 1st Division, including Ted Roosevelt Jr. Speaking on the steps above an old-world fieldstone courtyard brimming with his commanders, all eager to finally prove their merit and the merit of their troops in battle, Pershing reminded them that they had been the first American division to arrive in France, they had been the first to lose soldiers to the fighting in Europe, they had been the first to be sent into the trenches, and now they were to be the first to be thrust into the heart of battle. They were not just representing the American army in the Great War; they were also representing the whole nation, and the eyes of the world would be upon them. The long-awaited arrival of an American fighting force had come at last, and it was the 1st Division holding the line. "Our people today are hanging expectant on your deeds," Pershing told them. "The future is hanging upon your action in this conflict."

It was really no exaggeration to say so. War has its moments of incredible speed and lightning-quick brutality. It also has its moments of pregnant development, which the Allies had been experiencing for almost a full year now. In a war that had gone stale and incredibly cruel between massive armies along a massive front, it felt like something was about to give. The Germans had freed thousands of troops to fight in the West. To counter their potential impact, the Allies had the untried American troops who were now entering battle for the first time. The British and the French were exhausted by four years of war. The troops with the spring still in their steps were here now at Chaumont ready to take their turn in the great battle. And they would be led by the 1st Division, Ted Roosevelt among them.

It was about time, they thought. "They were delighted," Ted would write later of the prospects of going into battle. "Men do not like sitting in trenches day in and day out, and being killed and mangled without ever seeing the enemy . . ."[3]

The village of Cantigny rested on the farthest point west of the great line that divided the Central Powers and the Allied forces. It had been taken by the Germans in the March offensive and now represented the extent of their line. The 1st Division arrived to replace a French Moroccan unit that had tried and failed to retake Cantigny in several efforts through April. Now it would be the Americans' turn to try.

The village and the two German battalions holding it were positioned on a high plateau among farm fields that rolled along with the swales of the countryside, interrupted by small but thick woods, including one that backed Cantigny to the north. The town itself was at the tip of a salient that pushed the German front out toward the Allied lines. It had been occupied by Germans earlier in the war and had been subject to artillery fire then as it was about to be now, but not nearly to the degree to come. For now, it was still recognizable as a town.

The no-man's-land between the lines was littered with dead colonial troops. The 1st Division found shallow trenches and only a handful of dugouts—evidence of a newly created extension of the lines. As they moved into the valley below Cantigny, the French Moroccans told incoming Americans that they were not so much "turning over a sector, but a good place to make a sector." Until they created their own defenses, the 1st would be exposed to open fire.[4]

Spades furiously scraped the soil, and dirt flew. The 1st Division started to build defenses around the surrounding fields but did so under a steady barrage of artillery. Raids and counterraids were conducted. By the end of May, American forces were ready to mount the first large-scale attack by U.S. troops in World War I. Ted's old friend George Marshall, planning and operations officer for the 1st Division, was responsible for planning the assault. Because the Americans were so inexperienced, the objective of the attack was designed to be simple: the 1st Division, led by the 28th Infantry Regiment, was to take Cantigny from the Germans straight up the hill under artillery cover, in the teeth of the defenses. The 26th, including Ted Roosevelt's 1st Battalion, was to act in support on the far right wing of the attack.

On May 28, at 6:45 a.m., after staging an hour-long artillery barrage of its own, the 28th Infantry Regiment went over the top and charged toward the German lines, along with three machine-gun companies and a company of engineers. So heavy and effective had been the initial American artillery that French pilots observing German artillery before the assault reported that only four of some ninety German guns showed any activity. Germans manning the frontline trenches were assumed to be either dead or "in deep dugouts."[5]

Supported by a rolling barrage of artillery, along with a contingent of French tanks, the four thousand men of the 28th advanced up the hill toward Cantigny, moving at a pace dictated by the fire of American guns that led them forward: the thunder rolled out two hundred yards in front of them and then inched ever deeper into and beyond the German lines. No-man's-land was a curtain of smoke and dust. The village of Cantigny was essentially gone, smashed to smithereens, and the German troops holding it had been sent underground into cellars and dugouts to escape the bombardment. They offered little resistance to the advancing Americans.

Units to the north of the French village in the woods surrounding the town offered stout defenses, however, aiming heavy machine-gun and infantry rifle fire into the ranks of the American left flank. Troops from the advancing 28th Infantry hustled toward the abandoned German trenches in Cantigny and jumped inside to escape the murderous fire from the north. No matter that they were escaping deadly machine-gun fire; in a matter of minutes after jumping off, the 28th had reached the village and pushed the Germans out. Americans had taken their first objective in the war and now awaited the continuation of the rolling barrage to cover their advance beyond Cantigny.

The Germans were hardly done for the day. Most of the two battalions that had occupied the French village had simply pulled back as the Allied artillery commenced, waiting for the barrage to settle to look for their chance at counterattack. It came when American forces reached the village and began to occupy the trenches there. Now the Germans came out of the woods and struck hard at the 28th.

Roosevelt's 1st Battalion was soon drawn into the action in support of the assault. Joining the American line on the south side of the fighting— to the extreme right flank on the edge of a cluster of trees known as the Cantigny Wood—the battalion was hit heavily by German artillery, announcing the opening of the counterattack. Soon clouds of mustard gas enveloped their posts.

After the cascade, the Boche sent a wave of troops over the top back into no-man's-land, primarily pointed at the 1st Battalion's A Company, which was temporarily driven from its trenches. After alerting American artillery to this raid, A Company fought back with the assistance of Ted Roosevelt himself, who had gone to their sector to assist. Hand-to-hand combat followed, and the 26th was able not only to stem the raid, but also to run the Germans back to their own trenches, which they took, along with a number of Boche prisoners. Those members of the 26th who'd advanced encouraged others in the battalion to join them, but orders came quickly from the division for the reserve to return to their own lines so as not to get overextended.

The German counterattack was turned back by the 28th, and Cantigny was soon in American hands again. The artillery fire that opened the German counter turned out to be the most devastating fire faced by the 26th in the action. Roosevelt was himself blasted by a cloud of gas. Despite inhaling the noxious fumes and partially losing his sight when some of the gel got in his eyes, he refused evacuation throughout the subsequent fighting. Despite his miseries, he stayed through the day's fighting (and the next day's fighting and beyond; he would continue to suffer the effects from his gassing for weeks, according to Eleanor, who said that he couldn't lie on his back without having to quickly sit upright to clear his lungs).

Ted lost some key members of his 1st Battalion in the German raid, beginning with Captain Frey, his second-in-command, who was struck by artillery fire in the stomach and died. He also lost a trio of Irish American sergeants, Sullivan, O'Rourke, and McCormick, who had been stalwart leaders in the battalion. When Frey was hit, the stretcher bearers carried him past Roosevelt, and the captain shook Ted's hand. They said good-bye to one another, and as Frey was being carried away, he managed to bring himself upright on the stretcher, salute crisply, and in a delirium order, "Sergeant, dismiss the company," before passing on to the rear and a better life.[6]

The Germans were repulsed, but late in the action Ted's former aide

Charles Ridgeley, now commanding his own company, found himself on the right side of the line, outside the wire, in a shell hole. As a raid was ending with an artillery duel between the Allies and the Germans, Ridgeley's men scrambled back to the line in the midst of the explosions. Several soldiers were still missing, and as Ridgeley watched, a corporal appeared from the haze, his arm draped over the shoulder of a soldier Ridgeley at first did not recognize. It was only when they got nearer that he recognized his battalion commander, Ted Roosevelt, as the man bringing his corporal back to the company. "I guess this will be the last that will be coming back," Roosevelt said as he eased the wounded man down.

Ridgeley later told Ted that he wanted to recommend Roosevelt for a Distinguished Service Cross for his heroism. "If you do," Ted warned, "I'll not only kill [the recommendation] at Battalion Headquarters before it gets further, but will make you my adjutant again."[7]

German counterattacks continued throughout the first day of combat and into the second. In the end, however, Cantigny was taken by an American fighting force, the first U.S.-led victory in the war. It came at a steep cost: of the approximately four thousand Americans engaged, three hundred men were killed and thirteen hundred wounded. Still, there came a sense that a new and potentially powerful ally had proved itself in battle on the Western Front. And that was no small thing.

NINE

QUENTIN

Word of Ted's heroism in France arrived at Sagamore Hill through the newspapers. On June 24, the Associated Press reported in the *New York Times* that Ted had been cited for "conspicuous gallantry" in the capture and subsequent defense of Cantigny.

The citation, printed in full beneath the headline MAJOR ROOSEVELT CITED FOR BRAVERY, read, "During an enemy raid he displayed high qualities of courage and leadership in going forward to supervise in person the action of one of the companies of his battalion, which had been attacked.

"On the day of our attack on Cantigny, although gassed in the lungs and gassed in the eyes to blindness, Major Roosevelt refused to be removed and retained the command of his battalion under a heavy bombardment throughout the engagement."[1]

For a family as steeped in American history as the Roosevelts, the significance of having one of its sons participating in the first American action of the Great War was not lost on the patriarch, his sons, or anyone else in the extended family at Oyster Bay. To Ted, his father wrote, "Our pride even surpasses our anxiety. I had just written Kermit that it seemed as if he had the most interesting experience, but this of yours is *the* experience . . . you have won high honor by rendering great service; you have not only won it for your children, but, like the Chinese, you have ennobled your ancestors. I walk with my head higher because of you; and indeed whatever weight my words carry now it is chiefly due to the record of you four boys in the past year."[2]

Despite the distressing news of Ted's gassing, which along with Archie's earlier wounds indicated the growing costs of war to the boys, Theodore's pride in their service couldn't be dampened. Nor was his (or their) enthusiasm for continued action discouraged. There was no sacrifice too great to make for one's nation in a time of military crisis. This was the credo that Theodore lived by and this is the credo that he had instilled in all of his sons. Any doubts, any physical fears for their own safety or harm, that any of the boys may have entertained in the dark recesses of their minds were kept stowed, lest they be revealed to their father and each other. Theodore himself expressed his anxieties but would not dwell on them. "Black care rarely sits behind a rider whose pace is fast enough" was a familiar maxim of Theodore Roosevelt's, and his sons as well emulated the sentiment: they rarely shared their deepest uncertainties.[3]

Other war news over the past month had similarly excited Theodore. Word came in late spring that Quentin was finally going to the front. After months of delay the French Armée de l'Air had at last allowed Quentin access to shooting practice at an aviation school in preparation for actual combat missions—a fact that cheered Theodore greatly, but nonetheless failed to prevent him from a continued harping on the United States' lack of preparedness for the war. The word that Quentin was finally getting to fly planes in the war came in late May, and Theodore wrote Quentin of his pride, joy, and anxiety that after his long period of waiting, he had "started to the front."

Quentin was himself eager to get forward. Soon word came that Kermit too would arrive at the European front. He had asked for a transfer from Mesopotamia, where, like Ted and Archie, he had recently won a medal, the British Military Cross. Kermit decided that he wanted to spend the remainder of the war with U.S. forces in Europe. The fact that Kermit would soon be with his brothers in France, along with his new medal, had elicited even more chest-swelling pride from Theodore, and more encouragement for Quentin to get to the front.

Meanwhile, Eleanor had established a combination infirmary/R & R center at her home in Paris for visiting Roosevelt brothers, even as she continued to work for the YMCA in the city. Early in June, with Archie back recuperating in a nearby hospital, Quentin stopped in for a visit on his way to the front and ran into Ted, who was there with a pass from the front.

It was a nice reunion, however brief and tempered by the fact that Archie was not doing well. His arm had been so badly broken that central nerves had been severed, making movement nearly impossible and thereby slowing the healing process. Future active duty on the front seemed an unlikely prospect—a fact that got Archie down and compounded the difficulty of his recovery. His depression was becoming general and lugubrious. In low moments, he began to doubt that any of the boys would return from this war whole.

Archie had been offered a position as a staff officer at headquarters, a post that Ted urged him to accept. Unfortunately, Roosevelts were not inclined to serve behind the lines. Archie insisted he would only go on staff duty if Ted did as well, but of course Ted wasn't interested. "When an amateur goes into the war," he wrote to his father, "he goes in not for profit or advancement but for work and fighting." Ted explained that he, too, had been offered an opportunity to go to the staff school, which would have guaranteed advancement in the command structure, as well as "work in a comfortable town" and opportunity to see Eleanor frequently, but he declined. He would stay in the fight.[4]

Ted soon returned to the 26th Infantry and stayed with them in the Montdidier sector of the front, helping the 1st Division to solidify lines and maintain pressure on the Germans. He sent out patrols and ordered raids, while to the east, on the division's right flank, near Château-Thierry, the Boche began their second drive of the year. The American 2nd Division replaced the 1st as the principal combatant to the German advance. Ted and the 1st Battalion continued to man the line, not under constant attack, but under constant pressure, during which the 26th Infantry suffered a total of 122 killed and 712 wounded.[5]

Gas attacks continued with increasing frequency. Roosevelt described the uncertainties that came each time rumors of a German gassing came to the battalion: "reports come in from various sections that they are gassing Fontaine Woods, Cantigny Woods, and the valley between. You stand out on some point of vantage and listen to the shells singing over and bursting. As day dawns you see a thick gray mist spreading itself through the valley. The men have slipped on their gas masks. The question now is, what's up? Just meanness on the part of the Huns, or is it part of some ulterior design to straighten the salient and nip off the two points of woods we are holding? How heavy is the gassing to be? How quickly will the wind carry it away? A thousand and one other questions. You send your gas officer up to test. You go up yourself and generally know as much as the gas officer. Our general experience was the first gas casualties we had were the gas officers."[6]

Ted was becoming an exceptional battalion commander, respected by both his men and his commanders. He maintained a healthy cynicism toward staff officers who failed to gain any practical experience on the line. He moaned, for instance, about the amount of mapmaking that was required at the battalion level, and about the patrol reports that needed to be written for a command that might have been better informed if they just came to the trenches more frequently.

At the same time, however, Ted was himself an organized thinker. He was a concise planner, making his instructions and orders simple and crystal clear. One of his written raiding plans was so specific and direct, and carried out so crisply, that it became an instant model to other 1st Division commanders, copied and distributed among officers in the brigades. It would eventually become part of a text called *Infantry in Battle* written by George Marshall when Marshall was teaching tactics at the U.S. Army Infantry School in Fort Benning, Georgia, between the wars.

Ted's after-action reports were similarly models of narrative precision and solid, clear prose: "Lieutenant Dabney, leader of the C Party, saw an officer and rushed to take him. While he was seizing him, [Dabney] was attacked by three Germans. A private near him shot two and bayoneted the other with so much force that he pinned him to a tree where the bayonet stuck so fast that it had to be left, the only piece of ordnance lost by the assaulting party."[7]

Quentin got up in the skies for the first time on July 1, just days after leaving Eleanor and his brothers in Paris. On the sixth he fired his first shots at an enemy aircraft, and on the tenth he brought down his first German plane.

Flying out of a town near Reims, leading a small squadron of French-made Nieuport planes, Quentin was the top man in the formation when he found himself flying above three planes in the skies over Château-Thierry. Thinking the planes were part of his own squadron, he started to tail them when he spotted the markings of a German Fokker. After a moment's hesitation, he got in behind one of the enemy and started firing. "My tracers were shooting all around him," he wrote, "but I guess he was so surprised for a bit that he couldn't think what to do. Then his tail shot up and he went down."[8]

His father received word of this "kill" in a cable, and as expected was deeply proud. He spread the word among Roosevelt relatives that Quentin was now, like his three other sons, "blooded."[9]

In the world of flying aces, the average life span of a chase pilot at the front measured eleven days; time sped like a racing machine.[10] Just days after the triumphant cable, another telegram arrived at Sagamore Hill. It read simply that the family should expect news from the front soon. The brevity and vagueness of the message immediately suggested that one of the Roosevelt boys had been injured. Theodore and Edith immediately suspected it was Ted, whom they knew to be at the front. Then came word that it was Quentin.

On July 14, thirteen American planes were flying patrol about ten miles inside German lines above the Château-Thierry sector of the Western

Front, not far from where the 1st Division was braking to a stop, when the squadron encountered seven German aircraft and gave chase. Observers on the ground saw one of the American planes veer off in pursuit of two of the Germans during the dogfight, but suddenly the two Boche fighters switched positions on the single American, now attacking him from the rear. Machine-gun fire could be heard from below. The American plane was suddenly tumbling out of the sky, according to one report, streaming flames behind it; according to others, it simply fell in a spin toward the ground. It was assumed that the pilot was hit by gunfire, but in any case, Quentin Roosevelt twirled to his death on the unyielding French soil.

Quentin's personal popularity, his ability to make friends and find admirers everywhere he went, was evident in the outpouring of grief that followed the news of his passing. Old air squadron mates sent letters to the family, while the people of Oyster Bay set flags at half mast and openly grieved. Journalists who'd covered the family back in Washington wrote of Quentin's warm character and penchant for high jinks. They recalled the time when Archie was sick with diphtheria and Quentin sneaked his brother's pony onto a White House elevator and up to Archie's bedroom, thinking the horse would make him better. Washington insiders remembered when young Quentin, suddenly interested in the study of bees, had found a hive, and brought it with him on a crowded streetcar to take back to the White House for further study.[11]

Theodore issued a brief statement to the press: "Quentin's mother and I are very glad that he got to the front and had a chance to render some service to his country and to show the stuff there was in him before his fate befell him." Later, the mourning parents took a boat out rowing, just the two of them, and grieved privately on the waters of Oyster Bay.

It turned out that, indeed, Quentin was struck by a bullet in the head prior to his crash. He was buried in France by Germans, behind their own lines. After learning who this young pilot was, German aviators dropped a note onto American aviation camps to let their flying comrades know that the ex-president's son was dead.[12] Then they built a simple wooden cross with Quentin's name and the date of his death, and further marked the grave with a crude wooden fence surrounding the grave. A U.S. plane would eventually spot Quentin's grave, and when the land reverted to Allied occupation, it was guarded and would eventually serve as a site for pilgrimages from American soldiers remembering the war dead.

Before his burial, someone took photographs of Quentin with his fatal wound on full display. These shots were later hawked as souvenirs by unscrupulous vendors, and though efforts were made by the AEF to gather and destroy all copies, some leaked out of France and actually made it to Sagamore Hill. Curiously enough, the macabre postcard of Quentin in death that arrived at the Roosevelt home was not only saved, but also copies were made and distributed to family members to be stored in photo albums as a testament to his great sacrifice. The mangled axle of his plane wound up displayed in the trophy room at Sagamore Hill in a similar gesture. Years later, when on a visit to his old home, after it had been turned into a museum, Archie Roosevelt discovered that someone on the archival staff had hidden the axle out of sight from nosy tourists. Archie insisted that it be brought back out for public viewing: people ought to know the sacrifices the Roosevelt family had made in the war, no matter how gruesome the evidence, or perhaps the more gruesome the better. The Roosevelts understood their obligations, and thought the public should understand them as well.[13]

TEN

SOISSONS

In early July, the 1st Division was relieved and sent to an old village named Beauvais. It was soon moved to a town nearer to Paris and told it would get a month's rest. Everyone in the outfit was delighted. Their new location was built on rolling country, Ted remembered, "and its gray cobble-paved streets twisted and wound up hill and down through a maze of picturesque gray houses in whose doors well-dressed, bright-cheeked women and children stood watching us."[1] Running through the heart of town was a stream, where the war-weary soldiers enjoyed their first baths in more than two months. Billets were found for officers and enlisted alike, and at least one doughboy remarked to Roosevelt that the men were "sitting on top of the world" as they anticipated weeks of relief in the idyllic French countryside.[2]

The next morning, a motorcycle messenger roared into the village and handed Ted a note that read, "You will be prepared to entruck your battalion at two this afternoon." So much for the month's rest in their lovely hamlet.

The Huns were making another push at the front, trying to smash the French army near Reims, northeast of Paris. The 26th was needed to help stem the tide of attack. Soon the battalion was organizing to head north toward the fighting. A black humor inculcated the troops. With raucous laughter they sang "Hail, Hail, the Gang's All Here," and as they passed the village graveyard on the way to the trucks, someone joked that this would be the ultimate peaceful billets for the 26th.

They drove all afternoon and into the evening. No one was certain where they were going—some speculated that the Germans had broken through and crossed the Marne. Come morning, the trucks finally stopped near the city of Soissons, opposite the German right flank.

At the edge of dense woods, Ted Roosevelt's 26th Infantry, along with the rest of the 1st Division, hooked up with the 2nd Division, who'd similarly moved to this sector northeast of Paris. Also to participate in the counter-offensive was the French Foreign Legion. Overall command of the three units had been handed to a French general, Charles Mangin. Care was taken to limit movements of the gathering forces in the woods where they'd stopped: Mangin hoped for a surprise attack the next day that would see his fresh American and Foreign Legion troops surge through the French troops currently holding the line in front of the Germans, and smack the Huns with a powerful punch they wouldn't see coming.

It rained heavily the night before the battle, which helped quiet preparations. The attack would employ the open warfare techniques that the 26th Infantry had so diligently practiced over the past year at General Pershing's insistence. For the march into battle the 26th would be side by side with the 28th Infantry Regiment on the north, or left, flank of the 1st Division's advance. To the right of the 1st Division, the 2nd Division would advance along parallel lines, and the French Foreign Legion would man the right flank to the south of the 2nd, likewise attacking in parallel fashion. As at Cantigny, a rolling barrage of artillery fire would lead troops toward the German line, heading west to east over a series of rolling hills and deep ravines.

With no acclimation to the terrain or adjustment to their new circumstances, the Americans were to be thrust into the battle. "Apparently the idea was to stake all on one throw," Ted wrote. "Marshal Foch had decided on a counter-offensive in this part [of the front] and had delegated to General Mangin the task of putting it into execution."[3] Early on the morning of July 18, "the artillery skittered and strained into place. The tanks clanked and rattled up, breaking the columns and tearing up what was left of the road. It was so dark," Ted Roosevelt wrote, "you could hardly see your hand before your face."[4]

The 26th stood at the ready at 4:00 a.m., awaiting the artillery barrage that was to preface its attack. They were at the edge of a rugged and steep ravine, and the rain had ended. A pink dawn faced them to the east and eerie silence prevailed, interrupted solely by the chatter of early-rising birds. "Suddenly out of the stillness, without the warning of a preliminary shot, our artillery opened with a crash. All along the horizon, silhouetted against the pale pink of the early dawn, was the tufted smoke of high explosive shells, and the burst of shrapnel showed in flashes like the spitting of a broken electric wire in a hailstorm."[5]

At 4:35 a.m. the infantry surged forward. "The surprise was complete," according to Roosevelt. "Germans were killed in their dugouts half dressed." In just an hour's time, all of the first-day objectives were taken, the enemy's advance batteries were in Allied hands, and German prisoners were streaming back behind American lines. But as the day progressed, the 1st Brigade (the 26th and 28th Infantry Regiments) started to outpace the 2nd Brigade and Moroccan troops to their right flank. Well-positioned Boche machine guns began to take a toll on the 26th, which was partially echeloned on the right because of its advance beyond the 2nd Brigade.

Both the 26th and the 28th came to a halt when they reached the edge of a kilometer-wide gully called the Missy Ravine, which rested about forty meters above a swamp and stream below. Along the inside of the ravine, on its western edge facing east, a series of caves had been employed by the Germans to store ammunition. The Germans built corduroy roads into the caves to transport the arms across the swampy land of the ravine to gun batteries on the eastern side of the ravine.

The combination of the artillery and German machine-gun fire placed around the ravine took a heavy toll on the 1st Brigade as it advanced. Troops surged down the steep face of the ravine into the teeth of the gunfire. Some Americans, who hadn't noticed the caves as they plunged over the side of the embankment, took fire from Germans placed within these shelters now behind them. Even as they faced fire from all sides in the ravine, as well as from the caves, the 26th continued to advance through the course of the day. And with a French infantry division arriving on the scene to aid the brigade, the 26th and 28th were able to move forward six kilometers, allowing the 1st Division artillery to advance forward to support the next day's action. The Missy Ravine was ultimately taken, and along with it, thirty pieces of enemy artillery and fifteen hundred prisoners marching now with their hands raised, to the American rear.

The 26th bivouacked in what had been enemy territory at the start of the day. In the night, Boche airplanes flew above them, dropping small bombs and flares.

Charles Ridgeley, commanding 1st Battalion's D Company, had ended his day in a captured German trench sited toward the west, in the direction from which the Americans had come that morning. His company was waiting in the dark for food to come up from the rear. Getting a meal to those who needed it most, frontline troops about to lead the battle the next morning, was always a difficult proposition, made more so, on this first night at Soissons, by German planes "laying eggs all along the road" leading to the front—the very terrain that needed to be "traversed by our chow detail" in order for them to get fed.[6]

From out of the dark Ridgeley watched a lone figure approach. He recognized Roosevelt's voice calling out to him before he saw his battalion commander's face. Which company was he approaching? Roosevelt wanted to know. D Company, Ridgeley hollered, then said to his major, "You shouldn't be alone."

"I wasn't when I started,'" Roosevelt answered. His adjutant and a couple of runners had been hit along the road out here, he explained, and he'd had to go on without them.

Had D Company been fed? Roosevelt wondered. Told no by Ridgeley, Ted said he would "see to that" and then headed back into the night, with bombs still dropping. D Company would ultimately get its meal.[7]

★

The next morning's attack began once again with a rolling barrage that started as it had on the first day of battle. The 26th began its sweep across open fields that lay beyond the Missy Ravine. They immediately stepped into withering machine-gun fire with backing artillery. The battalion's first objective was a roadbed that might provide minimal cover at a highway running northeast to southwest, directly across the unit's path. By 9:00 a.m., the 26th had reached the road but stalled trying to take a hill behind it. The commander of the regiment's 2nd Battalion was killed taking the road; dead along with him were two of his company commanders. More infantry began to fall, but the 26th kept pushing forward until the hill was theirs, ultimately taken with the aid of French tanks that had moved up in support.

In the midst of the morning action, Major Ted Roosevelt Jr. led a charge against a machine-gun nest said to be "particularly annoying to the Americans" near the village of Ploissy. In his haste to get to the gun, Ted had gone over the top without his helmet, as if he were still playing a helmetless left end for the Harvard frosh. The stutter of the machine gun sprayed all around him and he watched comrades fall left and right before feeling the sting of his own wound and collapsing to the ground. He tried to keep going, but it was no use. Ted had been shot through the knee and his leg was useless.

The machine gun was ultimately taken by his unit, but Ted's role in the Battle of Soissons was effectively over. An empty artillery caisson soon arrived and carried him from the field for care behind the line. The artilleryman who drove the wagon said later that it was necessary to strap Ted to its bed to keep the major from climbing off in an attempt to return to the action.

In fact, the wound was serious, and care at the overwhelmed aid station was inadequate. Ted quickly determined that he would get better medical help in Paris, under Eleanor's supervision, than at the aid station. He got a sprinkle of sulfur on the wound, had it dressed, and then somehow found a soldier with a motorcycle and sidecar. He was soon jouncing over battlefields and rutted roads toward Paris. Before he left, someone pinned a note on his khakis that read, simply, "gunshot wound severe," and with one change of transportation, from sidecar to an automobile, that is how Ted arrived at Eleanor's home in Paris. She saw the sedan pull up to the curb, knew somehow that it was Ted, and came rushing to help him inside.

Ted tried to reassure his wife that the wound was minor, but he was also acting irrationally as he came inside. He called for a hot shower and a warm meal, insisting that he wanted black bean soup and broiled lobster. He then ran through a list of subsequent courses that he also expected, including clams, duck, roast beef, and a quart of champagne. Needless to say, Eleanor was having trouble dealing with Ted alone. She contacted her brother-in-law, Ethel's husband, Dr. Dick Derby, who happened to be in Paris at the time. He rushed to the Avenue du Bois de Boulogne to assist her, examined Ted's leg, and quickly determined that his brother-in-law needed to get to the Red Cross hospital immediately. Derby found two bullet holes: one in the front of Ted's knee, the other in the rear, both gushing blood. Seeing how much fluid Ted was losing, Derby recognized that there was a real possibility that Ted could lose his leg, and they rushed him to a waiting car.

Ted joined Archie in the same Paris hospital and underwent immediate surgery. His army surgeon described his injury as "a perforating wound of the popliteal space." A single bullet had entered the back of his knee and exited the front, leaving a gaping hole where tendons and ligaments had been joining muscle and bone just the day before. Wheeled to a recovery room after the operation, no longer calling for bean soup and champagne, and back nearer to himself, Ted was nonetheless a seriously wounded soldier.

A cablegram from Eleanor arrived at Sagamore Hill the day after Ted's return to Paris: "Ted wounded. Not seriously. Here with me. Not any danger. No cause for anxiety."

Eleanor's message arrived at Oyster Bay the same day as President Wilson's telegram officially confirming Quentin's death.

ELEVEN

THE COST OF WAR

The Battle of Soissons continued for four more bloody days after Ted's wound and evacuation. At the end of day two, the 26th had advanced all the way to a hill just south of Ploissy. It had taken prisoners from four different German divisions. The Huns were rushing more and more troops into the fight, but they were on their heels.

At the end of the third day, many in the 1st Division got to eat their first warm meal since the start of the battle. By the end of day four, the 1st Brigade had pushed all the way to Berzy-le-Sec, the village just beyond Ploissy, through which a vital railroad ran. At the end of day five, battalion strength had shrunk within the 1st to a fraction of what it had been at the start of the battle, but the infantry kept moving forward until they were finally replaced by a division of Scottish Highlanders at the end of day six. By this time the German army had been forced into its first general retreat since the Americans had entered the war. There was a sense up and down the front that the tide had turned against the Boche.

Casualties were heavy. "At the end of the battle," Roosevelt would later write, "companies in some cases came out commanded by corporals, and battalions by second lieutenants . . . the regiment lost most of the men that built it up."[1]

Roosevelt's immediate superior, Colonel Hamilton Smith, the commander of the 26th, was killed in the battle for Berzy-le-Sec, as were dozens in the officers' ranks. Hundreds more died among the infantry. The battalion commander in each of the four infantry regiments of the 1st Division was a casualty. Of 96 officers in the 26th Infantry, 62 were carried off the field; 3,100 enlisted men from the 26th had gone over the top on the first day of battle. At its end, on July 23, the 26th could muster only 1,440 soldiers for duty, and many of these were replacement troops who had entered the fight after the first day. There were 9,000 casualties from the 1st Division as a whole in the four days of fighting at Soissons.[2]

The observations of a veteran stretcher bearer with the 1st Moroccan Division, fighting on the 1st Division's right flank, give a sense of the manner in which the Americans did battle. Pierre Teilhard de Chardin was a young man in uniform, not the famed theologian and philosopher he was to become. In a letter to a friend, he described the fighting nature and character of France's newest allies on the Western Front: "We had the Americans as neighbors, and I had a close-up view of them. Everyone says the same: they're first-rate troops, fighting with intense individual passion (concentrated on the enemy) and wonderful courage. The only complaint one would make about them is that they don't take sufficient care; they're too apt to get themselves killed. When they're wounded, they make their way back holding themselves upright, almost stiff, impassive, and uncomplaining. I don't think I've ever seen such pride and dignity in suffering. There's complete comradeship between them and us, born fully fledged under fire."[3]

After the fighting, the 1st Division was withdrawn to a bivouac near Paris for rest and recuperation. Its wounds were grievous, and yet its fighting spirit remained undimmed. When the commander of the division, General Charles Summerall, was asked if he thought the 1st had any fight left in it, he replied, "Sir, when the 1st Division has only two men left they will be echeloned in depth and attacking toward Berlin."[4]

For all his unrelenting willingness to do battle, there were indications that Ted was pondering the deeper costs of war as he recovered from his wound. For the first time, he was able to consider the fact that he'd not only lost his young brother to the war, but also dozens of the men he'd trained and fought with over the past year. In addition, Archie was recovering at an achingly slow and distressing pace. Across the ocean, his parents and the rest of his family were trying to cope with the loss of Quentin and their fears over the brothers still battling in Europe. This was deep sacrifice and profound loss. The Great War was tragedy on a scale never dreamed of before.

Ted spent a few days in the hospital before being allowed to continue his recovery at home in Paris with Eleanor. He was forced to use crutches and then a cane to get around. If there was one benefit to his circumstances, it was this: his first opportunity to really explore the city. He and his wife, often accompanied by Archie, made frequent excursions to nearby cafés and other watering holes.

Kermit and his wife, Belle, arrived in the city, too—Kermit was about to begin training at an artillery school outside of Paris—and the brothers and wives shared several wine-filled and melancholy evenings carousing, recalling Quentin, reflecting on their own fate, and wondering if any of them would make it home alive. The existential turn their lives had taken led them—Ted, in particular—to seriously uncharacteristic behavior. In one drunken reverie, Ted and Archie played a pair of drunken strangers trying to seduce Eleanor on the Métro. In another, on the Champs-Élysées, Ted pretended to be a mental patient, picking butterflies out of the air. With Kermit, Belle, Eleanor, and Archie in tow, Ted burst into a marching song as they left a Paris restaurant one afternoon. His brothers joined in and as they careered down the street in locked-arms drunkenness, a group of Parisians began to sing as well. They all made a parade down the narrow street singing "Hail, Hail, the Gang's All Here" and shouting *"Vive la France!"*[5]

Kermit soon moved on to his artillery school, and Ted was assigned duty training officers while he continued to heal. There were continuing concerns that Archie would try to get back to the front, but he was finally convinced to head home to Sagamore Hill to get the benefit of a complete break from life in the U.S. Army. Ted sent a letter home to his father with

Archie, prescribing appropriate care for his brother. Archie needed "ordinary, plain upbuilding of physique," he told Theodore. He needed to be "thoroughly sensible" about getting back into the line. Archie still had an opportunity to work on the headquarters staff in France, but taking a staff position would probably mean the fighting war would be over for Archie, and Ted advised his father not to talk up this position with his third son. It would just make him itch to get back to the front. Ted also said that he was glad that brother Kermit was heading into artillery. "The dangers that he will run there are not one in ten as great as those of the infantry."

He reported that Eleanor had taken a leave from her work to nurse him. And there were discussions and remembrances of Quentin, particularly when Quentin's good friend, fellow flier, and Harvard and Groton classmate Hamilton Coolidge (who would himself die in a dogfight in two months) stopped by the Paris apartment.

He also reported that cousin Franklin Roosevelt was in Europe in his capacity as assistant secretary of the navy—his first visit to the front. FDR got a chance to see Belleau Wood and the Meuse and was invited to fire a 155mm howitzer when he happened by an artillery unit. He relished the opportunity.[6]

Franklin also stopped off at Eleanor's place in Paris to check on Ted and Archie. His presence in Europe encouraged Ted to think that his arrival signaled a greater sense of urgency from the administration in supplying the necessary manpower and matériel to end the war.

Finally, Ted closed the letter to his father by admitting that his leg was not yet capable of supporting him in battle. Yet it was "coming around." And all his worries on behalf of his brothers at the front were not concerns that he felt for his own well-being. "Four weeks should see me back in the line," he told his father.[7]

Late in his convalescence, a group of half a dozen officers from the 26th visited their comrade to give Ted an update on his men and the final disposition of the battle. As he rested his wounded leg on a settee in the parlor of the Paris home, his colleagues began to list casualties in the unit: Colonel Elliot; Captain J. H. Holmes; Captains Mood, Hamel, and Richards; Lieutenants Kern and Clarke; Majors Compton and Travis; and, of course, scores of infantrymen. As they listed the dead and wounded, Ted called to Eleanor and asked her to pour "something extra special for toasts." As the melancholy roll call wound down, Ted asked his men to raise their glasses first to the 26th Infantry and then to the dead of the regiment. That order of toasts has remained standard for all gatherings of the 1st Division and 26th Regiment ever since.[8]

For a time that summer, Theodore and Edith had gone up to Maine, where the colonel sadly and uncharacteristically spent an inordinate amount of his vacation staring at the stars in the night sky. One of the Roosevelt family maids found him alone in his bedroom one night that September, rocking in a chair and muttering, "Poor Quinikins! Poor Quinikins."

The Roosevelts had received a flood of condolences about Quentin at Sagamore Hill from friends high and low, including King George, many Rough Riders, and a barber from Brooklyn who knew Quentin when he was training to fly. He was "afraid of nothing," according to the barber, "the goodest kid I ever saw."[9]

Archie's arrival did little to lift the gloom. When he came home that fall to continue his recuperation on Long Island, he was subject to periodic bouts of depression and had trouble bonding with his infant son. He continued to think that there was a chance he might be able to head back to the war.[10]

TWELVE

ARMISTICE

The Battle of Soissons pushed the Germans back to lines they'd held prior to their spring offensive and prompted the beginning of an Allied counteroffensive in August that would continue to keep German defenders on their heels and leaning back toward the Hindenburg Line all September. A series of battles north and south along the front, collectively called the Hundred Days Offensive, took its toll on German forces led by General Erich Ludendorff. French and British forces continued to lead the attacks against the Germans, but Pershing's American forces were now fully mobilized and pouring into the fight. Ten thousand U.S. troops were arriving in Europe every day by midsummer 1918, and as fall rolled around they began to be funneled into the action at sites whose names would soon be familiar to all Americans, such as Saint-Mihiel and the Meuse-Argonne.

In early September, Ted was feeling well enough to go back to work, but he was judged not ready to serve at the front line. Still healing, still using a cane, he reported for duty as an instructor at the army's Line School, where, three days after his arrival, he was promoted to the rank of lieutenant colonel. Along with the upgrade came a citation for his bravery and leadership at Soissons from the commander of the 1st Division, General Charles Summerall. "Your services in the Division have been conspicuous for efficiency, energy and leadership," it read. "It would be difficult to convey to you my appreciation of the manner in which you led your battalion in the Soissons fight, and of the great assistance rendered by you in moving boldly ahead of the line, thereby greatly facilitating the general movement that followed on 19 July. The corps commander was present when the report was received of your enterprise in gaining ground under the most difficult circumstances, and he shared with me the relief and confidence that your conduct inspired. I think no one who has been a member of this Division occupies a higher place than you in the esteem of your comrades, and you will receive a warm welcome whenever it shall be our good fortune to have you return to us."[1]

Tired of his convalescence but still not certified for action and still hobbling with a cane, Ted decided to rejoin the 26th Infantry anyway. He went to his old friend George Marshall, still serving in the command of the 1st Division, and explained that he was eager to get back to the front line but was having trouble getting medical clearance. The cane was only a minor inconvenience, Ted claimed, and wouldn't hamper him in the field. Marshall advised him to "take the bull by the horns" and simply go back to his unit without medical clearance. Ted did just that—a move that made him technically A.W.O.L. for a couple of weeks. But as he rationalized, "they don't court-martial for A.W.O.L. if you go in the right direction."

That his commanders at the 1st had no trouble with this decision is evident in the fact that Ted was soon given charge of the full 26th Infantry Regiment, thus becoming the first volunteer officer in the whole AEF to be named commander of a regiment. Now, as colonel of the 26th Regiment, Ted Roosevelt Jr. arrived for the final act of the war.[2]

As at Soissons, the 1st was now moving in conjunction with the American 2nd Division, with French forces abutting them to the north, on their left flank. The Allies were asserting constant pressure on the retreating Boche army in what would become known as the Meuse-Argonne Offensive, which began late in September and would not end until the war was over.

Fighting in north-central France, Ted joined the 1st as it followed the 2nd on a nighttime march to the French village of Landreville. There he was astonished to find Kermit, newly graduated from artillery school and assigned to duty with the 1st Division; they would serve together through the end of the war. Also at Landreville, the brothers reunited with brother-in-law Dick Derby, who was serving as a surgeon with the 2nd Division. A night of reunion and family news was conducted near a field of battle still littered with day-old casualties.

Eighteen hundred new replacement troops filled the unit rosters of the 1st Division early that October. Fresh and enthusiastic new blood, they were able to keep constant pressure on the Germans, who continued to move backward toward Sedan, north of Verdun. The 1st Division soon swapped positions with the 2nd, taking the lead in a continuing pursuit of the German troops.

Colonel Roosevelt felt the stresses of his wound. Riding a horse on the pursuit turned out to be more painful for Ted than marching with his troops, so for five days, primarily moving at night, he got off his horse and hobbled on his cane over the rolling hills and woodlands of northeastern France toward the enemy. Roosevelt led the 26th in pursuit of the Germans, heading north, up the Meuse River. "There is a military phrase which has always irritated me," Ted later wrote of this march. "It is, 'At this point fresh troops were thrown into the action.' There is no such thing as 'throwing fresh troops' into action. By the time troops get into action they have marched night after night and are thoroughly tired."[3, 4]

The 26th nonetheless continued to engage the Germans in a running battle for six days, pushing them toward the French city of Sedan on the Meuse near the Belgian border. Sedan was a border city in the Ardennes and had a long history as the jumping-off point for German invasions of France. Now, however, the fight was out of the Huns as they retreated. Prisoners taken by the 26th were German boys so exhausted by their retreat that one of them told Roosevelt he'd only been awakened from a dead sleep in a foxhole by the prod of a bayonet from the 26th Regiment infantryman who had captured him.[5]

The doughboys smelled victory. Despite their deep fatigue and the still fierce fighting (an average of more than two thousand Allies a day were killed in the last days of the war), the endless march was carried out with renewed esprit de corps by the Americans.

Roosevelt hustled his troops onward, pushing them toward Sedan. Rain washed over the French countryside on both the fourth and fifth days of the march. The 1st and 2nd Divisions alternated taking the lead in clearing the area of Germans. The now experienced American troops "moved forward and with the easy precision of veterans found their positions, got their direction, and checked in as in place at the moment of attack."

At eight o'clock in the evening of their sixth day of marching, orders came down to Roosevelt to move his regiment into position for an attack the next day on Sedan. He roused the troops once more for a nighttime march to get into position. In the last stages of exhaustion, the infantry climbed to their feet. "All night long the men plowed like mud-caked specters through the dark, some staggering as they walked" to move to the edge of Sedan. By morning, they had reached a suburb of the city called Omicourt, where they encountered a unit of French soldiers on the heights above Sedan. The 26th brushed by the resting Frenchmen and prepared to attack.

Needless to say, the French troops viewed this maneuver with alarm. Sedan had been the site of the last crushing defeat of the French army by the Prussians in 1871; Germany had held the city through all four years of the Great War. Shouldn't the French, by rights and history, be entitled to take the city? Hurried messages were passed from one Allied command to another and then back to the front lines. Just as Roosevelt was prepared to send his men forward, word came from on high that the honors of receiving the German surrender of the city should go to the French. Sedan's history with Germany was just too meaningful to France. Only the intervention of the high command allowed its surrender to go to France and not to Ted Roosevelt. The 1st Division was pulled back and pointed south and east, toward the city of Metz.[6, 7]

For days now, there had been vague rumors of an armistice, but most of these whispers were discounted. "We had grown so accustomed to war that we could not imagine peace," wrote Roosevelt.[8] Some of the men were fearful that any terms of an armistice would be too favorable to the Germans. Now that the Allies had the Boche on the run, they wanted to see the fight through to a punishing end. Of course, a large number of the "Bills" simply wanted an end to the killing.

Gathered outside of Metz were four divisions of the AEF, including the 1st, waiting for orders. One rumored scenario suggested that the divisions would simply be sicced on the city with no stated objectives beyond allowing the quickest unit to attack to take the prize. In the midst of this atmosphere, Roosevelt heard one enlisted man tell another, "I hope those damned politicians don't spoil this perfectly good victory we are winning."

On the morning of November 11, an officer from 2nd Division headquarters in the rear rode up to Roosevelt and with no preliminaries simply told him that all hostilities were to cease at eleven o'clock that morning. In similar blunt fashion, Ted sent word up and down his column that armistice had come. Many doubted the announcement, which was met with only scattered cheers.

They marched once again that day, but when night fell and the endlessly shuffling feet halted, the men gathered around campfires to talk over the news. They soon grew confident that this was indeed the end. The very fact that they lit fires indicated peace; no one had ever lit campfires before in sight of the enemy.

For Roosevelt the certainty was made clear late that night when another messenger from the rear came forward. Oddly enough, this was a chauffeur in full cap and uniform now standing before Ted with the amazing word that Eleanor was sitting in a car in a nearby village, waiting to see him. Learning of the armistice and carrying news of which he wasn't aware—that she needed to return to the States to be with the children— she had come all the way from Paris, wanting to see him before she left. Could he be pulled away from the front for a moment?

They drove back with the chauffeur to a YMCA station some ten miles behind the lines and had chocolates and crackers. Not surprising in this surreal moment, Roosevelt did not record their conversation. He did note, however, that on the way back to his men, "through the night the sky was lit by fires of the men. On every side rockets were going up, like a Fourth of July celebration. Gas signals and barrage signals flashed above the treetops. The whole thing seemed hardly possible."[9]

THIRTEEN

NEWS FROM SAGAMORE HILL

In early December, Kermit received a letter from Sagamore Hill. "I suppose you are [now] marching through Germany on your war to the Rhine," Theodore wrote. "I really cannot overstate the pride and pleasure I take in what you have done." Archie, he added, was in fine spirits and getting along well, though "He will be crippled for some time to come." Archie had written a small book about the first year of the war and was going into the oil business with a friend of Quentin's at an annual salary of $5,000. Because of his condition it was important for Archie to get a good salary as soon as possible, his father told Kermit.

There were other matters on Theodore's mind that December, but it was good to focus on the details of Archie's circumstances. The fact was that Theodore's body was gradually giving way to his many infirmities, but he didn't want to concern the boys in Europe. He had returned to the hospital in New York in November with numerous aches and pains attributed to rheumatism and lumbago. With walking too painful to bear, he was bedridden and miserable.

In New York, Theodore was visited by an old friend, the writer Hamlin Garland, who made a proposal to the colonel: Garland and a few friends wanted to buy the plot of land in France where Quentin had died. They intended to turn it into a park dedicated to Roosevelt's son's memory. Theodore got emotional at the thought of it, but said he had to check with Edith. Ever the puritan, she ultimately nixed the idea, afraid that honoring her son would suggest that he was somehow more special than others who had given their lives in the war.[1]

Through his various illnesses, Theodore tried to keep working. He had employed Quentin's fiancée, Flora Whitney, as a stenographer in the hospital, and she and Edith along with a string of visitors kept him company during his convalescence. Remarkably, given his condition, there was still talk of his entering the 1920 presidential race, and among those contacting him in the hospital were Republican leaders sounding out his interest in running. He discouraged them.[2]

Eleanor, home from France, visited as well. They had a long, heartfelt talk during which she told him that Ted would probably walk with a limp for the rest of his life. Theodore rued the fact that Ted and Kermit could not come home on leave for the holidays. It would be so good to see them again.

Eleanor opened a door to a deeper subject that Ted simply could not bring up directly with his father. All of the years of trying his best to do as he imagined his father wanted him to do had led Ted nowhere but to a basic uncertainty. He knew that his father loved him, but even now, after all his bravery, after being gassed and wounded, Ted couldn't be sure whether he had been worthy of his father, if Ted had done all that he might to live up to the reputation of this man he adored. Striking now that the exchange could only take place between his father and his wife, that Ted would never hear Theodore's affirmation. "Worthy of me? Darling, I'm so very proud of him," Theodore told Eleanor. Then he used a phrase that he had before in reference to Ted: "He has ennobled his ancestors. I walk with my head higher because of him."

Theodore added a note that should have had some resonance with the son who once stared admiringly at his father from a camp tent at Montauk. "I have always taken satisfaction from the fact that when there was a war in 1898 I fought in it and I did my best to get into this one," he told Eleanor. "But my war was a bow-and-arrow affair compared to Ted's, and no one knows that better than I do."[3]

Back in Europe, with the war ended and peace settling over the Continent, Ted and Kermit marched in the 1st Division with the Third Army toward Germany amid the impoverished and starving populations of a string of French villages. Despite the miseries they encountered, the doughboys were greeted at every stop by celebrations and ceremony. In one small town the villagers presented Ted with a flag containing fifty stars—the two extra stood for Alsace and Lorraine, said the mayor who presented it.[4]

Luxembourg was equally pleased to see them. In one village, a corpulent official presented the keys to the village to Ted. The local band kept striking up a tune that Ted and his aides confused with the Luxembourgian national anthem—a song with which none of them was familiar. Each time the music played, Ted and his officers stood at rigid attention until they noticed that none of their hosts was doing the same. It turned out to be simply a popular tune in Luxembourg.

A couple of days later, in early December, the Americans reached the Moselle and crossed that river into Germany. They were the first U.S. forces to make that entry onto enemy soil and found much trepidation among the population, particularly the women, about what might happen to them. Roosevelt assuaged fears by having a local burgomaster explain that they need have no concerns because his soldiers were Americans and not Germans. He made sure the translation was given in just those words.

Ted and Kermit arrived at the Rhine in mid-December and were billeted near Koblenz a little less than a month later when word about their father's worsening condition reached Germany.

Just before Christmas, the former president began to run a high fever and showed signs of the pulmonary embolism that would soon kill him. He was afflicted as well by shortness of breath, chest pain, listlessness. He made it home from the hospital for the holiday but was unable to perform the duty that he'd served on Christmas for the past thirty years; Archie played Santa Claus for the family instead.

Alice, Ethel, Archie, Archie's wife, Grace, Edith, and the grandchildren were there for the occasion, and Theodore sat up to watch the presents being ripped open by the kids, but that was the extent to which he could participate. He soon went to bed.

Remarkably, in the few days he had left, TR continued to dictate articles for the *Kansas City Star*, for which he'd been writing for many months.

The last night of Theodore Roosevelt's life was spent in the company of Edith, who described his mood to Ted later in a letter. She said he spoke of his happiness at being home and "made little plans for me. I think he had made up his mind that he would have to suffer for some time & with his high courage had adjusted himself to bear it."[5]

He had been having difficulty sleeping because of his pains, so she asked his doctor if it was all right to give him a shot of morphine before bedtime. The doctor agreed, and Edith watched as a nurse administered the drug. Roosevelt's butler, James Otis, helped him into bed. Theodore's last words were to Otis: "James, will you please put out the light?"

He died early the next morning, January 6, 1919.

It was a fact many in the country had a hard time imagining. Though his illness that winter had been widely reported, as had his sicknesses and hospital stay the previous spring, his seeming recovery in the early summer had led to assumptions about his health that weren't true. In fact, he wasn't in good health; his body remained weakened by the infections that had struck in the spring; his heart was going bad.

But to the people of the country, Theodore Roosevelt was such a vital figure that the image of his vigorous body in perpetual rest was difficult to fathom. Even Edith, who had witnessed his decline all year long, had trouble acknowledging that it was over for her husband. Just hours before his death, she had accepted an invitation on his behalf to chair a New York State committee to welcome returning soldiers in the coming year.

It was said that the death of son Quentin and the wounds to Archie and Ted had taken their tolls on Theodore; yet it remained hard to believe that come spring he wouldn't be out on the stump somewhere, shaking his fist at the foes of progressive Americanism.

In keeping with Edith's deep sense that the Roosevelt family should be viewed as nothing more than typical Americans and her husband "as a quiet, democratic, Christian country-gentleman," the funeral service and burial were to be absolutely unostentatious. She asked that no flowers be sent, that no music be played, and that no eulogy be intoned. Just the "simple service of the Episcopal Church, conducted by the pastor, the Rev. George E. Talmage."[6]

Snow greeted the wide range of dignitaries and common folk who filled the Oyster Bay Episcopal Church the morning of January 8. Despite Edith's ban on flowers, arrangements came from the Republican National Committee, the American Academy of Arts and Letters, the Boone and Crockett Club, and several others.

Archie Roosevelt, in the full-dress uniform of the 1st Division and with a chestful of medals, including the Croix de Guerre, served as usher to the crowd. Serving with him were Nick Longworth and nephew Theodore Douglas Robinson. Among those attending were delegations from Congress, the U.S. Army, the U.S. Navy, French and British military men, General Leonard Wood, a weepy William Howard Taft, and Woodrow Wilson's vice president, Thomas Marshall. There were contingents of Rough Riders and citizens from Oyster Bay and some old acquaintances of the colonel's who typified the wide range of his interests and the basic humanity of his life: Harry Donovan, a New York chauffeur and the son of prizefighter "Mike" Donovan, was a great friend of the president's and had sparred with Roosevelt back in the day; Father J. J. Curran of Wilkes-Barre, Pennsylvania, had helped the president negotiate in the famed coal strike of 1902; and Russell Coles, who had gotten the colonel interested in the sport of devilfish harpooning and had just written TR to see if he would be available for a springtime outing. All came to pay their respects.[7]

The man was buried near the summit of a hill overlooking Oyster Bay, across the cove from his home on Sagamore Hill. A morning snow lingered on the ground at the cemetery, but melted quickly as the sun shone and the afternoon ceremony began. The narrow road to the grounds prevented the line of cars carrying mourners from entry, so the family and friends climbed out of their vehicles at the gate and made the climb up the hill to the grave. Dripping snow plopped off the boughs of evergreens dotting the grounds, dampening the hats and brows of mourners passing beneath. TR's flag-draped oak coffin was set on pine boards above the vault and the family, including deeply bereaved daughters Alice and Ethel—but minus Edith, who stayed at Sagamore through the burial— watched as Theodore Roosevelt was lowered into his final resting place.[8]

In Germany, Ted and Kermit spent the day together, remembering their father. Archie had sent them a cable with the news a couple days earlier, writing simply, "The old lion is dead."

That same day, Ted wrote his mother from France, "All our thoughts have been and are with you. We long to be with you. To us and to the country Father can never die. He is too much a part of us. In our best thoughts and actions he is represented."

Brother Kermit put his sentiments more poetically when he wrote Edith, "The bottom has dropped out for me."

FOURTEEN

LEGIONS

On February 15, 1919, twenty officers of the AEF, all of them from the National Guard or Reserve, arrived at a meeting in Paris to discuss with regular army officers from General Headquarters ways to improve conditions within the Allied fighting force in Europe. From the very beginning of U.S. involvement in the Great War, there had been discontent in the ranks about everything from the way troops were supplied, to the way they were trained, to the way they were billeted, to the way they were finally brought into the fighting. Now with the end of the war, there were loud grumblings about the achingly slow way in which they were being shipped home. Morale was sinking, and the AEF command wanted help in giving it a boost.

The difficulties of pleasing such a large and diverse body of soldiers drawn so quickly together, for such a difficult task, and now to be dispersed, were not immediately soluble. The AEF tried to help by suggesting more leave time, more entertainment, and more recreational events for the troops. That didn't seem to answer a basic need of the soldiers, however. Many of the men wanted to know if this was it, if they were now to simply go home and go about their business after such a monumental experience.

The officers soon found themselves drawn together in a cause, one suggested by a key member of their group. Over dinner on February 15, Theodore Roosevelt Jr. asked the men if they would be interested in forming an organization of veterans that would continue to capitalize on the camaraderie and esprit de corps currently found in the American soldiers in Europe. Why let such a powerful force dissipate back in America? Why not form an organization, similar to the one created by Civil War veterans, the Grand Army of the Republic (GAR), to continue to foster the connections made in Europe and enhance the idea of national service back home?

Ted would later credit the idea of forming a veterans' organization to a sergeant he met in passing while in the hospital tending to his wounded knee the summer before. Roosevelt asked the man, Sergeant William Patterson, also wounded, what he was planning to do once he got home. Patterson said he wanted to form a group of fellow veterans in his town: "We've been together in the bad times; let's stick together in the good ones."[1]

In truth, a veterans' organization had been talked about by a number of soldiers stationed in Europe before the war was over, but none had the name, the savvy, and the military and political connections necessary to get the ball rolling. Just thirty-two years old at the end of the war, Ted had already become a figure of national prominence. He was a bona fide war hero, the eldest son of the revered and now recently deceased ex-president of the United States, and a man of striking youth and vigor. He had become a familiar figure at Allied headquarters, knew Pershing and Marshall, and was seemingly conversant with everyone in the 1st Division. By dint of his name and reputation as a frontline fighter, he was also well-known and popular among the doughboys. He had been in the newspapers all his life and continued to garner press, almost always in praise of whatever he was doing.

Over dinner, the twenty officers, most of whom were of a similar rank to Ted, discussed just what sort of principles the new organization should be founded upon. Before the evening was through, they had agreed on three basic tenets, and all smacked of Ted Roosevelt's interests: the first was that there should be no distinction made between those who had served overseas and those who had not; "the desire to serve was what mattered." (The VFW, Veterans of Foreign Wars, founded after the Spanish American War, had excluded those who had not been shipped to fighting in Cuba or the Philippines—a continuing sore point to those veterans in 1919.)

The second principle was that the veterans' organization needed to be democratic in style and function. There would be no ranks among its members; "privates would get a chance to tell generals what they thought of them."[2]

The last tenet pertained to politics: there would be no political affiliations in the group—"the organization should concern itself with policies, not with partisan politics."

The first two issues were straight from the Progressive Era thinking of his father. The last principle emerged from Ted's own rectitude. It would have been hard for Ted, in the wake of his own military career, not to think of how his father had made hay of his Cuban heroics. Surely the memory of seeing the first Roosevelt colonel, accepting the accolades of his soon-to-be deactivated Rough Riders in that Long Island camp back in 1898, on the brink of being nominated for governor of the state of New York (and from there to the office of vice president, and from there to the presidency)—surely it must have crossed Ted's mind that his political future could be just as bright with the backing of an organization such as this. Others certainly thought so.

But Ted's sense that it would be wrong for him to take political advantage of his standing in a veterans' organization such as the one being formed ran deep. From his days back in Groton, when he had balked at the title of "first boy," through his cares on the Harvard football team that he get no special favors, through his first job at the Connecticut carpet factory, Ted had exhibited concern about getting special favors for his status as a Roosevelt. Now he wondered if people would say that he'd been involved in the founding of this veterans' organization simply to organize his own political backers. Already Ted had a political career in mind, and his name would certainly provide him benefits, but he didn't need or want the sort of work he was doing here to cause the organization any taint. He would continue to balk at using the organization as a means to advance his own political fortunes.

The Paris meeting ended with the formation of an organizing committee and a to-do list. Ted was named chair of the committee and was joined by Eric Fisher Wood, soon to be the first president of the American Legion. Also on the founding committee was Bennett Clark, son of the Speaker of the House in Congress, Champ Clark. The organizers decided to hold two separate caucuses, one in Paris, headed by Clark and Wood, intended to gather, lobby, and organize large numbers of veterans still in Europe into forming the group. A second meeting, headed by Roosevelt, who was on his way home, would organize veterans who had not made it to France—those who had remained in the States for the duration.

The Paris meeting took place in March at the American Club and was a rousing success. Because enlisted men had a harder time getting leave and couldn't simply ask their commanders for time off to go to a meeting in Paris, a number of devious means were used to get the doughboys to the caucus. A number of the officers attending drafted privates and noncoms to serve as their orderlies for the event. In some divisions officers took up collections to defray the cost for enlisted men. Almost two hundred men arrived on the fourteenth to discuss the organization, which soon had the name the American Legion. They also quickly adopted the three principles set out by Roosevelt and company at the initial meeting less than a month earlier. There was particularly strong sentiment in favor of the provision that eliminated all rank from the Legion. They decided that each would call the other "comrade" instead—ironic, perhaps, given the strength of anticommunism that would soon dominate the organization.

The U.S. meeting was scheduled for May in St. Louis. Ted arrived back in the States two months before the gathering, and helped open a Legion office in New York. From there, he and others in the fledgling organization sent out feelers to veterans in all forty-eight states, asking of their interest in a veterans' group and whether they could gather state

contingents to come to the meeting in St. Louis. Working with Clark,
Wood, and his brother-in-law Dick Derby, among others, Roosevelt began
to make connections all around the country. In April he put notice of the
gathering in the *New York Times,* calling the organization "an association
which should keep alive the principles of justice, freedom and democracy
for which these veterans have fought."[3]

The American Legion was not the first veterans' organization in the
country, and those that currently existed—the fast-dwindling members
of the GAR, and the VFW—had not done so without serious criticisms.
The fact that a Roosevelt was at the heart of this new organization, however, gave it an undeniable credibility among the public. The name Theodore Roosevelt was still golden, and it didn't matter much if its chief
bearer was now Ted Jr. The pairing of Roosevelt, whose Republican lines
ran deep, and Clark, whose family members were lifelong Democrats, lent
more bipartisan, or nonpartisan, authority to the organization even before
the St. Louis meeting. "It is a pleasure to know that Lieutenant Colonel
Theodore Roosevelt, the worthy inheritor of a beloved American name,
has called a meeting of soldiers and sailors at St. Louis," wrote the *New
York Times* in an April 10 editorial. Of Roosevelt and Bennett Clark, the
editorial continued, "These two gentlemen, associated in a patriotic movement, indicate by their names its common national purpose, apart from
politics and partisanship."[4]

By the time the doors opened at the St. Louis convention on May 8,
1919, the excitement of the attendees could hardly be contained. A new
generation of young veterans had returned to the United States to take a
role in the nation's civic life after having endured a horrible war.

A din rose up to the vaulted ceiling of the Shubert-Jefferson Theatre
in downtown St. Louis, beginning a full half hour before the assembly was
gaveled to order. Mostly young men filled the auditorium to its balcony.
They were bright-eyed and lively, happy, and a little astonished to be
home from the war and together again, now safe and sound, feeling an
intense camaraderie. They were soldiers who had just spent endless months
together in rat-filled trenches, donning masks against fearsome breaths of
mustard gas, going over the top into the sputtering spray of machine guns

in no-man's-land. Somehow they had escaped death and were now miraculously here in this auditorium in the good old U.S.A.

And they had a mission. They were here to do something for their country, to make a difference in their own future, to take charge of their own circumstances in a way that had been denied most of them for the past two years.

A good portion wore dress uniforms, but an even greater number were happy to be in civilian suits and ties, the war suddenly and blessedly behind them and with it all of its trappings. The enthusiasm for the gathering was general and loud, and though it was only two thirty on a Wednesday afternoon, more than a few of the delegates had already indulged in the brew that made St. Louis famous.

Placards denoting the various state delegations were held on sticks by members seated in the audience. Comrades sidestepped through the theater rows to join their proper groups. Up on the stage and arrayed in three tiers arced around a simple table were more veterans, the chief organizers of this gathering of a group calling itself the American Legion. It was a consciously egalitarian organization, whose members individually called themselves Bills, just as the next generation of soldiers called themselves Joes. A full nine hundred strong from every state in the Union filled the theater.

In the center of it all was Ted Roosevelt Jr., the chairman and unofficial leader of the tumultuous crowd out in the theater, raising a gavel that had been given to him expressly for this purpose. It was a mallet carved from wood taken from the rudder of the steamship that had delivered Admiral Peary to the North Pole in 1909, the S.S. *Roosevelt*.

The crowd was so loud that Ted's first crack of the gavel on the table at the front of the room sounded not at all. The second whack only prompted more drowning noise. The third brought howls and more cheers from the crowd for its own disobedience. "Roosevelt, demanding order," said the official history of the gathering, "had just about as much chance of getting it as the Kaiser has of making Prince Joachim [the kaiser's youngest son] King of the Bronx."[5]

After a full two minutes of deafening noise, Roosevelt's gavel finally garnered enough order for his shouted voice to be heard over the din. "Gentlemen," he called. "Gentlemen. A little order! Let us proceed to the first order of business. The floor is open for nominations for permanent chairman of this caucus!"

But the chaos continued. A delegate from the State of Washington rose and was recognized by Roosevelt. "In behalf of the State of Washington," the man said, "and representing the men of the rank and file of the Pacific Northwest, it gives me pleasure at this time to place for your consideration the name of a sterling patriot . . . [a man who] proved himself to be a one hundred per cent true blooded American when his country's honor was assailed. He was among the first who placed himself in the front-line trenches, he was wounded twice, he was ready and willing to make the supreme sacrifice in order that this world might be made safe for democracy. I deem it an honor and a privilege, and the Pacific Northwest deems it an honor and a privilege, to place in nomination the worthy son of a worthy sire—Theodore Roosevelt."

The crowd anticipated his final words long before they could echo through the hall. Ted's nomination was drowned out, but his name was picked up in the chant that followed: "We want Teddy! We want Teddy!"

The legion of men once again topped its own volume, and Roosevelt was helpless to call the caucus to order. He began to pace across the front of the room, the gavel tapping silently in the palm of his own hand. Finally, after several minutes, someone seconded the initial motion, which set off another demonstration. There was more shouting, more cries of "We want Teddy!" To any who'd ever witnessed a national political convention, the pandemonium was comparable to the moment the convention's leading candidate is introduced in the hall.

It was entirely possible at the moment to imagine Ted Roosevelt riding this wave of popular support to whatever heights he cared to. Here was an army of political backers; here was the youth and vigor of a new generation of American leaders, all shouting his name and imagining him as the man who could lead them into a future of righteous civic virtue, just as his father had led his generation at the turn of the century.

Ted stood at the front of the room with the famous broad Roosevelt grin stretching ear to ear. Feet spread wide, elbows out, with the backs of his hands resting on his hips, his whole body suggested confidence and command.

The only problem was that Ted wasn't ready to assume the role of leader. Not in the way his father had been, not yet. What was more, Ted knew it. He was just thirty-three years old and had never held a political office in his life. Aside from being his father's son, he had no real political experience. He had worked in business, he had been a soldier, but he simply didn't know the ins and outs, the give-and-take, the horse-trading and compromise of life in a political party, be it in Albany or in Washington.

When Ted was finally heard he announced his withdrawal from consideration. "It is my earnest wish . . . it is my determination," he told the crowd.

They wouldn't let him continue. "We want Teddy!" they chanted. "We want Teddy!"

"Teddy" turned them down again and again. He would not accept the nomination, and if he was drafted, he would immediately resign. The wide Roosevelt grin remained on his face throughout the demonstration as he paced back and forth in the auditorium before the chanting crowd. His time would come; of that, he was certain. Just not now. Ted Roosevelt had a plan for his future, but it didn't begin here.

"The most amazing incident of the gathering so far undoubtedly has been the refusal of Lieut. Col. Theodore Roosevelt to accept the chairmanship of the organization pending the national convention in November," reported the *New York Evening Mail*. "It took him an hour and a half to make his will prevail over the delegates who demanded he should be the leader of the new organization.

"He remained adamant, and in doing so put an end to the criticism which maintained that the foundation of the American Legion was mostly a scheme designed to further his political ambitions.

"As a matter of fact Col. Roosevelt emerged from yesterday's extraordinary proceedings a national figure in his own right. There are plenty of delegates from states not usually Rooseveltian who are willing to credit him with having the genius of real leadership."

The paper continued in this glowing vein, calling his continued refusal of the honor of being nominated "an almost superhuman feat for a young man"; describing his "iron purpose" as he paced the stage during the shouts of "admirative—and indeed affectionate—clamor" from the delegates.

"The man who could turn so much popularity aside for the sake of principle is destined to go far," the report continued. "To anyone who witnessed those dramatic scenes, when hard-muscled men who have gone through all the cynicism of war gave vent to an almost boyish hero-worship for so young a man, the conclusion is irresistible that he will go, barring accidents, as far as his ambition beckons him."[6]

FIFTEEN

AMERICANISM

In August, Ted began a monthlong twenty-three-city speaking tour on behalf of the American Legion, where again he was hailed for his bravery and principled leadership—as well as for simply being his father's son. In Los Angeles, Ted was greeted by a large crowd of servicemen, including some from the 26th Regiment, along with the mayor and prominent citizens. A reporter for the *Los Angeles Times* wrote, "Those who watched him saw many of the mannerisms which made his father famous throughout the nation. The colonel's son, himself a fighting lieutenant-colonel of infantry in the 1st Division during the war just ended, in talking often heartily exclaims, 'By George,' and 'That's fine' as did his father."[1]

From L.A. he went to San Bernardino, then to San Francisco and on up the West Coast before heading to the Midwest. Ted left the American Legion caucus without an official post in the organization, yet without doubt, he was its most famous and highly regarded organizer. In the months ahead, before the Legion's first convention in November in Minneapolis, Ted would continue to publicize and foster the organization of the group.

He had other projects as well. Ted was elected to the executive board of the Boy Scouts of America that summer, marking the beginning of lifelong service and dedication to that organization. That same summer, he began to write his reminiscences of the war, which he would publish before the year was through under the title *Average Americans*. Aside from being a compelling account of the fighting as experienced by his regiment, the book offered a continued rationale for the "Gospel of Preparedness" espoused first by Ted's father and now by himself. Ted called it American-ism, which was a term also used by his father and Leonard Wood to describe a similar philosophy and political policies. In Ted's book, he tried to make it his own, writing the last chapter like an essay that might serve as the grounding for a political career.

The war had been successful on one level, wrote Ted, in crushing the brutal military power of Germany. But it would be a hollow victory, he thought, if the citizens who fought in this war did not learn its deeper meaning. "More important and more far-reaching than the military vic-tory," he wrote, were the lessons learned through the course of the war. The first of these was the serious unpreparedness of the country. Like his father, he was harsh with the Wilson administration: "We permitted in the past," he wrote, "a policy which substituted fine words for fine deeds, the pen and the voice for action. . . . Those who went to Europe saw blood shed unnecessarily through lack of supplies, inefficient organization, and untrained leadership. At no times did our equipment compare favorably with that of either of our major Allies. At all times in Europe we were to a greater or lesser extent equipped by them."

The institution of a compulsory draft had helped Americans overcome the deficit with which they began the war, Roosevelt wrote. The draft now should continue in peacetime. It was the only way to make certain that the next war would not see the sort of unpreparedness that caused Americans to spend the first year of their involvement in the war learning how to be soldiers.

Ted espoused the old democratization ideas of his father. Universal training would help restore the physical welfare of American youth. Turn them into the fit and healthy youths who could continue to build the republic beyond their service. A continued draft would be a boon for the impoverished and uneducated. "For the person who lives where every modern convenience surrounds him it is difficult to believe the conditions which exist in parts of the country," Ted wrote. Teaching conscripts simple rules of hygiene, the care of feet and teeth, and eating habits could help society as a whole, he argued. As those who had been called to service went back to their homes "in the poor sections of any great city . . . [or] the mountain districts of Tennessee or North Carolina," they could spread the gospel of good health and diet. They would learn of a wider world, too, of cities and learning, where achievement could be won through hard work and education.

The benefits of compulsory training would serve all classes. The democratic nature of the service would help upper-class citizens get a broader sense of the varied classes in the country. Draftees would be treated alike in service—a thing that was not happening in the nation's public schools. "It is a rare thing for the sons of the wealthy to go to the public schools. Compulsory training would be a very real benefit to them."

Roosevelt ended his essay with a long list of soldiers who exemplified the values that he saw at the core of his ideas. Men born in Ireland, Italy, Greece, and Poland. Germans, Jews, and French Canadians—in the wake of the war experience, "All of these men were straight Americans and nothing else. All of these men thought of themselves as Americans."[2] On the other end of the spectrum, men like himself, from Wall Street and the Ivy League, were humbled and made aware of the leveling force of service to a greater cause. More straight Americans.

It was Rough Rider principles on the grandest scale, a national program to preach the gospel of vigorous righteousness to young men across the country.

The idea of Americanism evolved into a number of ideologies over the next few years that tended to diverge from Rooseveltian notions centered on democratization and shifted, in the case of the American Legion, to an emphasis on patriotism. Instead of stressing the principle of national service as an instrument of democratizing the diverse groups of the nation, the Legion developed a bedrock stance against the internationalism of the Bolshevik movement and the IWW—the "Wobblies"—as well as of revolutionary socialists and anarchists. In fact, over the next few years, the Legion often became the bulwark by which right-wing capitalist forces fought against leftist causes in the nation.

On the very day that the American Legion opened its inaugural convention in Minneapolis came the most notorious incident in the organization's history. It was the first anniversary of Armistice Day, November 11, 1919, and out in Centralia, Washington, a group of about eighty newly minted Legionnaires was marching at the tail end of a commemorative parade with other townspeople, including service club members and Boy Scouts.

An IWW union hall was housed in an old hotel in Centralia. The IWW had advocated against the war throughout its course, and the hall in Centralia had been the center of patriotic hostility toward the "Wobblies" a number of times during the conflict.

Now as the parade began to pass the hall, the group of Legionnaires bringing up its rear came to a halt and surrounded the building. At the sound of a whistle from the Legion commander, the men began to advance against the Wobblies inside.

The Wobblies were armed, however, and shots rang out from within the building. Two legionnaires quickly fell and two more would be killed before the bloody scene ran its course.

For their part, the Legionnaires ran to a nearby hardware store to arm themselves with whatever tools they could pull from its shelves. They returned to the hall, overpowered the Wobblies within, and beat many to a bloody pulp. One of the union members escaped out the back with a gun in hand. Wesley Everest was followed by an unarmed Legionnaire, whom Everest shot as he was about to be apprehended. The union man was not saved.

A crowd of Legionnaires soon caught up with him, beat him severely, and hauled him off to the town jail, which provided only a temporary reprieve. That evening, the Legionnaires came back to his cell and dragged him out of it and to a bridge over the Chehalis River. They tied a rope around his neck and tossed him over the rail. Everest was not immediately killed in the process, so the Legionnaires hauled him back up and repeated it, finally executing the man the second time around.

Ted Roosevelt managed to sidestep involvement in this and other Legion controversies in the following years by maintaining a separation between his Legion affiliation and his political career. In the fall of 1919, he had decided to officially enter the world of politics and chose as his first step to walk directly in the trail his father had blazed forty years earlier. He would earn his political spurs in the New York State Assembly. Ted was nominated and ran for a seat from the 2nd Assembly District in Nassau County, where his Oyster Bay home was located. He won election on November 4, 1919, with the largest majority ever given to a candidate from that district. On the same day, Eleanor gave birth to their fourth and final child, a son whom they named Quentin, of course, for the brother Ted had lost in the war.

To some the Assembly seat might have seemed a baby step for some-one of Ted's name and growing renown, but to him, it was a necessary rung up the ladder of New York politics. There was no denying the fact that his political ambitions, and the ambitions of the Republican Party for him, would eventually lead him to seek national office. But his climb would most likely take him to those heights through the governor's office in Albany; and for the moment, he needed seasoning, education in the ways and means of state government and party politics. He quickly had his first lesson.

Heeding the anti-Bolshevist sentiment sweeping the nation at the end of the war, in the opening days of the 1920 legislative session, Roosevelt's own Republican Party voted to invalidate the election of five Socialist assem-blymen from New York. Liberal politicians from both sides of the aisle protested the move. Ted initially waffled on the matter, though he ultimately rose to make his first speech in the legislature in support of the expelled legislators and against the wishes of his fellow Republicans.

According to a New York political journalist of the day, Henry Prin-gle, Ted was "like all first time legislators, lonely and nervous." He was "well liked ... modest and unassuming" and liked to seek out advice from veteran journalists on legislation under consideration. Unfortunately, he also suffered in their estimation by comparison to his father. In Ted's mind, he'd made a principled stand in favor of men being ostracized by their association with a politically unpopular movement. But if he expected plaudits from GOP leaders for his courage, he was sadly mistaken. After his speech in defense of the legislators, the Republican Speaker of the Assembly stood and excoriated Roosevelt for his vote, saying his father would be aghast at his son's response. According to Eleanor, Ted's vote in favor of reseating the legislators was extremely unpopular in his district and across the state as well—"He received so many abusive letters that we thought his political career might be over before it began."[3] It didn't matter to the leaders of his own party.

Nor did liberals rise to his defense. Ted was criticized from the left for not being forceful enough in his defense of the socialists. "He was enough his father's son so that he did not bow to the machine," wrote Pringle. "But he was not good enough to serve as a leader for liberalism and the Socialists were ejected."[4] The sense was that Ted needed a lot more seasoning to skillfully navigate the committee rooms and chambers of the state capitol in Albany.

Ted survived this first battle, and his small rebellion was ultimately forgiven by the Republican Party. He won reelection to his Nassau County seat in the fall (terms were for a single year), and due largely to his last name, he quickly became one of the most popular speakers in the country on behalf of the GOP presidential ticket in 1920.

Ted's role in the campaign turned out to be an important one for the national party, helping him rise above the often petty politics of the statehouse in Albany to become a voice of wide interest. He was drafted into the party's service to offer a clarification on behalf of the GOP: the Republican ticket was headed by Warren Harding for president and Calvin Coolidge for vice president. The Democratic candidates were James Cox for president and in a surprise nomination, Ted's cousin, former assistant secretary of the navy Franklin Delano Roosevelt, who was plucked from a long list of would-be candidates to be the party's nominee for vice president.

Many people across the country assumed Franklin was a son of the recently deceased and still immensely popular former president Theodore Roosevelt, an idea that no one in the Democratic Party was quick to correct.

Ted's role was simple: he was to set the populace straight about who was the true heir. In the process of clarifying, he helped open a breach between the two branches of the Roosevelt family that would have consequences in American politics for years to come.

SIXTEEN

RIVALS

Through most of the first twenty years of the twentieth century, the Roosevelts of Oyster Bay and the Roosevelts of Hyde Park had maintained the sort of sociable relationship of distant cousins who shared the same interest in politics and similar connections to the social circles of New York culture and society. To the Oyster Bay Roosevelts, the Hyde Park family looked a little effete; to the Hyde Park Roosevelts, especially Franklin's mother, the Theodore Roosevelt clan was a little crude, especially the boorish patriarch. In the games played at Sagamore Hill, Franklin stood out as stiff and unathletic, as did his future wife, Eleanor, who as a first cousin to the Sagamore Hill Roosevelts was the most direct bridge between the two families. The differences between one set of Roosevelts and the other were not enough to keep Franklin from relishing his visits to Oyster Bay or to prevent Theodore from heartily blessing the union of his niece Eleanor to Franklin in 1905, and in fact walking her down the aisle.

Nor did Franklin share his mother's low opinion of Theodore. Though a Democrat from cradle to grave, like his own father, Franklin had long been an admirer of his fifth cousin and Theodore's progressive politics. In fact, he emulated Teddy's career, first running for and winning a seat in the New York State legislature and then accepting the position of assistant secretary of the navy in the Woodrow Wilson administration. Franklin served in Washington beginning in 1913 and extending all the way through World War I, and all of his achievements were made with the approval and endorsement of Theodore.

There were some hiccups in the relationship: Theodore and his family had been disappointed that Franklin had not joined them in the colonel's 1912 Bull Moose presidential campaign, instead choosing to remain with Wilson in the Democratic Party—loyalty that helped Franklin earn the invitation to the Department of the Navy in Washington after the election. The Roosevelt boys had also been typically touchy about the fact that Franklin had not resigned from his office and donned a uniform to serve at the front during the war. Few sins were graver to Ted and Archie than shirking, and though Franklin had obviously served his country during the war, he'd never had bullets flying past his head.

Coinciding with Franklin's absence from the war in the summer of 1917 was the beginning of his affair with Lucy Mercer, a Washington socialite and the Roosevelt family's former nanny.

Alice Longworth, who seemed to know everything there was to know in Washington, was well aware of Franklin's romance. As the wife of the House minority leader (Nick Longworth would soon rise to majority leader and then Speaker of the House) and the leading socialite in Washington, Alice was privy to gossip of all kinds, political, romantic, and scandalous. She also frequently socialized with Franklin, which made his affair with Lucy difficult to hide—Alice even invited him and Lucy to dinner with her and Nick.[1]

Under the circumstances it was not surprising that rumors of the romance reached the boys in Europe, who were predictably disgusted to think that while they were suffering in uniform, cousin Franklin was gallivanting around Washington with someone other than his wife. At the height of the romance, which coincided with Franklin's tour of Europe during the war, he made sounds as if he might actually enlist, perhaps trying to expiate his sins, but the idea of his assistant secretary of the navy resigning an important post in Washington for the symbolic gesture of getting into battle seemed ridiculous to Woodrow Wilson, who quickly put the kibosh on the notion.[2]

The troubles between the branches of the family grew more serious after the war when Franklin's value began to rise in the national Democratic Party. The 1920 presidential election would turn out to be a mismatch, with Democrats suffering from a number of factors related to the outcome of World War I and party leader Woodrow Wilson. Chief among them was the fact that Wilson had suffered a debilitating stroke on the heels of his failed efforts to have the United States join the League of Nations. Also a factor was the general upheaval that inflicted the nation in the wake of the war.

Veterans had returned to the States in chaotic fashion, many wondering just what had been the purpose of their service, others demanding bonus compensation. A Red scare was sweeping the nation, and reactionary forces, including the attorney general of the United States, were jailing socialists across the country on trumped-up charges. To protest these right-wing attacks, anarchists had bombed Wall Street, killing 38 and injuring another 140 people.

By the time the Democrats met for their party's national convention in San Francisco in July 1920, Wilson was a presence in name only. Ohio governor James Cox won the presidential nomination on the forty-fourth ballot, and Franklin Roosevelt, a lowly assistant secretary of the navy but a man with a golden surname, was put forward as the candidate for vice president.

The press was quick to note the connection between FDR and cousin Theodore. The Democratic Party tried to be subtle about the relationship; in a campaign biography of Franklin, party publicists failed to mention that he was a relative of the colonel. But then again, they didn't have to. In fact, the less obvious they were about Franklin's ties to the still revered Theodore, the better it might have been. More than a few voters out on the stump were quick to assume that FDR was just another of the many boys sired by TR. Franklin himself was none too quick to clarify his relationship, frequently invoking his cousin's name, and even tossing phrases such as "square deal" and "bully" into his speeches.[3]

The purposeful confusion irked the Oyster Bay Roosevelts not only for the obvious reason that they felt FDR, a Democrat, was taking advantage of their father's name and reputation, but also because they now had a family member with high political ambitions of his own. Ted wanted no confusion about who was the real son of Theodore Roosevelt.

Despite the fact that he was in his early thirties and had completed only a single term in Albany, Ted Jr.'s name was already being bandied about as a future candidate for the U.S. Senate or the governor's office in New York. Sister Alice, a staunch opponent of Woodrow Wilson and his League of Nations, had begun to make it clear that she had political ambitions on her brother's behalf. She was not about to let Franklin usurp the power of the Roosevelt family name in the service of the Democratic Party.

Ted arrived at the Republican National Convention that summer of 1920 as a force in his own right. Though both he and Alice supported the nomination of their old family friend General Leonard Wood for president, they were quick to get behind Warren Harding when he left the convention with the party nomination. Further, Ted volunteered to go on a speaking tour in support of the nominee. It was then that the party gave him what others might have considered the distasteful assignment of shadowing his distant cousin. Ted was to be the truth-teller, following Franklin out on the hustings, to clarify for the electorate just who was and who was not the son of the revered former president.

Matters between the Hyde Park and Oyster Bay Roosevelts quickly got nasty. Speaking to a group of Republican women in Kansas City, Ted gave a rousing speech in which he obliquely reminded his cousin of the fact that he hadn't served in combat during the war. Not only Franklin, but not a single member of the Democratic administration had been in range of gunfire during the late war, Ted said. When someone in his audience hollered out, "Hit him again, Teddy," Ted, warming up to his own subject, hollered back, "I like to hit them when they deserve it."[4]

Ted was joined by other members of the family in his efforts. Alice, Aunt Corrine, brother-in-law Nick Longworth, and even his mother, Edith, got into the fray. Longworth called Franklin "a denatured Roosevelt." Edith said he was "nine-tenths mush and one-tenth Eleanor." In a speech in Wyoming, Ted said that Franklin "didn't wear the brand of our family."[5]

In Franklin's defense came his mother, a furious Sara Roosevelt, who claimed that the animus of the Oyster Bay Roosevelts came primarily because her side of the family, the Hyde Park branch, had "all the looks!"[6]

It's doubtful that the relative closeness, or lack thereof, of Franklin Roosevelt to Theodore Roosevelt had much bearing on the outcome of the election—the Democratic ticket was soundly thumped by the Republicans and probably would have been had Franklin actually been a son of Oyster Bay. Within the family, however, a Rubicon of political politeness had been crossed. From now on squabbles between the Roosevelt family in the political arena would be conducted with bare knuckles.

SEVENTEEN

WASHINGTON

Ted's reward for his speech making and support of Warren Harding was the federal post that had grown to be something of a political sinecure for aspiring members of the Roosevelt family: assistant secretary of the navy. That he was following in the footsteps of his father was a source of pride for Ted Jr.; unspoken was the fact that he was following in the footsteps of his cousin Franklin as well.

Ted was appointed in February 1921 and arrived in the nation's capital soon after. Years down the line, Ted's wife, Eleanor, would write, "Although we were to have bad trouble in Washington we enjoyed Ted's tour of duty there. We were young and life was fun. His work was absorbing."[1]

Edward Denby, his boss, the secretary of the navy, was frequently out of Washington, during which time Ted was in charge, and he liked those periodic moments of increased power, liked rubbing elbows with cabinet members. Harding did not overly impress him (nor did he overly impress anyone else: "To call him second rate would be to pay him a compliment," said Ted's sister Alice).[2] But Ted found the political climate of Washington to be alluring, and he and Eleanor had the ears and elbows of the city's most connected couple: Alice and her husband, the newly elected majority leader of the House, Nick Longworth.

Alice continued to keep a vigilant eye on Ted's future political career in New York. She encouraged his friendship with New York senator Jim Wadsworth, a power in state Republican Party circles, and introduced him to the Washington social scene. Ted was immediately pegged as an up-and-coming political star, with inevitable comparisons to his father. The fact that he and Eleanor now had a houseful of four children to bring to Washington—Grace, Ted III, Cornelius, and the two-year-old Quentin—along with his assignment in the Navy Department, only added to the perception. Nostalgic visions of a large and youthful Roosevelt family occupying the White House once again danced in Republican eyes.

Alice and Nick were frequent companions of Ted and Eleanor at dinner parties, card games, and evenings at the Belasco, a theater in Washington where they all saw Will Rogers one evening and collectively approved of his poking fun at Harding—"A President who went aboard his yacht on Thursday," said Rogers, "did not come back until Tuesday, and played golf on Wednesday."[3]

That Alice and Nick had one of the most notorious relationships in the city did not seem to impinge on their closeness to Ted and Eleanor. Nick was an unabashed philanderer and boozehound whose regular poker games were well-known for their wild drinking and general naughtiness. Alice's affairs with, among others, but most singularly, Senator William Borah of Idaho, were likewise carried out with little to no regard for discretion.

Ted was no paragon of virtue, particularly around alcohol, and he was always sociable; but he had a deep moral streak as well. "I dined with Sister," he recorded one night in the diary he kept during his tenure at the Navy Department. "We had no one but Tom Miller from the outside. I am very fond of Tom, but he has the morals of any ordinary barnyard rooster. He is one of those character combinations you run into in both men and women. He is devoted to his wife and children, and he will run after any girl he sees. He never can quite make up his mind that I am not the same type of man. He merely thinks I am clever in concealing it."[4]

Miller, a friend of Ted's from the war and one of the founding members of the American Legion, was a crony of Harding's as well. He headed the administration's Alien Properties Division and would wind up in prison for eighteen months in 1927 for corruption in running that office.

Ted entered his new office with no prior experience in U.S. Navy matters. He had always been a diligent student of any enterprise he entered, however, from carpeting to bond salesmanship to soldiering, and he quickly became a highly regarded, well-informed figure in an administration that otherwise proved a swamp of mediocrity. His largest task in his first year in office was to help craft ways and means of reducing U.S. Navy ship tonnage to comply with the Conference for the Limitation of Armaments, a gathering of diplomats from Great Britain, France, Italy, and Japan intent on curtailing future arms races like the one that had precipitated the Great War. Ted's role was to work between Secretary of State Charles Hughes and the U.S. Navy Board to negotiate a genuine reduction of American naval arms, one that Hughes could realistically bring to the gathered nations as a meaningful offer, and yet not leave the admirals of the U.S. Navy faint at the thought of the battleships they would be losing. It would become a familiar dilemma in twentieth-century cabinets, and Ted managed to carefully walk the tightrope and received praise from both Hughes and his father's old secretary of state, Elihu Root, for his efforts.

After the conference concluded, Ted's principal duty for the navy became to defend it from further cuts from a growing contingent of the public who felt that military funding ought to be more seriously reduced. Ted spent much of the spring of 1922 in congressional hearings, trying to prevent a further reduction of navy personnel from eighty-six thousand to sixty-seven thousand seamen.[5] He called himself a "hard-headed peace lover" as opposed to the "soft-headed pacifists" who were arguing for a crippling dismantlement of the navy.[6]

Even as he plugged away in Washington hearings, Roosevelt kept an eye on the political happenings in Albany. In May rumors that Ted Roosevelt was in line for the GOP nomination for U.S. Senate in New York prompted a lengthy article on the matter in the *New York Times*. He was seen as a progressive alternative to the Republican incumbent, conservative William Calder. Ted was thought to be "the most popular vote-getter the Republicans could put up for either governor or senator." The problem was that the Republican governor of New York, Nathan Miller, wanted to remain in office, and any intraparty attempt to remove him would be bloody. On the Senate side, ex-governor Al Smith was rumored to be the Democratic candidate for that office, and he would be an extremely formidable foe for any Republican. The question was whether the GOP wanted to send an untried but potentially strong candidate so quickly into the ring against either of these savvy opponents.[7]

Through much of the summer and into the fall, Ted kept a finger to the winds of Albany politics, waiting until the September convention to find out just which way they were blowing. Not in his direction, as it turned out. Miller ran for governor and Calder for the Senate, which in the end was fine with Ted. He could bide his time and run for one of the offices in two years. The fact that the election turned out to be a disaster for the Republican Party, with both of its candidates losing handily, only served to heighten Ted's value within the party. The year 1924 would be one to wipe clean the slate and bring forward a new rising star, the son and namesake of the former president, the man the *New York Times* liked to call "Young Roosevelt."[8]

It was just then, however, that the "bad trouble in Washington" that Eleanor alluded to began to bubble like a well of crude oil.

The name Teapot Dome first came to Ted Roosevelt's attention back in 1921, when he learned that the Harding administration was interested in transferring control of a pair of federal oil fields from the Navy Department to the Department of the Interior. The navy had held these reserves in Elk Hills, California, and a place called Teapot Dome, Wyoming, as a future source of fuel for its fleet; but word reached the administration from the large oil companies that were developing those fields that wildcat operators had moved into the areas and were illegally draining oil from the lands. This prompted the Harding administration to issue an executive order shifting management of the fields from the navy to the interior. The latter had long experience in leasing lands for mineral rights and oil deposits, while the former didn't.

Roosevelt was a little dark on the particulars of the deal, and was uncomfortable with the move. On principle, he felt that oil reserves first created for the potential use of the Navy Department ought to remain under its control. He was told by Secretary Denby, however, that while his opinion was noted, the decision had already been made.

This is where matters got sticky. These federal oil fields would be opened to development by Harry Sinclair of the Mammoth Oil Company, a subsidiary of Sinclair Oil, and Edward Doheny, a well-known Los Angeles businessman and oil operations man—two giants in the industry. Secret negotiations with the secretary of the interior, Albert Fall, had secured the leases for Sinclair at Teapot Dome, and Doheny at Elk Hills, all on the down low, even from Ted. Anyone sniffing might have smelled a rat.

Prior to being appointed to his cabinet post, Fall had been the first U.S. senator from the new state of New Mexico when it entered the Union in 1912. Before that he had had the distinction of being the attorney who successfully defended the accused killer of Sheriff Pat Garrett (coincidentally, an old friend of Ted's father). Fall had also been accused in a number of shady frontier dealings involving various factions, political and business, in the world of New Mexican settlers. Depending largely on where a person stood regarding his pioneer dealings, Fall was either corrupt going to Washington in 1912 or corrupt by the time he headed back.

In his years in the Senate, Fall began enjoying the company of friends of Warren Harding who were dubbed the Ohio Gang. This group of Harding cronies liked to gather at a house on K Street in Washington for poker, drinking, and, according to later testimony in hearings about what was eventually dubbed the Teapot Dome scandal, discussions of how to make the most out of their positions in the Harding administration. Among its members were Secretary Fall, Attorney General Harry Daugherty, and Ted's boss, Edward Denby.

The scandal broke in the spring of 1922, when some wildcat oilmen in Wyoming complained about the drilling being conducted at Teapot Dome by Sinclair Oil. How had Sinclair gotten the leases when no one else was aware of any sort of bidding? Coincidentally, observers in New Mexico noted that Albert Fall's ranch was undergoing a serious renovation with an obvious and deep influx of cash. Ted was drawn into the matter when Fall requested that he send a few Marines to the Teapot Dome area to clear out the wildcat oil squatters from the Wyoming land so that Sinclair could operate unencumbered in the fields.

Ted agreed to send a handful of men to the oil fields, though he continued to remain in the dark about how Sinclair had "won" the leasing rights to Teapot Dome. He hadn't been privy to any of the negotiations.

When the press started reporting on the squabbles between the wildcatters and Sinclair in Wyoming, the administration announced officially, for public consumption, that Harry Sinclair had leased the fields in Wyoming and Edward Doheny in California. As a result, stock in Sinclair Oil skyrocketed and Ted, who had been on a fishing trip in Pennsylvania when all of this broke, came rushing home to Washington in an utter panic.

Harry Sinclair was not only an old friend of his, but also Ted's banking firm had helped finance Sinclair before the war and Ted had served as a director of the company before severing ties during the war. Not only that, but in 1919 Ted had gotten a position with Sinclair for brother Archie, whose continuing depression and war wounds had rendered him a difficult man to employ since the end of his service.

There was one last thing: he and Eleanor owned $1,000 in Sinclair stock, which had just taken a ten-point leap in the stock market. The implications were apparent to Ted; when word got out of his connections to Sinclair, "My political career is over and done with," he told Eleanor.

He rushed back to Washington to find that he could rest easy in at least one sense. For years Eleanor had handled their day-to-day finances. When he had accepted his position in Washington a year earlier, Ted decided that she ought to handle all of his money and gave her power over his investments. One of her first decisions, she told him now, was to sell his Sinclair stock to pay a tax bill. He was safely divested, but would soon hear more on the matter.[9]

Democratic senator Thomas Walsh of Montana, head of the Senate Investigating Committee, began to look closely at the Teapot oil fields in the coming year, but Ted had no involvement in the story through the rest of 1922 and into 1923. The Harding administration, however, began a long, slow, embarrassing decline through the seemingly endless testimony that began to outline its corrupt practices. In time it was revealed that not just the Interior Department, but also the Justice Department, the Office of the Alien Properties Custodian, and the Office of Veterans' Affairs had been crooked. Harding himself was viewed, at best, as an ineffectual leader, more interested in maintaining ongoing romantic affairs (he fathered an illegitimate child while in the White House) and his golf game than keeping an eye out on his appointees. Though Harding, in public, was an advocate of Prohibition and kept the bottom floors of the White House dry for all parties and state functions, upstairs in the private rooms of the mansion, you could get any cocktail you wished. Even Alice Roosevelt, hardly a teetotaler, was appalled by this hypocrisy.[10]

In the summer of 1923, Harding set out on a long journey to the Western states, on what he dubbed "A Voyage of Understanding." He entrained to the West Coast, visiting Yellowstone and Zion National Parks along the way. He shipped north to become the first president to visit the Territory of Alaska, and stopped in Vancouver on the way home, becoming the first president to visit Canada while in office. By the time he reached San Francisco, he was exhausted and suffering from both an ongoing heart condition and pneumonia. While recuperating in the Palace Hotel, he suffered a cerebral hemorrhage and died.

Ted had a friendly relationship with Harding and liked him (so did Eleanor, who referred to him as "that kindly, ineffectual man"), but Harding was hardly a powerful presence in his life. The new president, Calvin Coolidge, on the other hand, was a total mystery to Ted. In his diary he wrote, after hearing of Harding's death, "What the future may hold is prophecy. Coolidge becomes President. In so far as I am concerned, he is a sealed book." Ted admitted that he had no personal relationship with Coolidge and remarkably didn't know of anyone in the cabinet who did. "Though I sat for more than two months in cabinet with him," Ted wrote, "I never heard him express his opinion on major questions. I hope he's for a good navy, but I don't know."[11]

Despite the fact that Walsh's investigating committee was continuing its hearings in Washington, Ted Roosevelt's concerns about the taint of any scandal touching him were so diminished that he began to earnestly plot his political future once again. On a trip to New York in the fall of 1923, he spent a long train ride listening to Senator Jim Wadsworth outline a course of action over the next four years that would lead Ted not just to Albany, but also to the White House. The initial step would be for the two of them to gain control of the Republican Party in New York over the next few months, and then for Ted to run for and win the governor's race in New York in 1924 and again in 1926. From this seat, and with a New York power base, Ted could make a strong case for the Republican nomination for the presidency in 1928. Of course, there were many obstacles on the path to higher office, but Ted confided to his diary, "it is sound tactics" even if "I don't know quite what to make of all this."[12]

Unfortunately for Ted and his aspirations, Teapot Dome soon raised its haunting head once again.

Through the remainder of 1923 and into the start of the New Year, Walsh's committee had bogged down. Missing in the details of the oil deals among Secretary Fall, Harry Sinclair, and Edward Doheny were what a later generation in a presidential scandal to come would call "the smoking gun": the committee had thus far failed to uncover concrete evidence of a bribe being offered by the oilmen and taken by Fall for the rights to the Teapot Dome oil. Through all the months of innuendo and hearsay evidence, no one had ever proved that Fall had lined his pockets with oil money.

That was about to change, and the agent through which the big revelation came was none other than Ted's brother Archie, the Sinclair employee.

In late January 1924, Ted got a call from Archie in New York. His brother's voice was urgent: he needed to talk, privately, and soon. When could Ted be in New York?

As it happened, Ted was already on his way to the city on other business, and the two brothers met as soon as he arrived. Archie was in a panic. He had just learned from Harry Sinclair's private secretary, a man named G. D. Wahlberg, that at the time Sinclair was signing the lease for the Teapot Dome oil reserve, Wahlberg had seen a check for $68,000 in Fall's name from Harry Sinclair. What legitimate reason could there possibly be for a check of that size to be written in Fall's name from Sinclair's account? Here it was finally, proof positive that the secretary of the interior of the United States had been paid off by Sinclair. Archie had not actually seen the check himself, but now he knew of its existence. What should he do?

Ted immediately brought Archie down to Washington and contacted both Nick Longworth and Senator William Borah for advice. At Ted's house, in the company of Eleanor, all agreed that Archie needed to voluntarily go before Walsh's committee to testify against his boss, Sinclair. To confirm his story, Archie also needed to make sure Wahlberg testified.

When Archie called Wahlberg back in New York, he found that the secretary was deeply frightened at the prospect of losing his job if he told the committee of Sinclair's shenanigans. According to Eleanor, when Wahlberg balked, Archie handed the phone to Ted, who told Wahlberg in no uncertain terms the committee would send for him if he didn't show, and further, "It's your plain duty as an American citizen [to testify]."[13]

The press learned of the impending dramatics, and the next morning the committee room in the Senate Office Building was wall-to-wall people waiting to hear the incriminating testimony of the two Sinclair employees, one of them a son of Theodore Roosevelt. Archie offered witness first, telling the story that he'd told Ted two nights earlier of Wahlberg's confession to him about Fall, Sinclair, and the $68,000 check.

A plainly nervous Wahlberg took the stand next. Speaking in a voice barely above a whisper, he denied Archie's testimony. When asked directly by Walsh about what Archie Roosevelt had just testified to, he suggested a juxtaposition that strained credulity. "Mr. Roosevelt is mistaken," Wahlberg said. "I never mentioned a check for sixty-eight thousand dollars. What I said was that Mr. Sinclair had sent Secretary Fall a present of six or eight cows and bulls."[14]

The incredulous guffaws were audible. While the "smoking gun" remained missing for Senate investigators, this blatant misrepresentation was galling enough to set off a fury in Washington. Heads finally began to roll: first, Fall resigned and then Edward Denby. The money trail would ultimately lead to bribes of $100,000 from Doheny to Fall and a little over $400,000 from Sinclair to the secretary.

Ted did not escape further scrutiny. In fact, every connection that he had with the Sinclair Oil Company was looked at through the prism of this obvious duplicity of members of the Harding administration. The public was reminded that Ted had once been on the board of the Sinclair Oil Company, that he had obtained a position for Archie with Sinclair, that he had sent U.S. Marines to Teapot Dome to defend Sinclair Oil Company drillers, and that he had owned a thousand shares of Sinclair stock.

For this son of Theodore Roosevelt, a man who in many ways was more righteous than his father, there was nothing so painful as these public accusations against his character. A man proud of the fact that he'd been able to earn enough in his years on Wall Street to support himself and his family for years to come—so tight with a buck that he drove an old Model T long enough for his neighbors at Oyster Bay to call it "the colonel's historic relic"— he was personally embarrassed by rumors that had him profiting by bribes.

All of which put him in high dudgeon in mid-March, when Nick Longworth called asking for specific details about the Sinclair stocks Ted and Eleanor had owned: How many were there? When were they purchased? When were they sold? How much were they sold for? As it turned out, a congressman from South Carolina, William Stevenson, was making a speech on the floor of the House, accusing Ted of making money from the sale of his Sinclair stock as the leases were being signed with Secretary Fall. He was demanding Roosevelt's resignation from the Navy Department.

Details of the legitimate sale were quickly provided by Eleanor and arrived in Longworth's hands on the House floor, and he was able to rise and defend Ted with hard facts.[15, 16]

Ted, who had been visiting Albany when all this transpired, wasn't satisfied. When he returned to Washington early the next morning, he was furious enough with Stevenson that he made plans to visit the congressman in his Capitol Hill office, and like the pugnacious Groton schoolboy he'd once been, beat Stevenson up. Eleanor could not dissuade him at home and in a panic called Alice. Alice asked to speak with her brother, who came immediately on the line, spitting fury and threats. Did he know, Alice said as calmly as she could to Ted, that Stevenson was a little old man, well into his seventies, who wore glasses? No, he didn't know that. "Remember to have him take them off before you hit him," she said.[17]

Dissuaded from punching out the congressman but still steaming, Ted grabbed a pencil and an envelope and sat at the family breakfast table, with the kids crawling around him, to write a response to the Stevenson attack on the back of the envelope. He explained the history of his association with Sinclair, how and why he got the job for Archie, and the fact that Eleanor had sold their stock at a loss. For all his temper, it was a reasonable and measured response, but he didn't spare his critics. "Every crook," he added, "should be punished regardless of politics or position. Equally crooked, however, with those who take bribes is he who, cloaking himself in Congressional immunity, misrepresents facts in an endeavor to injure an innocent man. Regardless of politics, such a man should be held to strict account, and such a man is Congressman Stevenson of South Carolina. I call on all Americans, Democrat or Republican, who stand for honor, fair play and Americanism, to make it their business to drive from public life slanderers of this type."[18]

His statement went to the press and helped stem the tide that was pounding him. His reputation had been hurt, but Ted remained his father's son—a popular and prominent figure in the political world. A resolution in the Senate asking for Ted's resignation was brought to a vote a few days after Stevenson's attack. It was badly beaten.

Even as he was spared more disrespect in Washington, talk of Ted's running for governor of New York in the fall went to the back burner, a fact that did not disappoint Franklin Roosevelt and his key adviser, Louis Howe. Or, for that matter, Franklin's wife, Eleanor, who was, with the guidance of Howe, becoming a greater political presence in New York politics than she'd ever been before, serving more and more often as a stand-in for Franklin. Franklin, at the time, was in Florida, trying to rehabilitate his polio-stricken legs. There he received periodic updates on Ted's situation from Howe, who viewed the junior Roosevelt as the most dangerous political rival to Franklin in New York and national politics. Like the Oyster Bay Roosevelts, Howe felt there would be room for only one Roosevelt on the path to the White House, and in his estimation that needed to be Franklin. During the height of Ted's Teapot Dome imbroglio, he sent articles detailing the scandal to Franklin, sailing in Florida. He jotted a gleeful note on one newspaper story, much to Franklin's delight: "I'm sending you clippings from which you will see that little Ted appears to be down and out as a candidate for governor. The general position of the newspaper boys is that politically he is dead as King Tut, for the moment at least."[19] The fact was that despite his innocence in the scandal, Ted had not shown much leadership or political astuteness through the whole affair. Through each step of the process— from the transfer of the oil reserves from the Department of the Navy to the Department of the Interior, to the negotiations among Fall, Sinclair, and Doheny, to the deployment of U.S. Marines to protect the Sinclair leases in Wyoming—Ted had raised no questions or alarms within the administration about the dealings. When Archie got involved, and Ted's and Eleanor's Sinclair stock sales were questioned, Ted's behavior and openness were generally above reproach, but prior to that, as one New York reporter put it, Ted was "Filled with faith in Republican human nature, no shadow of suspicion crossed his mind.... Thus he was ... made the tool of the era of corruption."[20]

A cooling-off period followed. Ted remained a powerful figure in Republican politics but stepped back from the limelight. At the National Republican Convention in June in Cleveland, he worked with Jim Wadsworth, his sister Alice, and the New York delegation to help find a suitable vice-presidential nominee for Calvin Coolidge. Alice's lover, Borah, was not interested in the job, which ultimately went to Charles Dawes. Ted noted that "In so far as the governorship goes, there was a good deal of talk about me, but there was also a great deal of opposition. The organization really does not want to nominate me."[21]

As he awaited a final consideration on his political future, Ted continued his duties at the Navy Department. One of these turned out to be dealing with a request from Kermit on behalf of Kermit's shipping company for a naval contract. Ted felt deeply uncomfortable even discussing such a proposition, coming as it did on the heels of the Teapot Dome scandal. He felt that Kermit's very request was insensitive to Ted's position. For his part, Kermit was angered because he felt the request was a legitimate business proposition and that his brother was not taking it seriously precisely because it was coming from Kermit.

Through a series of meetings, lunches, and tennis matches, and mediation by Alice in July of 1924, ruffled feathers were smoothed and Kermit came to understand the delicacy of Ted's position. The matter was dropped, and on a visit to Washington a month later, Kermit stopped into Ted's office and all seemed forgiven. But Ted revealed a deeper sensibility about Kermit and his own growing fatigue with his work in Washington in a diary entry after the visit. Of his time with his brother, Ted said, Kermit "was as delightful and inconsequential as ever. He told me he thought he would have to go to the orient this winter. How I do wish I were able to do the same myself!"[22]

EIGHTEEN

WHO TOLD ME THAT?

Despite daydreams of adventure through the summer of 1924, the tug of politics stayed strong in Ted. A day after last visiting with Kermit, he went up to New York in advance of the upcoming state GOP convention. He took in a Yankee game against the Senators and watched Babe Ruth belt two home runs. The Senators made a remarkable comeback, however, knocking in eight runs in a single inning to win the game. More important to Ted, in the fourth inning, when he stood up to walk from one section of the stands to another, he was pleased to note later in his diary, "the whole grandstand recognized me and cheered and clapped."[1]

The fans at Yankee Stadium foreshadowed his reception at the New York State Republican Convention the next month. Ted's star was ascendant in the weeks before the gathering with support from his old friend Senator Jim Wadsworth and Ted's sister Alice, who both spent considerable time whispering in Republican ears that Ted would make the most formidable Republican challenger to Democrat Al Smith.[2]

Two major issues animated the gathering in Rochester: What was to be the Republican gubernatorial candidate's position on Prohibition? And how was he to deal with the Ku Klux Klan? The Klan was a political power all over the nation in 1924, and had strength in some areas of the state.

Elsewhere the KKK allied with Democrats, but in New York, it had hooked up with the GOP, particularly in upstate regions. It got nowhere with Ted Roosevelt, who had already made a strong statement against the Klan prior to the convention, repudiating any endorsement they might consider offering. He would contentedly live without any support from Klan elements in the Republican Party.

The wet/dry support was a trickier question. Al Smith was a decidedly wet candidate. Ted's stance was that Prohibition was a foolish law, but as a law, it needed to be enforced. Not the sort of ringing endorsement that the Republican drys in upstate New York wanted to hear. Nor did it appeal to the many silent wets in the city who secretly (and not so secretly) wanted an end to what history would judge an ill-advised law.

Reports of the Teapot Dome scandal were also heard in anti-Roosevelt camps at the convention, as was talk that Ted had been too long away from the politics of Albany to be sufficiently aware of state issues. Al Smith would chew him up and spit him out in debates on local matters, went this argument. For good measure, Smith would also "smear [Ted] in oil,"[3] even if Ted's role in the Teapot Dome scandal was ultimately judged "as innocent as it was thick-headed."[4]

All concerns were waved aside at the convention. With Wadsworth's support, Ted was named the gubernatorial candidate on the first ballot. His accompanying platform included a strong condemnation of the Ku Klux Klan, stating, "The Republican party now, as from the beginning of its existence, recognizes neither color nor creed nor race as a test of good citizenship or as a disqualification for any form of national service or national honor. It could not do this and remain either Republican or American."[5]

Odds against Ted were long: Al Smith was the incumbent governor, serving in that office first in 1918, then again in 1922 (he lost in 1920). He was also a national leader in the Democratic Party and had just come from a nearly successful bid at the party's 1924 national convention to be the Democratic nominee for president (he would be selected by the convention four years later). Before becoming governor, Smith had served in the New York State legislature since 1904, rising through the ranks of Democratic Party politics.

Smith's long association with the party stretched back to the days of Tammany Hall corruption, a fact that Republicans had tried to exploit with decreasing effectiveness through all of Smith's elections. Ted opted not to emphasize Democratic vice and instead chose as his principal tactic in the race to outwork, outhustle, and outcampaign his Democratic rival. Soon after the Republican convention, Roosevelt announced that he would begin a speaking tour the likes of which no one in the state had ever seen. Beginning with a ceremony in Oyster Bay at which the Republican State Committee would officially notify Roosevelt of his nomination for governor, Ted would quickly travel by train to upstate New York and wind his way back to the city after giving 185 speeches in 18 days.

"Bands playing 'Over There' and 'It's a Hot Time in the Old Town To-night,' World War veterans, Spanish War veterans, Civil War veterans, gold star mothers, parades, flags, bunting and a small, excited, perspiring, dark-haired man making twenty to twenty-five speeches a day; such was the exhibition given by Theodore Roosevelt in 1924," wrote reporter Henry Pringle of the campaign.[6] Ted on the campaign trail was the spitting image of his father: exuberant, fist-waving, fist-pounding, with that wide Roosevelt grin flecked by a couple of gold crowns, a "bully" here and a "d-e-e-e-lighted" there. Ted spoke with a distinctive frog-voiced bellow that carried to the far reaches of an auditorium, or could fan out wide to listeners gathered behind the back platform of a train. He tried to make political hay of the record of the Coolidge administration while other Republican speakers traveling with him reminded the audiences of Roosevelt's sterling war record and his beloved father. From daises in Legion halls to podiums in school gymnasiums to the back car of his train, Ted whistled-stopped across the state, with a campaign that began to pick up steam by mid-October.

Smith, meanwhile, was peculiarly quiet about his opponent, suggesting to his allies that battering the candidate, whom he was always careful to call "the young colonel"—emphasis on the "young"—would only encourage voters' sympathy, particularly if he mentioned Teapot Dome.[7]

Smith had a surrogate for that job. "From all we heard no one mentioned oil except Ted's cousin, Mrs. Franklin D. Roosevelt," wrote Ted's wife in a reminiscence that still rankled thirty years after the campaign. And exactly how Franklin's Eleanor brought up the subject was boldly original.

Eleanor was flexing new political muscle. With her husband down in Florida, still rehabilitating his legs, Eleanor had jumped full-fledged into the governor's race on the side of Al Smith and against her cousin Ted. It didn't take much for Louis Howe to convince Eleanor that Ted Jr. was Franklin's chief rival both in New York and in federal races to come. And to many it seemed that the more distant she was from her husband, the more confident and independent Eleanor became. At the Democratic National Convention in 1924, Franklin gave the nominating speech for of Al Smith, but then went back to Florida for more rehabilitation. Smith lost his bid for the presidency in a chaotic convention deeply influenced by Klan issues. As Smith returned to New York to focus on the governor's race, Ted took to the road. He was soon followed by a truck covered by an enormous papier-mâché teapot labeled for anyone too dense to catch the symbolism "TEAPOT DOME". The car turned out to be the work of the unpolished ex-newspaperman Howe and none other than Franklin's Eleanor. As unlikely a team as they were, he and she, along with Eleanor's daughter, Anna, had constructed the TEAPOT car and sent it on the road to counter Ted's campaign.[8] If the Hyde Park and Oyster Bay Roosevelts had been distant before, they lived in different worlds now.

Ted soldiered on, continuing to gain ground. He turned out to be a solid campaigner, an engaging man with that broad Roosevelt grin and energy almost as electric as his old man's. According to the *New York Sun*, a speech in Syracuse drew the largest political crowd in the city's history. There were overflow crowds in Binghamton and Schenectady as well. As befitted an inexhaustible Roosevelt, Ted campaigned everywhere around the state, making ten speeches a day in every corner of New York. The nonstop schedule, however, worked against him one day at Colgate University, where he made the mistake of congratulating students on the football team's recent win against Cornell. When he was informed that the team had actually lost the previous week's game, and it was against

Nebraska, Ted turned toward the aides congregated behind him and said, "Who told me that?"

Finally it was time for Smith to get in on the fight. He picked up on the miscue and sent out word to his campaign to highlight it. Every misstatement or error made by the Roosevelt team during the rest of the campaign was met with the mocking cry "Who told Teddy that?" Smith himself gave a speech soon after in which he went through a litany of Ted's blunders during and before the campaign, including his excuses about the oil lease negotiations. After each item, Smith paused to ask the rhetorical question *Who told Teddy that?* By the end of the speech, the crowd needed no prompting to fill in the response.[9]

In his last week of campaigning, Ted made another rousing speech condemning the Ku Klux Klan before a large group of African American voters in Harlem. "I would never stand for any group, organization or individual which at any time endeavored to distinguish between American and American on any other ground except whether that man or woman was a good citizen," he told the crowd. "No race, no religion must ever be permitted to come up when American is meeting American."[10] It was no mistake that he ended his campaign in New York City. It was here that he needed votes if he was to stand a chance against Smith. He told Eleanor again and again that all would depend on New York City, where Smith's base lived and in which he would certainly take a majority of the votes. The question was how big that majority would be.

Ted wound up sweeping the vote upstate, taking fifty-six of the state's sixty-two counties. But he lost heavily in the city, particularly in the Bronx. When the votes were finally tabulated, Ted had done well, pulling within 100,000 votes of the incumbent Smith, 1.6 million to 1.5 million. But Theodore Roosevelt Jr. would not follow in his father's footsteps on this occasion; Al Smith was reelected governor of New York.

Among the many letters of consolation that arrived at Oyster Bay came one from Tientsin, China, where Ted's old friend from the war, Colonel George Marshall, was observing the beginnings of the Chinese Civil War. "I am deeply disturbed," Marshall wrote, "that the intelligent people of New York state did not turn out and select you for their leader.

While it is probably true that you had for an opponent the most popular man in the Democratic party, yet mere popularity should not determine such matters."

A month later, Ted Jr. responded: "Many thanks for your letter. The election was the fortunes of war. After all, we old soldiers know that it is what you fight for and how you fight that is the vitally important consideration. In true First Division style, I am digging in where I halted, waiting for replacements and waiting for a chance to go over the top again."[11]

NINETEEN

POLITICAL ANIMALS

While Kermit had a long history of making expeditions with his father—first to Africa in 1909, and the second on the famed River of Doubt exploration in Brazil in 1914—Ted was a novice to worldly adventure. He had traveled extensively through the United States, but except for the war, he had never ventured out of the country on a lengthy trip. Yet the spirit of adventure coursed through the family's blood, and now, after a disappointing defeat, it seemed a good time for a long and serious journey. As Eleanor put it succinctly, "What to do next? That was Ted's problem at this time."[1]

He wasn't interested in any political appointments, and for all his bravado in suggesting to Marshall that he was waiting to "go over the top again," running for elected office was hardly an option at the moment. In fact, his political future was in limbo, and there was nothing he could do to revive it anytime soon. His star had taken a significant dip in the New York GOP firmament. The measure of any future leader in the state Republican Party was whether he could defeat Al Smith, and it was plain now that Ted could not. While the party recognized that Ted was a great boon to the GOP because of the Roosevelt name and style, he was also a bit too independent to strictly toe the party line. As his father had often shown, a Roosevelt could be more trouble than he was worth.

Beyond that there were whispers that Ted simply did not have the stuff of his father. The way he had campaigned, the style of his oratory, his forcefulness, his energy had all suggested the old man. But his issues were not issues of passionate politics; he was not raining hellfire down on the plutocrats of Wall Street or the timid politics of William Howard Taft or Woodrow Wilson, as his father had done. When he tried to link Al Smith to the corruption of Tammany, it seemed like stale coffee to his listeners, a connection that was far more meaningful twenty years earlier. And he got no one's heart thumping campaigning as he did on the Republican record of Calvin Coolidge. The one political passion that Ted could speak about with heartfelt certainty—the Americanism that he felt so deeply—was an issue that had been spread thin in 1924, so diluted by different interpretations that it could only be argued in the negative, by suggesting what it was not rather than what it was, as Ted did in the case of the KKK's unsavory definition of true-blooded Americanism.

For all the downsides to Ted's political standing at the end of the governor's race, however, there were a number of strong positives to counter the negative. The first was his age: just thirty-seven years old when he lost to Al Smith, Ted figured to have years and years of electoral eligibility to come. If he traveled now, he would be back in New York in time for the next gubernatorial race in 1926, still not forty years old, and fresh and tan from a world adventure. Young and bully, he'd be around for the next general election in 1928, when Al Smith might possibly be the Democratic candidate for the presidency.

On top of this was the fact that the Republican Party was not exactly loaded with quality candidates in New York or at the presidential level— witness the fact that "Silent Cal" Coolidge might be the presidential standard-bearer for the rest of the decade.

Perhaps most encouraging from Ted's future political perspective was the fact that his cousin's future in New York and national politics seemed doubtful. Despite Franklin's diligent efforts to literally get back on his feet, his polio remained an intractable obstacle. In the world of Roosevelt family politics that meant it was Ted's future in politics that remained brighter, even in the wake of his defeat by Al Smith.

Whatever the psychological cost Ted's defeat might have brought to him—and no doubt, he was a man who didn't like to lose—on many levels his "involuntary holiday" was welcome. A "hard trek" was a respite from the frustrations of campaigning, the past stresses of dealing with the Teapot Dome controversy, and the often mundane world of running a Washington, D.C., bureaucracy. Roughing it had been second nature to Ted's father and a natural response to political loss.

Besides jaunts to South America and Africa, as well as wartime in Mesopotamia, Kermit had made a solo journey across the Sonoran Desert in Mexico, had hunted tigers in India, and had made several trips to Korea and Japan, once riding the Trans-Siberian Railroad across the Soviet Union to Moscow. If Ted was the responsible oldest son, dutifully following his father into the family business of politics, Kermit was the great adventurer, never quite settling down but always colorful, full of tales of travel and experience. For all of Ted's sense of responsibility, at times he was pulled by an intense desire to do just the sort of wandering that inspired Kermit. They were, in other words, a nicely matched set, brothers looking forward to journeying together.

Native to the mountains of central Asia, the *ovis poli* is a great-horned sheep, a larger relative of the bighorn sheep of the American West. Its long, spiraling antlers are the lengthiest of any sheep in the world, measuring up to sixty inches. First spotted by Marco Polo on his journey to China in the thirteenth century—and subsequently named for him—the animal lived in virtual obscurity for nearly six centuries until the British colonization of the subcontinent rekindled interest in the ovis in the West. Even then, only a few hardy British adventurers were able to trek to the largely inaccessible region of the world where the ovis live, and consequently no mounted specimens could be found in any American natural history museum. When Ted and Kermit found out that the Field Museum of Natural History in Chicago was interested in building a diorama centered around a group of ovis poli, they had found the quarry upon which to focus their journey. They quickly contacted Stanley Field, the president of the Chicago museum, who in turn contacted James Simpson, chairman of the board of Field's own Marshall Field Company. Simpson agreed to fund the expedition.

In the company of zoological collector George Cherrie, who had been with Kermit and his father on their epic exploration of the River of Doubt, and a photographer, distant cousin, and longtime friend of the two Roosevelts, C. Suydam Cutting, the brothers began to plan the details of the trip.[2] They would sail to India in late spring and travel over the Himalayas at Karakoram Pass before pushing into the Pamir region, to Turkestan, across the Chinese plains, and into the Tian Shan Mountains. They would then circle back to the Pamirs and the Himalayas before winter closed the Himalayan passes back into Kashmir.

In offering a preview of the journey to its readers in a May 1925 *Science* magazine article, the editors wrote, "Newspaper accounts have, perhaps, borne heavily on the idea that the region to be visited is wholly unknown and quite unexplored. This is of course not justified, for although it is remote and difficult of access, sportsmen and travelers, mainly British and less famous than Marco Polo, have traversed much of it and various books and maps have been published. Many parts of it, however, offer wholly new fields for the zoological collector and carefully made collections are particularly desirable at this time to supplement those being made somewhat farther north by Roy Chapman Andrews and the Third Asiatic Expedition in connection with which the American Museum and the Field Museum have a cooperative agreement."[3] In other words, the Roosevelt boys would be trekking in rough and fresh territory, but ground already mapped. The true novelty of their journey would be in what they shot, skinned, and brought back for the natural history displays that were so popular at the Field Museum.

Aside from the arduous task of supplying the trip and arranging for transport, the Roosevelts dealt with scores of would-be adventurers from all over the world who wrote to them asking if they could join the expedition. They ranged from legitimate outdoorsmen to cranks, and even to a stenographer who thought his skills might be valuable. All were turned down; not only did the brothers think it best to travel with just Cherrie and Cutting, but for financial reasons, "they had to cut personnel to the bone." They also would have to cross multiple borders and secure passage from a number of governments, including distant China and the Soviet Union, which had no embassy in the United States at the time. Ted and Kermit would have to wait until they got to London before they could obtain visas from the Soviets.[4]

For reading material, Ted packed *Pilgrim's Progress*, the Bible, Shakespeare, the poetry of Kipling (a friend of both Roosevelt boys), the poetry of Edward Arlington Robinson (another friend), *Plutarch's Lives*, the comedies of Molière, and "a number of others selected equally at random." The brothers also decided to transport a pack of four cougar hounds, two from Montana and two from Mississippi. These were to be used in case Ted and Kermit found themselves hunting what Ted called "the varmints" of Asia, meaning, in particular, a rare tiger found in the region, which might present dangers to the brothers. The dogs turned out to be far greater nuisances than any "varmints" on the journey.[5]

Ted, Kermit, and Cutting sailed for England on April 11, 1925. After picking up their Soviet visas, they traveled through Paris, Marseille, the Mediterranean, Port Said, and Aden before landing in Bombay exactly a month later, on May 11, in the early stages of the hot season in India. Cherrie had already arrived with the dogs in tow. All entrained now to the famed Vale of Kashmir, and in seven days, the expedition had left all motor power behind. A long train of sixty ponies was gathered and the group set out for Zoji La Pass between Srinagar and Leh in the western Himalayas of northern India. In the words of Kermit, they made this first major crossing "serenaded by avalanches."

As they trekked, they passed from the world of Islam to that of Buddhism. In preparation for their trip through Islamic territory, the Roosevelt brothers had been growing beards since the beginning of the journey—a natural feature on the faces of Muslims, but not on Buddhists. At Leh, however, they were advised by the shikaris (local hunting guides) in their train to shave for their ceremonial visit with the local Buddhist officials they would now be visiting. The brothers along with Cherrie and Cutting opted to keep their beards, and instead dressed in "store" clothes—long pants with cravats tied over their hunting shirts—to honor the dignitaries. No offense to their unshorn faces was taken by the locals. After tea, the group was welcomed at a polo match staged for their pleasure.

Outside of Leh, they began hunting for burrhel, a smaller relative of the ovis poli, about the size of a donkey. After shooting enough for the purposes of the museum, they moved deeper into the mountains, and Ted and Kermit soon found themselves at the highest altitude either of them had ever climbed, 17,800 feet. Ted confessed to being winded by the ascent, though he didn't experience altitude sickness until beginning the downward hike. There were higher passes to come shortly, including the famed Karakoram, which separated India and China.[6]

It should be noted that Ted had done little to get himself physically in shape for this journey. He was a heavy smoker—both cigarettes and pipe—for all his adult life, and he also contended with the fact that he'd taken a bullet through the knee less than ten years earlier. That wound bothered him throughout his life, and it undoubtedly did now in the mountains. Nevertheless, he made few complaints about the difficulty of the trip except to record that at 17,000 feet the heart beats "like a trip-hammer" and sleep was difficult. "You wake every few moments, struggling for breath, and feel as if you had been long underwater. The severity of the journey is mutely witnessed by the bones of pack animals which lie everywhere."[7]

They camped on glaciers and snowfields, forded rapid-flowing mountain streams. They found out from meeting other caravans heading back toward Leh that Karakoram Pass was in good shape for a crossing. On the way up, however, they saw ominous-looking dead horses and donkeys, even a few camels. "The tracks of wolves were everywhere," wrote Ted.[8] The Roosevelt expedition itself lost a pack pony on the last ascent to the summit of the pass—the eighth animal thus far lost—but they made it over Karakoram.

There were several more harrowing Himalayan passes before the party began the descent from the mountains down to the Turkestan plain to the north. Once there, they followed the Yarkand River and made good time across the flat landscape toward the Tian Shan Mountains to the north. Along the way they separated from Cherrie, an ornithologist by scientific training who would now collect birds and smaller mammals of the region for the museum's holdings. With Cutting along for company and photographic witness, and working at a slower pace, Cherrie trailed the Roosevelt brothers for a time, but would eventually break off permanently and head out of the region by way of Russia through western Turkestan.

Ted and Kermit kept on, passing through the territory that Marco Polo made famous as a trade route to China, through desert landscape to the north, pushing for big game. They skirted and then entered the westernmost portions of China and acquired an overweight government official as an official but cumbersome and unwanted guide through the desolate territory.

Ted admired Kermit's skinning techniques on one desultory trek through the desert. As boys, Kermit and Ted had made a very Rooseveltian hobby of taxidermy, at which Kermit became better than proficient. Despite having little practice in preparing small mammals since the days when the Sagamore Hill icebox invariably held a dead rodent or two, Kermit retained enough expertise to be able to pin out and skin the carcass of an Asian mouse against his saddle as he continued to ride his small pony through the flat land. An impressive skill for just this sort of expedition.

Eventually the brothers began to climb out of the plain. And after a day's ride into the foothills of the Tian Shan Mountains they found a more pleasant landscape, stopping at a yurt on the edge of a spruce forest beside "a glade literally frosted with snow white blossoms," Ted wrote. Just beyond the dell, now four months into the journey, they spied the mountains themselves.[9]

Ted and Kermit were eager for serious hunting. In hours they sighted the first ibex of their journey, which, after the ovis poli, was the brothers' (and the museum's) most sought-after game. They went exploring for game and soon brought down roe deer and wapiti. Their best Kashmiri shikaris—a pair of brothers, Rahima and Khalil Lone, who would become famous in Kazakhstan for their subsequent work guiding Westerners on trips like these—spotted a group of fifteen or sixteen ibex sipping in a stream bed about two hundred yards distant "like a row of brown stones." Kermit won a coin toss and got the first shot; he fired and the ibex scattered, but not before Ted shot as well. No animal fell, but both brothers were confident they'd hit something and followed. Two blood trails went straight up the nearby mountainsides, an almost perpendicular ascent. The trails split, and the brothers did as well. As darkness came, Ted finally gave up his hunt while Kermit kept after his goat, ultimately bringing it in late that night. It took a second search the next day, but Ted finally found his, too, and brought a second ibex into camp.[10]

They continued the hunt from their idyllic spruce forest, shooting wapiti and Asian bear in the Tian Shan. They failed to find the ovis poli, however, and to make it the long distance back over the Himalayas before winter arrived, they had to swing back toward the Pamir region to have a chance at bringing home the big-horned sheep. Turning back over the Yarkand flatlands on their return journey, Ted and Kermit witnessed the colorful rituals of a Mongolian wedding, complete with a horseman groom swooping down across the plain to capture his bride, who was riding double with her father on the back of a pony. They continued to hunt for various big mammals as they skirted the Mongol plains to the east and the Tian Shan to the west, but they knew they wouldn't have a chance to find any poli until they got back to the Pamir.

Anxiety grew among the members of their train as the days and weeks passed on the way back to the big mountains. In everyone's head was the ticking clock of the seasons. No one wanted to be trapped on the wrong side of Karakoram Pass for the winter. Heading due south now, the expedition finally began to climb the foothills of the Pamirs, whose bare red buttes reminded Ted of the landscapes of Colorado. It was now October, and the weather was getting cold—bitterly cold in the mornings. There were occasional flurries; up ahead in the high mountains, they could see the snow lying thick near the summits. There were no trees in the Pamirs and thus no firewood to warm their mornings.

They switched from ponies to yaks as their principal beasts of burden. "Not an uncomfortable beast to ride," wrote Ted, "but patience is necessary. . . . He moves over obstacles with the same deliberate unconcern with which I have seen a tank in the war negotiate a shell-hole." For all its barrenness there was quite a bit of wildlife in the mountains: they saw wolves, vultures, snow buntings, and hawks.[11]

A few days into the Pamirs, the brothers passed a lake full of geese and flushed a drove of bouncing hare. A few moments later, Khalil Lone jumped off his yak and cried *"Goolja,"* the native name for ovis poli, pointing up at a slope six hundred yards ahead. With spyglasses quickly pulled, the Roosevelt brothers scanned the hillside. There in the distance they spied the sheep, running toward the summit. Ted and Kermit quickly determined that these poli were too small to shoot. To fulfill their own standards for the museum grouping the brothers were searching for a near record length of horn, ideally in the neighborhood of sixty inches. They were also hoping to find two pair of poli, both male and female, to round out the grouping for the diorama. Later that same day, they saw a group of female sheep but determined not to shoot until they had first got their horned rams. They went back to camp, thrilled to have sighted their quarry at last.

The next day Ted and Kermit headed toward the mountains surrounding the lake. As they climbed, they found a difficult ascent, up to sixteen thousand feet on snow and slippery rock, but one of their shikaris had spotted poli ahead, so they plowed forward until they reached the summit. There, late in the afternoon, they spied eight poli, with horns that ranged, by their estimates, from forty-five to fifty-five inches.

To make the climb to the top, the brothers shed their winter coats, but once at the summit, they were freezing, damp with sweat, chilled to the bone, and shaking from the cold. They agreed that they had no chance to make the sort of accurate shot necessary to bring down a ram at a distance of hundreds of yards. It began snowing as they headed back down the hillside to the spare comfort of a yak-dung campfire. Ted slept with his shoes in his bedroll to prevent his feet from freezing in the night.

Up at four thirty, they reclimbed the mountain, and two hours later spied their game once again. The rams saw the hunters as well, and took off up the mountain. Ted, Kermit, and the Lone brothers watched until "At last they breasted the crest, showed for a moment outlined against the sky, and then disappeared on the other side." The hunt was on.[12]

The brothers climbed alternately through loose shale and waist-deep snow until they had reached an altitude of seventeen thousand feet. When they paused to rest, Ted collapsed and stretched out full on the ground, his chest heaving. They had reached the same crest where the poli had been outlined against the sky, and once again they saw sheep about a mile away across the valley below, as if taunting them, ever receding from their hunt.

To get their shot required another five-mile stalk, which was waged over two more mountaintops, over more loose shale, more snowdrifts and boulders. A fog began to roll in, and at one point Ted and Kermit were forced to toboggan down a steep slope on their own backs, almost starting an avalanche in the process. Once again they were sweating heavily and simultaneously chilled by a sharp wind. Six hours had passed since they'd first spied the rams across the valley, when finally the fog lifted and they were able to once again see the poli, at a distance of about eight hundred yards.

Now they crawled closer, looking for their shots. Ted had won the coin toss for the privilege of firing first, and at four hundred yards he rested the rifle in the crook of his left hand, steadied his breathing, and took aim at one of the animals. He slowly exhaled as simultaneously he squeezed the trigger. Kermit opened fire moments later. As the crack of gunshots echoed across the mountains, the rams bolted, running right toward Ted and Kermit, who raced closer. The sheep were running single file and came around the bend of a huge rock on the mountainside, now only 250 yards away. "Their great spiral horns flared out magnificently, their heads held high." Ted quickly took off his gloves and fired at the two leaders. "First one and then the other staggered."

But they weren't done yet. The wounded poli pulled themselves upward and continued on. The Roosevelts quickly picked up the blood trail and followed. Again they were negotiating waist-deep snow and scree, and time slowed to an achingly heavy pace. They were stuck in white tar, knowing that their long-sought-after prey was made for these conditions while they were not. Suddenly the wind picked up and snow began to fall, adding to the depths they were already mired in. Darkness was coming, and the Roosevelts knew they would have to resume the search the next day. Certain they had mortally wounded two animals, they worried that wolves would find the game in the night. The beautiful horns would have made fine trophies, but they needed the whole of the skin to make museum pieces, and no pack of wolves would leave enough of a poli skin to make the animal recognizable to schoolchildren wandering through the Field.

Their tents that night were stiff with ice and snow. They slept restlessly, shivering through the windy darkness, waking up anxious and eager to find the trails once again. For the whole day they searched for any sign of the big sheep. As evening came they reluctantly went back to their tents. One determined shikari who knew the mountains particularly well stayed out looking. He returned well after dark, having discovered the two dead animals; but just as they had worried, wolves had found the sheep in the night and stripped the flesh, leaving just the heads and curving horns. The man presented these to the Roosevelts, but without the animals' bodies they were simply trophies. It was small consolation to learn that one of the racks was more than fifty inches, and the other, just under.

Time was running out on their journey. The Kashmiri guides were getting extremely nervous about being caught on the wrong side of Karakoram Pass as winter neared. The brothers made a hasty decision to move eastward toward the Russian Pamirs in Kyrgyzstan, and pulled up stakes on their camp.

They got lucky in the process. A half day's hike from the lake, they came upon a village of four yurts and learned from the natives that poli were thick in the nearby mountains. The Roosevelts left word that their caravan, trailing behind them, should stop in the village, and without pausing, they set out for the mountains to continue their hunt.

Almost immediately one of the Kyrgyz villagers, who had now joined them, spotted a herd of poli, both male and female, grazing in a valley. An easy stalk brought the hunters to a hillside above the sheep. They caught their breath and fired into the group, killing one ram outright and wounding two others. Leaving Khalil Lone to skin the dead male, Kermit and Ted separated and trailed the two wounded sheep, eventually bringing them both into camp.

The next day, they set out again from the village yurts, and at noon they found their prey: a large herd of females accompanied by four rams. They all judged the horns to be about forty inches and angled up a hillside to get their shots. Unfortunately, the animals took off as the hunters moved, and the Roosevelts had to swing out wider into the mountains to head them off. Cresting a ridge above the valley, they inched out to see the poli below. There was no time for any more stalking: Kermit fired, and Ted did as well; each brought down a ram. Ted stayed to skin the sheep while Kermit set out after a third poli.

The horns on each were about forty inches—a disappointment to Ted. The animals, however, were each good-sized poli, and he quickly realized that the museum taxidermists could place the heads of the larger rams, killed at the lake camp and scavenged by wolves, on these skins to make their display. A good thing: not only had Kermit rejoined Ted empty-handed, but also the western sky had turned a dark purple as a fierce snowstorm began blowing in.

The yaks arrived to bear the burden of the poli skins, and the party headed back toward the village. The Kyrgyz suggested a shortcut over a mountain to get back toward the train quicker, but that meant climbing a steep slope already covered in snow up to the bellies of the yaks. Halfway up the hillside, a blizzard broke on top of them. Ted could barely make out the rumps of the yaks, "white-crusted . . . [looking] like moving snow-drifts," as they climbed over boulders and through the thick snow. An hour after the climb began, they crested the mountain and began a slippery, sliding descent to the valley below, where another hour later, the yurts suddenly appeared out of the howling storm.

"We had our sportsmen's trophies, the two big heads," Ted wrote later. "We had our group of poli for the museum."[13]

Standing before the fire in the relative warmth of the yurt, Rahima Lone pronounced the end of their journey. "All right, good morning, going!" he said.

A few weeks later, they made their way back over Karakoram Pass without incident.

Part of the agreement in letting their husbands make this journey was that the Roosevelt brothers' wives, Eleanor and Belle, would get their own trip to India. At its outset, they made plans to greet Ted and Kermit in Kashmir in early November. Consequently, they traveled together to the sub-continent, following the same general route as their husbands, and arrived in Srinagar, in the northwestern Kashmir area of India, remarkably enough, on the same day that Ted and Kermit were just finishing their last leg of the expedition. In fact, they met their spouses on the road outside of Srinagar coming down the mountain from their three-thousand-mile journey.

Sporting sheepskin coats, boots, caps, and thick beards, Ted and Kermit were hardly recognizable. "After dinner," Eleanor wrote, "Belle and I had but one idea, to get their beards off as fast as possible, as we made them sit one at each end of the table while we worked over them with sharp scissors. After twenty minutes of shearing the table looked as if we had been making over a rather poor quality mattress, and it was a great relief to see their faces again."[14]

The two couples spent a reunion month hunting in Kashmir, where both Eleanor and Belle set out in pursuit of a native deer called barasingha. Shooting was a skill that each of the wives had acquired through years of being married to Roosevelts. They were hunting at six thousand feet "wearing all the sweaters we could find," Eleanor would later write; Ted was with Eleanor in one party, Kermit with Belle in another. Eleanor's excitement caused a missed shot the first time she spotted a stag; a second effort was no more fruitful.

On the third day out, word came from Kermit and Belle's camp that she had gotten her barasingha that morning, an eleven-point stag, and Eleanor was determined not to be upstaged by her sister-in-law. They were leaving the next day at noon, which gave Eleanor just the morning to get her deer.

They fell behind the hunting guides on the start of the climb, and Ted gave her one end of his muffler and helped pull her up the hill until they saw the guides paused on a ledge with field glasses, indicating they saw barasinghas ahead. Eleanor hustled to get to their location but was too winded to shoot. "An easier shot could not have been imagined. But it was no use. I was still so winded by the climb that I could not even point by rifle, much less sight it. . . . The stag disappeared behind the rocks. Now I wished I had taken a chance when I realized that now I had to run uphill for some distance in order get another, much harder shot!"

Somehow they got up the hill, but the deer had spotted them and was running toward the crest of the hill. "It was now or never," Eleanor wrote. She shouldered her rifle and fired off six shots "just as fast as I possibly could." The barasingha stumbled but kept going. Eleanor lay down on the hillside with her face in the soil, thinking, "No power on earth could make me move until I could breathe." It was just then that Ted and one of the Kashmiri guides grabbed her by the elbows, a third member of the party pushed her from behind, and they kept on. "According to Ted I kept saying, 'I wish I were dead!'" Eleanor recorded. "'Oh, how I wish I were dead!'"[15]

But she made it to the top of the ridge, and just beyond it was the stag. Eleanor caught her breath, aimed, and fired true. The deer "plunged down the hill stone-dead, and I very nearly did the same."

She had her barasingha, a ten-pointer, just one less than Belle's, though Eleanor was careful to note that the length and spread of the antlers were larger than those on her sister-in-law's deer.

The many prizes from their journey were shipped in the spring of 1926 to the Fifth Avenue mansion of Suydam Cutting's father, a wealthy Wall Street financier. More than a thousand specimens needed to be sorted through before they were shipped to the Field Museum in Chicago, including bears, boars, ibex, and the barasinghas that Eleanor had shot, along with hundreds of smaller species and, of course, the prize ovis poli. The skinned animals were placed in a large room in the Cutting home in mounds of unsorted bones and hides with bits of dried flesh still clinging—and decaying—on the bones. The smell of the festering remains literally caused a stink among the Cuttings' upscale Upper East Side neighbors. The Roosevelt brothers, George Cherrie, and Suydam Cutting all sat down to sort through the treasures of the expedition and suffered even more intensely than the neighbors before the skins and bones were separated and sent to the New York Central Railroad for shipment to the taxidermy department at the Field.[16]

The ovis poli made their debut, with Ted and Kermit in Chicago accompanying them, on April 17, 1926, before ten thousand visitors at the

Field Museum. The brothers offered alternating lectures to discuss their trip. "We were fighting the elements of nature every day," Ted said. "The mountain streams in the Himalayas were running torrents from the melting snows, and the avalanches were far more numerous than they would have been had we delayed two or three weeks. But that was impossible. We were fighting time as well as nature."[17]

Eleanor wrote of "the great excitement and much publicity about the expedition" in the pages of the New York and Chicago papers. Other observers, however, noted a slight undercurrent of mockery about the journey that suggested the two Roosevelts had been on a political-minded lark as much as an adventure. In taking note of the prize catch of the trip, Will Rogers wrote, "You don't know what an *Ovis Poli* is? It's a political sheep. You hunt it between elections." When a photo appeared in one of the Chicago papers that showed Ted and Kermit along with the Lone brothers, with the ovis poli between them, the caption writer did not recognize the Roosevelt brothers beneath their heavy hunting beards. The cutline read: "The Ovis Poli with four natives."[18]

TWENTY

OFF THE MAP

Returning to New York in the midst of another gubernatorial election year, Ted considered running for office again. Unfortunately, any thoughts of gaining political capital from the hunt were quickly forgotten. The humorous snarking about their adventure undercut its drama and seriousness, and the fact that the biggest prize to come from their adventure was a big-horned sheep might have been fine for the purposes of the Field Museum, but thrilled few others.

Though Ted remained an appealing figure with the GOP faithful, his popularity rested more in the country as a whole, where the Roosevelt name still carried some magic. In New York, however, the name Theodore Roosevelt Jr. had gone stale. The state Republican Party, at least, was unenthusiastic about pushing him toward a run. He was, put simply, damaged goods as a candidate. Journalist Henry Pringle wrote of Ted, "He would have been game, no doubt, for another spanking from Al Smith. Even the New York Republicans are aware, however, that it is bad psychology to enter a defeated candidate against his conqueror."[1]

Ted had a should-I-or-shouldn't-I consultation with Calvin Coolidge before making a final decision about running for governor in 1926. The president was discouraging, telling Ted simply that the time was not right for a run. Some suggested that Coolidge was cool to the idea because he was grooming Ted for a position in his administration; others whispered that he was personally put off by Ted's "vivacity." His boisterous style was not compatible with the taciturn Vermonter, and no appointment was forthcoming. Nor did Ted throw his hat into the race for governor.[2]

Had the year out hunting in the wilds of Turkestan dampened his political prospects? His mother was concerned enough about Ted's future to send him a cautioning letter about being relegated to a figurehead position in the GOP. Don't let the party "send you around to all the doubtful districts and county fairs to speak for the other men," she warned.[3]

But despite Edith's cautionary note, the man against whom he continued to measure his political career, cousin Franklin, seemed no closer to Albany or the White House than he. Ted was not yet forty years old; there still seemed plenty of time for him to get back into politics. Franklin, meanwhile, five years older than Ted, had ensconced himself at Warm Springs in Georgia to continue his polio rehabilitation. He seemed no nearer to a return to politics than he'd been before.

Ted would need to do some work; he would need to reinvigorate his image; he would need to ingratiate himself again with the state's Republican Party; he would need to keep the Roosevelt name in the papers. In modern terminology, he would need to rebrand himself to challenge Al Smith in 1928. But it all could be done if he put his shoulder to the wheel.

Instead, Ted retreated to Oyster Bay and New York City. He commuted to an office in Manhattan on most weekdays, from where he dictated *East of the Sun and West of the Moon*, a book coauthored with Kermit about their adventures in pursuit of the ovis poli. He also wrote *All in the Family*, a combined reminiscence on his childhood at Sagamore Hill and tutorial on how the Roosevelt family had lived and been guided through his early years. During this same period, he wrote *Rank and File*, which was a collection of true stories of the Great War.

Ted also did a lot of hanging out with brother Kermit at the Knickerbocker Club in Manhattan. A floor in a nearby brownstone served as an annex to the club, and here the brothers, alongside other clubmates, escaped the strictures of Prohibition at a nice mahogany bar. Ted was a politician without portfolio, and he did little to ingratiate himself to a party that just wasn't that interested in his candidacy. He had shown once before that he couldn't beat Al Smith, and nothing had happened since to improve his prospects.[4]

Writing of those long days, sitting with Kermit at the Knickerbocker Club, probably sipping cognac, Ted began to sound like a character from his and Kermit's friend Rudyard Kipling:

"More than a year drifted by without our noticing it. Then strange but familiar voices began whispering to me. Spirits of the high places of earth, from the barren boulders and snows, hinted of days when the driving storm caked ice on beard and face; spirits from the desert sang of blowing sand and blinding sun. For a time I put them resolutely aside.

"Then one evening Kermit and I were alone together. I found he too had been hearing these voices. That was the beginning of our downfall. Soon we began to lunch more frequently with the brown lean men who drift quietly into New York, not those who go tourist-like across Africa in automobiles, camping each night in richly upholstered luxury, but foreloopers, who trek to lonely places where food is scant, travel by foot, and danger a constant bedfellow."[5]

The brothers soon began to plot another adventure. Consulting maps of the world for unexplored regions, they focused on an area of Asia northwest of Indochina, where the eastern slopes of the Himalayas began their descent to the tropical jungles of Southeast Asia and where five great rivers, including the Mekong and the Yangtze, had dug long and twisty paths to the sea. Szechuan was not only a largely uncharted region of west-central China, fitting the Roosevelts' desire to wander in territory largely unexplored by Westerners, but it also held an animal that Ted called "the Golden Fleece of our trip."[6]

The giant panda had first come to the attention of Europeans in the 1860s, when a French missionary and biologist named Père Armand David discovered it through the indigenous people of the Szechuan region. They brought to him the striking skin of a dead giant panda, which he transported home to France. Its unique coloring made it an instant and sought-after novelty, but it remained elusive. A handful of skins of the animal

were secured from native hunters by a Russian expedition in the 1890s—
one of these wound up in the British Museum, where it was mounted (to
be soon joined by a second skin). A number of Western hunters and scientists made journeys after the giant panda and were able, through conversations with indigenous hunters, to map its territory and learn that
bamboo shoots were its primary diet. Some skins were reported to be used
as rugs in a few Chinese homes, but actual sightings of the animal by
Westerners could be numbered on a single hand and all were questionable.
A German zoologist, Dr. Hugo Weigold, did as much research on the giant
panda as anyone working in the field, but even he failed to sight the animal
in the wild. Weigold accompanied native hunters into the giant pandas'
habitat and "found the chase a most arduous one, up and down over the
roughest country and through tunnel-like trails in the dense thickets. . . .
In much hunting, the nearest he had come to a sight of the game was the
appearance of waving bushes as they closed behind a fleeing animal."[7]

In other words, while there was scientific interest in the giant panda,
common knowledge of the animal was minimal. No children played with
cute stuffed pandas; and its eye-catching coloration and soft, rounded
features were only on display in a few natural history museums in Europe.
In fact, because the animal was usually designated as a bear, and a large
bear at that, there was no certainty that, when discovered in the wild, it
wouldn't be some sort of fearsome creature (anecdotal evidence from local
inhabitants who had actually seen and hunted the great panda suggested
they were harmless—but that was anecdotal evidence).

Even in China itself, the animal was unstudied and essentially
unknown, particularly in the more cosmopolitan regions of the country.
One recent scholar of the animal writes that "While there are tantalizing
stories implying that one Chinese Emperor or another knew all about
panda . . . there's one great mystery. Why is there not a single rendition of
this endearing beast in any of Imperial China's illustrated natural histo-
ries?" Its modern-day identity as a symbol of the nation was a thing of the
future in 1928, at least forty years to come.[8]

All in all, the prospects for the Roosevelt brothers actually encountering
a great panda were long—so long, in fact, that they kept the true intent of

Alice and Ted, circa 1888–89.
LIBRARY OF CONGRESS

Ted and his father, 1891.

Theodore Roosevelt playing with children at Sagamore Hill, circa 1894.

The library at Sagamore Hill.
LIBRARY OF CONGRESS

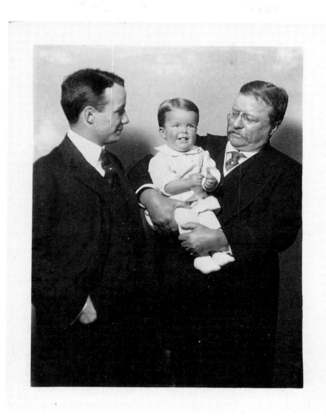

The three Theodore Roosevelts:
Ted, Theodore III, and TR in 1915.

Ted with his first deer, 1901.

Ted and Edith, 1903.

Ted, in a 1905 portrait by Edward Curtis.

Ted (*center*) v. Yale, 1905.

The Roosevelt family in 1907:
(*left to right*) Kermit, Archie, Theodore, Ethel, Edith, Ted (*standing*), Quentin.

Ted, being helped from the field in Harvard's game against Yale, 1905.

Ted and Eleanor, a week before their wedding, 1910.

Ted and Eleanor during the Great War.

Eleanor Roosevelt (*center*) knitting sweaters for the soldiers in France, 1917.

The Roosevelt family's sacrifice compared to the Kaiser's
in the wake of Quentin's death.

Ted and Eleanor in France, November 1918, just after the Armistice.

Ted promoting the American Legion, 1919.

Ted prior to the 1920 presidential campaign.

Ted, flanked by Warren Harding (*second from left*),
Mrs. Harding, and Edward Denby (*in a naval cap*), 1921–23.

Ted and his brother Archie during the Teapot Dome scandal, 1924.

Ted and Alice at the U.S. Capitol, 1932.

LEFT:
A cartoon lampooning
Ted's being left in the
Philippines by Herbert
Hoover, 1932.

BELOW:
Ted with George Patton,
1943.

Ted with his Rough Rider jeep in France, 1944.

their journey under their hats with the press. If they made loud noises about their search, and came back empty-handed, the mockery would be intense. Not that it mattered hugely to their quest. Ted and Kermit were deeply hooked. They had found their goal: to be the first Westerners to see a giant panda living in the wild, and bring it home for display in Chicago.[9]

With their connections to the Field Museum still solid, financing for the trip was secured—this time through William Kelly, another generous patron of the museum. The Kelly-Roosevelt-Field Museum Expedition was about to begin.

But first there were more political matters to deal with. Nineteen twenty-eight was a presidential election year—one in which (it seemed like a long time ago now) Ted had once been considered as a possible candidate. Despite the fact that, as the year progressed, Al Smith looked likely to step out of the New York political picture to make a run for the White House, Ted's standing with the state GOP did not improve, and he had forgone the necessary politicking in Albany that might have improved his chances at the nomination.

He was further stymied by the reemergence of his cousin Franklin on the New York political scene. Three years of hard conditioning in the Warm Springs spa that he had purchased in Georgia and turned into a sanitarium for victims of polio had resurrected his spirit and constitution, even if it hadn't improved his polio. For the most part he did his best to hide his disability: campaigning as often as he could from the back of an open sedan, or at a podium, with his legs locked in heavy steel braces, Franklin projected an image of a tall, strong candidate in good health and good humor. The fact that he did not receive the nomination until Al Smith handed it to him, after Smith accepted the national Democratic nomination for the presidency in September, meant a relatively short public campaign was waged.

Ted watched the developments with dismay. As the Democrats waffled over whether to nominate Al Smith as their presidential candidate, New York Republicans were left in limbo not knowing if their candidate for governor would be facing Smith or Franklin Roosevelt. Ultimately they decided that in either case, Ted would not be the opponent. In the end, cousin Franklin got the nod from the Democrats and was about to take a decided step forward in the Oyster Bay–Hyde Park family race to decide who should wear the political mantle of Theodore Roosevelt.

There was some talk of pairing Ted with the anointed Republican presidential nominee, Herbert Hoover, as a vice-presidential candidate, but it was determined by national party leaders that a Midwestern figure was needed to balance the ticket, and Senator Charles Curtis of Kansas got the nod. None of this constrained the Republican Party from asking Ted to go to bat for Hoover out on the hustings, where the name Theodore Roosevelt still raised large and enthusiastic audiences. Ted dutifully did his speech making in the fall of 1928, thinking that perhaps his work would result in a cabinet appointment from Hoover that would keep his name alive in party circles. But it was all a deep disappointment to Ted. No one was talking of his political potential anymore; no one talked of his youth.

Good thing that his mind was already on the other side of the world, as his body would soon be, too. By the time Franklin was inaugurated as the new governor of New York and Herbert Hoover president of the United States, Ted and Kermit were off to China for their next great journey.

TWENTY-ONE

GIANT PANDAS

In many ways, the trip to Indochina was a more arduous journey than their first hunt. In November, the brothers, once again accompanied by Suydam Cutting, sailed to England and followed the same basic path to Bombay. In India, they were able to secure a third Lone brother, Mokhta Lone, to go along with a few other trusted Kashmiris from their first journey as shikaris. They also picked up a Chinese American naturalist from San Francisco named Jack Young, who would serve as a guide, collector, and translator on their trip into Szechuan.

From India, they set out first for the Chinese province of Yunnan, tucked in a landlocked pocket among the eastern Himalayas, Burma, Laos, and Vietnam. From there, they would journey north to Szechuan, to the land where Père David had first spied the giant panda. After hunting the animal in the bamboo forests, they would head out of China toward Hanoi, Vietnam, where they would hook up with the scientific half of the expedition, headed by a young zoologist from Harvard named Harold Coolidge. As the Roosevelts were hunting big game in the mountainous regions of Yunnan and Szechuan, Coolidge would be collecting small mammals in Indochina (primarily Cambodia, Laos, Siam, and Vietnam).

The Roosevelts had two options to get to Yunnan from India: the northern route would take them over the mountains into eastern Tibet and down to Yunnan; the second route was through Burma by train into Yunnan. The Tibetan authorities failed to respond to their request for passage through the Himalayas in time, so the brothers made their way through Mandalay on the way to southwestern China, pausing at train stops along the way to dine and gather information from various Brits living in the outposts of the empire. On the day after Christmas, the train stations ended and the Roosevelts began the hike from Burma into Yunnan.

Their long pack train of ponies, mules, and local inhabitants was heaving with supplies as they set out through a terrain that alternated between dense jungles and high ridges. The Taping River Gorge separated the two countries, and its sight lines, narrowed by cliffs and tall trees as they trekked, reminded Kermit of the claustrophobic landscape along the River of Doubt in South America. At this point the group was collecting only birds and small mammals that they caught in traps put out each night. After four days, they reached the Chinese border, which, according to Kermit, was marked by a grass hut and two Chinese soldiers, "one lying down cooking himself an opium pill for his pipe, while the other tended a pot of greens boiling over a small fire. Neither so much as lifted his eyes as we passed."[1]

The journey through Yunnan was marked by slow progress. They picked up a contingent of four Chinese soldiers who were to guide them through the villages and protect them from the many bandits who occupied the Yunnan hills on the road north. Along the way, the Chinese soldiers held little sway with the government officials, who invariably required bribes and coaxing to let the caravan pass.

The expedition passed cultivated fields and thick forests; it passed the Mekong River; Kermit got ill, either from the water or something he ate, and the whole party was forced to lie up for a couple of days. Jack Young was sent to find a Chinese doctor, who could do little, according to Ted, but "say nothing and look preternaturally grave."[2]

Kermit recovered and they kept on. A couple of days later, they encountered their first evidence of bandits up ahead. At a village they were warned about a huddle of thieves lying in wait, so they veered off the trail to circumvent trouble and quickly found themselves in a wilderness. "As far as the eye could reach in every direction forested peak succeeded forested peak," wrote Ted.[3]

The population thinned out and they came to a village that was emptied and nearly leveled by outlaws. They were in the thick of dangerous country and adopted "the approved military formation for guarding a baggage train" learned from their war days. Ted took the lead, while Kermit protected the center, and Suydam the rear: all were fully armed and alert.

So it went through Yunnan, the course of their march dictated by the lawlessness of the region. They arrived at the city of Lijiang in late January and found a region of pine-covered hills and lakes, with snowcapped mountains beyond. The weather turned bitterly cold and they ran into delays because of incompetent mule skinners and lost some of their pack animals as they reached the Yangtze River.

A few days beyond, they were finally able to do some hunting: for a local mountain animal called a serow, which looks like a cross between a goat and an antelope, as well as for a sambhur, which is a more deerlike horned animal. Kermit brought in a serow but put off preparing it until the next morning. It was so cold at night, however, that when he went to skin it the next morning, he wrote later, "It was frozen stiffer than an Argentine steer in cold storage."[4]

They spent the Chinese New Year with the brother-in-law of the king of the Mulis, who over dinner made inquiries about the Roosevelt family, and actually recognized the boys' father when Ted hauled out a family photo from his kit. The Roosevelts left the king's brother-in-law as fast friends and traveled on into the high country, where they camped at "a treeless gut, fifteen thousand feet high, between two bare peaks."[5]

On and on they marched through northern Yunnan from one "unnamed pass on an unnamed mountain" to the next. Time and again local hunters promised big game for the museum but except for Ted shooting another sambhur, prized animals were elusive.

January turned to February, February turned to March. They finally arrived at Muping (Baoxing), which had been Père Armand David's home when he became the first Westerner to discover the existence of the giant panda in the 1860s. Muping was in the southwestern corner of Szechuan Province, near the border of Tibet. Its population was a mix of Tibetans and Chinese, with the Chinese ascendant, primarily due to the town's proximity to the large Chinese city of Chengtu, just to the east. It was from Muping that Ted, Kermit, and Suydam Cutting planned to base their camp as they set out to hunt both the giant panda and the takin, another thick-wooled goat-antelope native to the eastern Himalayas, and the second most coveted creature on the Kelly-Roosevelt Expedition.

The brothers sent out requests for local hunting guides, and chose a number of Chinese scouts, a few of whom had claimed to have hunted and shot panda in the recent past. Their first trip out, the Roosevelts bagged a group of golden monkeys for the museum exhibit and soon after they came upon signs of the great panda in the midst of the densest jungle Ted had ever been in. "It was of bamboo six to eight feet tall, interspersed with hemlock and beech. The slope [of the hillside] was forty-five degrees. We had to climb up on hands and knees. Deadfall blocked us every few feet. The dust from the dried bamboo leaves got into our lungs and eyes. The stems and vines through which we had to force our way tripped and clung to us like the tentacles of an octopus. The sweat ran in streams and caked the dust. It was impossible to see twenty feet."[6]

They were disappointed in their quest, as they would be time and again in the Muping area. There was nothing to track. In the process, they began to dig deeper into the guides' stories of their panda-hunting exploits and discovered that their prowess was not quite what it was cracked up to be: any pandas that were credibly claimed to have been hunted by the guides turned out to have been bagged years earlier. It all seemed like a bit of a fool's errand to the Roosevelt boys, and for a time they went off to the city of Yashow and then to Luchinsa, where they received cables from home, one of which held the disappointing news that President Hoover had named his cabinet, and Ted was not in it.

They went back to Muping. Their guides still insisted that the panda were out there, but luck was not working in their favor. They took out local dogs to help them find the animal, to no avail. Day after day in March, they set out through the dense bamboo forests. Ted, Kermit, Suydam, and fourteen native hunters—"not one member of the party [saw] a wild animal of any sort."[7]

In April they headed north to the village of Litzaping (Liziping), where they set up a new base. They were now heading into Lolo (Yi, in Chinese) country—Lolos being a reputedly fierce local tribe who were known to shoot Chinese people on sight and who worshipped the giant panda. The Roosevelts were warned to beware by, among others, Roy Chapman Andrews, but they found the Lolos to be friendly and helpful, if a little fearsome in their habits. Their dress was anything but frightening: they wore colorful tunics and shawls, and one of their traditional hats was a conical lid that looked like a brightly beribboned snare drum placed on top of their heads. They told the Roosevelts that while there were just a few takin in the region, panda could be found nearby in Yehle (Yele) district, just to the west. Again the Roosevelts set out, this time for Yehle. And despite their feelings about the giant panda, or because the Roosevelts emphasized their interest in takin, several Lolos joined the hunt as guides.[8]

Rain was falling as they followed a steep mountainside path above the Nanya River. Twice they had to stop to shore up the path and dig out landslides that had obstructed the trail. "At length," wrote Kermit, "the valley opened up and we had easy going. The country became more and more lovely; giant pine trees grew beside the path, and we finally rode out onto a great mountain meadow, with a wide grassy valley, hemmed in by well-crested mountains terminating in barren snow-clad peaks. We felt that we might almost be back in the paradise of the Tian Shan."[9]

They arrived at Yehle and spent a fitful night, knowing that the rainy season was nearly upon them and that they had only a few days before they would have to exit the region. The next morning, April 13, the Roosevelt party left the hamlet early. Just beyond the Yehle, the magnificent old pine trees became less spectacular; a number had been cut to build the village and fuel the cabins in winter. There were also a number of lightning-damaged or rotted and dying trees. But as the hunting party headed down the river valley, the tall canopy evergreens reappeared, overhanging a dense and lush jungle of bamboo.[10]

Three or four miles of hard hiking later, the group turned off the valley and up into a ravine. Almost immediately they came across giant panda tracks in newly fallen snow. Some of the Lolos were hesitant to follow due to religious scruples, but three remained with the hunters and took the lead into the ravine. Local dogs were accompanying them, but they proved poor and easily distracted trackers, heading for a time after the scent of a boar, whose tracks were also visible in the ravine. The sun came out for a moment, and Kermit and Ted worried that it would melt the panda trail in the newly fallen snow.

For two and a half hours, they trailed the giant panda through bamboo and alders. Kermit and Ted briefly separated: Ted joined by one of the Lolos; Kermit with Mokhta Lone and a Lolo guide named Sujiu Shila. The dogs suddenly started yapping below the ravine, down in the valley, but Kermit was uncertain if they had picked up the trail of the boar or the panda. A few steps later Kermit heard a clicking chirp, which he thought might be bamboo snapping, but he remembered back at Muping, the natives getting very excited by hearing a similar noise.[11]

The Lolo guide, Sujiu Shila, darted quietly forward and about forty yards ahead, wide-eyed and silent, excitedly waved Kermit and Lone to join him. Once by his side, Kermit saw the panda peeking its head out of the hollowed-out bole of one of the giant evergreens about thirty yards away. Leaning over the top of a dead tree trunk, with its big round black spectacled head, black collar, and white upper quarter visible to the hunters, it looked around "dreamily" like it had just been awakened from a sound sleep.

Kermit didn't want to take the shot without Ted, who was close enough to be waved at and came as quickly as he could after getting the high sign. For months they had dreamed of this moment; for months they had trudged over miserable trails, through jungles and mountains, past bandits, and along more than a thousand miles of trail since they'd left the train just east of Yunnan. Now here they were, the first Westerners to definitely sight a giant panda in the wild. One loud move could startle the animal fully awake and in an instant he would be gone. To Kermit, it seemed an eternity before Ted arrived, but when he did, neither brother wasted a moment. They raised their rifles and fired simultaneously. "Both shots took effect," Kermit wrote. The panda, "not knowing where his enemies were," turned toward them and floundered in their direction. He was five or six feet away from Mokhta Lone when the brothers fired again. Though he staggered a few more yards, the panda was dead.

They moved up to the animal, touched it with a boot or two, and then knelt silently, reaching out to feel the great panda. The quest was over; they would now bring this creature home for mounting.

"The shikaris, the Lolos, and ourselves held a mutual rejoicing," Kermit wrote, "each in his own tongue."

It's extremely difficult not to cringe at the thought of the Roosevelt brothers blasting a giant panda, peeking its sleepy head out from an afternoon nap in its own bamboo thicket in Szechuan. Today it seems barbaric to think that the first instinct of humans on a mission financed and sponsored by one of the leading natural history museums in the country would be to shoot and stuff an animal that no one from the West had ever seen in the wild, particularly a mammal so downright precious as a giant panda. Without pretending to justify the slaying in a present-day context, the hunt, in the sensibility of the times, was never condemned for its brutality. In fact, by bringing that panda home, Ted and Kermit not only helped educate the world about this bearlike animal (which turned out to be more closely related to raccoons), but also helped set off the first panda "mania" that ultimately brought a mountain of attention to the animal, both scientific and humane, and could be said to have helped foster the very adoration for the giant panda that makes its death today feel so gruesome.

Their explorations in China encouraged other adventurers into the region, including an unlikely explorer who brought back the first living panda to the United States, just seven years after the Roosevelts' journey. Ruth Harkness, a New York fashion designer and socialite, was married to adventurer Bill Harkness, the wealthy son of a New York attorney who went to China before his wife. His intention was to find and capture a giant panda. When Bill Harkness took ill and died of cancer in early 1936,

Ruth determined that she would continue her husband's pursuit. With the help of Jack Young, the Chinese American anthropologist who accompanied the Roosevelts; Jack's wife, Su-Lin; and his brother, Quentin, Ruth set out for panda country in southern Szechuan.

Harkness and the Youngs were able to find and capture a baby panda in the wild and bring it back to the United States late in the fall of 1936, where it made a sensation across the country. Ruth Harkness named the panda Su-Lin, after Jack Young's wife, and housed it in Harkness's own Manhattan apartment. She offered the panda to the highest-bidding zoo in the country, which turned out to be in the Bronx. As Harkness and Su-Lin awaited for final arrangements to be made for the panda, they entertained visitors eager to see the baby. These included Ted Roosevelt Jr.; Kermit; and Ted's seventeen-year-old son, Quentin. While Su-Lin sat in Ted's lap in the apartment, another visitor present suggested that Su-Lin might one day wind up stuffed and mounted in the Field Museum next to the Roosevelts' trophies. Far from his own trip to Yehle and obviously won over by the very cuteness of the little panda in his lap, Ted said, "I'd just as soon think of stuffing Quentin and putting him in a habitat group."[12]

TWENTY-TWO

THE WRONG ROOSEVELT

By the time the expedition ended in Vietnam, Ted was seriously ill with malaria and had a violent case of dysentery. When he met Eleanor in Saigon at the end of the trip, he was feverish and slightly delirious, and had dropped forty-two pounds from an already slight frame. He weighed just over a hundred pounds when he was put to bed.

Kermit had left the expedition several weeks earlier to return to New York, where he had to attend to a crisis in his shipping business, which had been hit hard by the looming economic depression. Like Ted, Suydam Cutting got sick and was forced to go home early. Ted was left to bring the expedition out of Southeast Asia, and in the process he wore himself out.

The problem now was that Ted needed to get back to the States. In late May 1929, while Ted was still in Vietnam, President Hoover had appointed him governor of the Commonwealth of Puerto Rico as a nod to Ted's work on Hoover's behalf in the past presidential campaign.

Puerto Rico was not a prime appointment for Ted. He had hoped for the far more prestigious post as colonial governor of the Philippines, and at first he declined the office in San Juan, letting members of his family know that he felt it was beneath him. Eleanor argued that he ought to take

the position. She subtly pointed out the ill effects of his political exile after
the last expedition, that his absence from politics had helped to place him
in this current predicament and ought to be avoided a second time. Puerto
Rico might not be the most exciting post, but he would still be in the game.
He finally agreed. "You are absolutely right. I have got to get into the line
of officeholders again or I am going to be forgotten."[1]

As he recovered from his malaria, Ted continued to arrange for the safe
shipment of all the specimens that had been collected by the expedition, and
then he and Eleanor shipped themselves home by way of Shanghai and Tokyo.

They arrived in the Caribbean in the midst of difficult times. It was
October 1929, just days before the stock market crash, signaling the beginning of the Great Depression, and Puerto Rico was hard hit by the economic
disaster.

Nonetheless, Roosevelt proved to be a popular and effective governor,
appreciated by the natives for his interest in the Puerto Rican people and
the local culture. On the cruise back from Asia, before assuming office,
Ted had boned up on his schoolboy Spanish, and though he never became
entirely proficient with the language, his efforts at speaking it with the
people of Puerto Rico were much appreciated. Also appreciated were his
efforts at lobbying the president and Congress to supply more aid and
loans to the islanders, and his work at trying to link the economy of the
commonwealth to the United States as a whole. He went into the countryside to personally talk with struggling farmers to see how agricultural
trade might be improved. He also tried to boost industrial commerce
and tourism, which had somehow missed out on a general boom in trade
in the Caribbean in the 1920s. To help increase the number of cruises
stopping at the island's ports—just thirteen had visited in 1929—Ted and
Eleanor held receptions for arriving tourists at their home, La Fortaleza,
a palace-like structure that was the oldest gubernatorial residence in U.S.
territory, dating from 1629.

Ted wrote a deeply sympathetic account of the trials of the children
of Puerto Rico, telling of their high rates of poverty, hunger, and under-
treated medical suffering, for the *New York Herald Sunday Magazine*—an
article that prompted protest from Washington, including within the

Hoover administration itself, which wanted to believe that such depriva-
tion could not exist in a protectorate of the United States.[2]

In November 1931, Ted was in Washington visiting with the president
when he learned that one of the major banks of San Juan had closed, pre-
cipitating circumstances that might lead to a run on other banks, perhaps
all of them, on the island. Like a George Bailey, he immediately flew back
to Puerto Rico and ordered the commonwealth treasury to deposit
$100,000 into the struggling financial institution and backed the money
from his own pocket. He then went on the radio and announced to the
people that the treasury had secured the bank and to please have confidence in the commonwealth economy. According to Eleanor, the loan was
about a quarter of the family wealth.

In her own right, Eleanor was deeply involved in helping the mission
in Puerto Rico. She started a needlework business, employing Puerto
Rican seamstresses to make delicate embroidered linens for customers in
high-end shops in Manhattan. She not only used her own connections to
place the island merchandise at Saks and other businesses; she also enlisted
her aging mother to take orders and make sure that samples got to interested shops.[3]

Ted's work in Puerto Rico received kudos in many quarters. A Baltimore newspaper called him "one of the finest, and perhaps the finest,
colonial governor in our history." When President Hoover visited the
island in the summer of 1931, he heaped praise on the job that Ted had
done, remarks that elicited "so prolonged [a] demonstration [from the
audience] that the Governor, sitting by Mrs. Roosevelt, was obliged to
rise and bow his acknowledgements."[4]

Unfortunately for Roosevelt, Puerto Rico was not proving to be a
stepping-stone to a better position within the Hoover administration. Two
years into the job, Ted felt that he'd done his duty and it was time for a
greater reward from the administration. He was pushed toward this sensibility by his sister Alice, who often in Ted's political career exhibited at
least as much ambition on her brother's behalf as he showed on his own.
She was afraid that Ted was mired in a nowhere position just as he needed
to be in the thick of the scene in Washington.[5]

Ted's ambitions were not helped by the state of the GOP. Nineteen thirty had been a disastrous election year for the party through much of the nation. The miseries of the Depression were heading toward a deep trough, and blame naturally flowed toward the party in power. In Congress, the GOP, which had held both the House of Representatives and the Senate by large majorities for much of the previous decade, suddenly lost power in the House to the Democrats. Meanwhile, in New York, cousin Franklin had not only won reelection as governor by a landslide, but he was already being touted as the likely next candidate for the presidency. And if the economy did not improve, it was hard to see Herbert Hoover returning to the White House in 1932.

The Oyster Bay Roosevelts were beyond concerned and heading toward panic at the thought of Franklin and his Eleanor moving into the old stomping grounds of Theodore Roosevelt and his boisterous family at 1600 Pennsylvania Avenue. Ted wrote to his mother in the wake of Franklin's 1930 gubernatorial reelection, "Well, as far as I can see the ship went down with all of us aboard. Your cousin Franklin will now, I suppose, run for the Presidency, and I am already beginning to think of nasty things to say concerning him."[6]

When finally Ted got his diplomatic promotion—in January 1932, he was named by Hoover as the new governor-general of the Philippines—concerns with the state of the upcoming election remained paramount. Even as Ted and Eleanor sailed to Manila and he assumed his duties on the islands, he kept one eye on the state of the presidential race back home.

As he had in San Juan, Ted made an immediate and positive impression on the people of the Philippines. Arriving in Manila in late February, he greeted an immense crowd of Filipinos in Tagalog, their native tongue. He eschewed being sworn in to his office in Washington before leaving the States, the traditional means of assuming the post, in order to be the first American governor of the islands to actually be sworn in on Philippine soil. As he had done in Puerto Rico, he began his term by touring the many islands of the commonwealth to meet its natives and get a better sense of the land. A newspaper applauded him as a governor-general "who does not mind being bitten by a mosquito." Ted also got points for visiting a leper colony filled with sick Boy Scouts, where he shook each and every hand.[7]

Knowing his reputation for hunting skills, natives asked Roosevelt at one stop to go hunting with them for carabao, a type of water buffalo that had long since been domesticated in the Philippines. So many of the animals had escaped into the wild, however, that now it was considered sport to shoot them. Ted was caught between his reluctance to shoot an animal that he didn't consider "game" and his desire to appear amenable to his hosts. The hunt turned into an elaborate event, complete with spectators, reporters, and natives driving the carabao toward Ted. He was grateful to down one of the animals with a single shot, thus putting a quick end to the hunt. The natives were duly impressed by his marksmanship and gave him the nickname "One-Shot Teddy." He told Eleanor later that he was just grateful that no brand was found on the hindquarters of the poor buffalo.[8]

Even as he was transitioning into office in the Philippines, however, Ted was feeling once again as if he were playing a very deep outfield position as far as the Republican Party was concerned. He had been a part of every national presidential campaign since 1920 and had proved an effective campaigner for the GOP. He had also heard rumors that Vice President Charles Curtis was thinking of stepping down, and Ted felt that he deserved a shot at the position. He had been getting praise, once again, for his diplomatic work, this time from the *New York Times*. In addition, Alice was prodding him from Washington. Aside from urging Ted to return, she was whispering in President Hoover's ear as well, reminding him how valuable the name Theodore Roosevelt would be to him on the campaign trail.[9]

As summer neared its close, and Franklin Roosevelt headed toward the Democratic National Convention with the most committed delegates, Hoover decided to recall Ted from the Philippines. The president had come to agree with Alice that a Roosevelt was needed on the campaign trail to counter Franklin, and her brother was again tapped to battle their cousin on the stump. Suddenly, however, Ted was reluctant to rush home,

fearful about appearances: how would it look for him to vacate an important position for obvious political reasons, just months after taking it?

Ted finally succumbed to the pleas of his sister and the president. On
August 22 he announced to the Filipino people that he was returning to
the United States "for a brief period" but would return to the Philippines
the first week of November.[10]

Ted turned out to be prescient regarding the negative impression his
return prompted. An early September *Time* magazine story dripped with
irony: "This year Republican leaders felt that their Hoover campaign
would not be complete without young T.R., now Governor General of the
Philippines. They thought they needed him to counteract Democratic
use of a Republican name. Cablegrams passed between Washington and
Manila. Alice Roosevelt Longworth, whose dislike for the Democratic
Franklin is intensely real, implored her half-brother to return from his
provincial post to take to the stump."

When he agreed to do so, however, "Filipinos squawked regretfully
at their Governor's proposed departure. U.S. businessmen in Manila shook
their heads sourly at the demands of mainland politics. The U.S. Press
generally mocked the idea that Governor General Roosevelt would promote President Hoover's reelection."[11]

Just two weeks later, the Hoover administration announced an about-
face. Prior to Ted's planned departure, the White House made public a
cable sent to the governor in Manila: "The President has reached the
conclusion that you should not leave your duties for the purpose of participating in the campaign."

Having urged Ted out on the limb, Hoover had proceeded to cut it
off, without an explanation beyond the obvious: that it didn't look good.
Ted tried to make the best of an embarrassing moment, but sounded lame
in the process. Of Hoover's supposedly selfless insistence that Ted stay in
Manila, Roosevelt told the press, "That's a striking illustration of the
President's devotion to public service. He's the man America needs and
must have as President in this national emergency."[12]

As the presidential election neared, and Ted remained helpless in the
Philippines, he waffled between "a hopeful feeling . . . that Franklin is such

poor stuff it seems improbable that he should be elected President" and despair about his own political career: "I believe that the Governor-Generalship of the Philippine Islands may well mark the end of my active career in public service."[13]

Not only was cousin Franklin elected in a walk, but he also arrived in Washington that November with a mandate to reform the nation like no other president had in the twentieth century. The Oyster Bay Roosevelts were bowed but unbroken. Right after FDR's election, Edith, Ted's seventy-one-year-old mother, made the trip halfway around the world to visit Ted and Eleanor in the Philippines. It was a show of solidarity with her son, long deemed by her as the true successor to Theodore. Despite the fact that Franklin had won the Roosevelt family race to the White House in decided fashion, her vote would always be with Ted.

The fact of the matter was, however, that her son, still only forty-five years old, was already well on his way toward the political bench, and even she knew it. That he was still a relatively young man only heightened the difficulty of his circumstances. For the next four years at the very least, Franklin and the Democrats would hold political power in Washington and across the country. Hoover and the Republicans had been so badly damaged by the Great Depression and the 1932 election, it would likely take another four years after that before the GOP could seriously challenge the Democrats for the presidency. And would the electorate, at that point, after eight years of one branch of the Roosevelt family in office (presumably), be excited to turn around and send another branch of the Roosevelt family back to the White House in 1940?

Of course, adding to the misery of these circumstances, in Ted's eyes, was the ongoing sense that it was his cousin Franklin who had robbed him of his birthright. FDR had, from the very beginning, usurped the Roosevelt name, usurped the Roosevelt reputation, usurped the Roosevelt accomplishments to appropriate the office and home—the White House—that belonged, rightfully, to the Oyster Bay Roosevelts. It was, at this moment of high triumph for Franklin and his Eleanor, a bitter pill indeed for Ted and his.

And then it got worse. Soon after his mother arrived in the Philippines, Ted received a letter from brother Kermit, who admitted that he had accepted an invitation for a postholiday Caribbean cruise on a yacht owned by Vincent Astor. Only after accepting, Kermit wrote, did he learn that the newly elected president would also be on the cruise.

Kermit's claim was not quite true. Not only had it been known for some time that FDR would be on the Astor cruise, but in fact Kermit had been flirting with his cousin for weeks. Shortly after the election he wrote Franklin a note in which he said, among other flattering smooches, "I have been a Republican all my life [but] I am tremendously relieved and pleased that you were elected." Compounding the hurt for Ted was the fact that Kermit's letter arrived just a few days after he learned that Franklin was going to recall him from his post in Manila.[14]

The newspapers picked up on the fact that Kermit and FDR were yachting together, and speculated that this might signal some sort of peace between the branches of the family. Not likely, given the mood of the Roosevelts gathered in the Philippines. At a public luncheon in Manila, Ted was asked why his brother was at that moment cruising with the president in the Caribbean. His mother, Edith, took the microphone to say, "Because his mother was not there."[15]

A few weeks later, after his letter of resignation had been accepted by the new administration and he and Eleanor were in the process of leaving the Philippines, Ted got in his own bons mots. The press was there again, and this time a local reporter asked the governor-general what his exact relationship was to the new president. "Fifth cousin about to be removed," he said.

TWENTY-THREE

FIFTH COUSIN TO THE PRESIDENT

At the end of his term in the Philippines, Ted was without a job, without a political future, and without a home that he and Eleanor could call their own. Their children were fast growing up. Grace, his oldest, was now twenty years old and unmarried. Ted III was a freshman at Harvard, where Cornelius would be an entering student in the fall of 1933. The youngest, Quentin, was in his third year at Groton. The Roosevelts had lost some of their wealth in the stock market over the past few years, and money was tighter than it had been—but not so tight as to prevent them from taking a long and circuitous sightseeing tour on their way home from the Philippines.

They went to Bali, Batavia, west to Agra, up to Afghanistan, to Peshawar and the Hindu Kush, to Teheran and then Baghdad; they traveled to Jerusalem, the Holy Land, up through Istanbul to Italy; Venice, Rome, and over to Monte Carlo. Son Cornelius and a friend of his joined them in France, where they spent a week in Paris before heading off for London. They traveled by train, plane, and automobile. Reaching England, they joined Rudyard Kipling for lunch in Surrey, where the famous writer asked Ted if there were any more trips in the works. Ted replied that he was thinking of an expedition to Tibet. "Aren't you getting a little old, Ted?"

Kipling quipped. "Really, you should leave that sort of thing for younger men."[1]

It was time to settle down. By September Ted and Eleanor were home at Oyster Bay and Roosevelt took a job, first as a director and then chairman of the board for American Express, a post arranged by Winthrop Aldrich, chairman of the board for Chase National Bank, who was married to a first cousin of Eleanor's.[2]

Ted did not give up on politics: among a plethora of volunteer positions he either acquired or reassumed upon his return to the United States was a position as president of the National Republican Club, which had lost half its members after the 1932 election. He reassumed his duties at the National Council of Boy Scouts, becoming its vice president in 1935; he was on the board of the NAACP, director of the National Health Circle for Colored People, and a trustee of Bethune-Cookman College; he was on the board of the National Conference of Christians and Jews; was instrumental in raising relief funds for China in the late thirties and early forties; and when Irving Berlin decided to donate all future royalties for his song "God Bless America" to the Boy and Girl Scouts of America, Ted, along with boxer Gene Tunney and journalist Herbert Bayard Swope, administered the funds.[3]

Ted made one more hunting trip in 1935, but one not nearly as grand as those with Kermit to Asia. On behalf of the American Museum of Natural History in New York, Ted went to the Mato Grosso in Brazil and shot a 340-pound jaguar. He was near the same wild land that his father and Kermit had traveled to reach the headwaters of the River of Doubt twenty-one years earlier; but he and his brother were now estranged. Kermit's sins with Franklin remained unforgiven; in addition, Kermit had taken up with a mistress and begun a long slide toward alcoholic dissipation.

Back from his last hunt, Ted accepted a job from another old friend from the Knickerbocker Club, Nelson Doubleday, at Doubleday & Company, a book publisher. Widely read, an international traveler with a broad circle of friends and connections everywhere, Ted fit well into the literary world of New York. Among the list of writers with whom he worked were

Pearl Buck, Vachel Lindsay, H. G. Wells, and William Allen White. He wanted to publish a biography of Oliver Wendell Holmes by Justice Felix Frankfurter, and corresponded with Frankfurter about a possible series of books on notable American Jews. Ted also asked for advice from Frankfurter on how to approach Justice Louis Brandeis on the possibility of doing an autobiography. "The best way to approach Mr. Justice Brandeis is to approach him directly," replied Frankfurter, "but of one thing I am sure and that is that nothing is farther from his mind than the writing of an autobiography."[4]

Ted and Eleanor grew tight with a group of friends who were part of the Algonquin Roundtable crowd, particularly critic, *New Yorker* writer, and radio commentator Alexander Woollcott. Known for his biting wit and eccentric dress and behavior, Woollcott was a talented journalist, but as his friend James Thurber wrote, he had "nothing particular to say." The Roosevelts (and Thurber) were frequent visitors at Woollcott's summer home on an island in an isolated lake in Vermont called Bomoseen. Here they drank, swam, played cards and parlor games, and traded quips with other frequent visitors, who included Thornton Wilder, Charlie MacArthur, Helen Hayes, Alfred Lunt and Lynn Fontanne, and Harpo and Susan Marx, with whom Ted and Eleanor got particularly close—Ted and Harpo were bass-fishing pals up on the lake.[5]

Ted and famed broadcaster Lowell Thomas captained an annual summer baseball game that rotated between Oyster Bay and Thomas's Connecticut home. Composed of teams drawn from a Who's Who of New York stage, publishing, radio, and sports, Ted's 1938 team included Robert Ripley of *Believe It or Not* fame, sportswriter Grantland Rice, boxer Jack Dempsey, composer Richard Rodgers, cartoonist Rube Goldberg, and baseball legend Babe Ruth, recently retired from the Yankees and quite a ringer for the team Ted dubbed the Oysters of Oyster Bay. On Lowell's team were famed flier Jimmy Doolittle, golfer Gene Sarazen, columnist Westbrook Pegler, boxer Gene Tunney, NBC's David Sarnoff, future founder of the OSS William Donovan, and journalist Heywood Broun. Players and their families arrived for the two thirty game, then adjourned afterward for a swim and supper, with many spending the night at nearby inns. The '38 game was filmed by a newsreel team and broadcast on radio as well.[6, 7, 8]

Of all the circles of friends that Ted engaged with in his lifetime—Washington and Albany politicos, Wall Street business types, Harvard chums, ranking officers of the U.S. Army—he seemed most comfortable with the literary, sports, media, and entertainment circles in New York. So often he had to play the role of the Roosevelt family leader or the candidate, the governor-general, or the commander, but with this crowd he could just relax and have a few laughs and drinks. He was a naturally gregarious and genial man with that winning Roosevelt smile and an easy head-thrown-back laugh. People liked him, even those who were predisposed not to, including those who didn't care for his politics or the "Roosevelt style."

Of his children, Grace was the first to marry and settle down outside the family. She and her husband, William McMillan, were also the first to provide Ted and Eleanor with a grandchild, a little girl named for Eleanor. After graduating from Harvard in 1936, Ted III decided to follow in his father's footsteps and look for an entry-level position at a corporation. He went to Wilmington, Delaware, and took a factory job with DuPont. Cornelius went to Harvard for a couple of years, but ultimately transferred to MIT, where he took a degree in engineering. In the late 1930s, the youngest son, Quentin, who was still at Harvard studying art history and anthropology, traveled in the footsteps of his father to Yunnan Province in China. He had become interested in the funeral scrolls of the Nakhi tribes, examples of which Ted had brought back with him from his visit to Lijiang, when he and Kermit were pursuing the panda. Quentin had arranged with Harvard and the Boston Museum of Fine Arts to make the trip on behalf of the museum. He traveled initially with his mother, who went at Ted's request to pick up a book manuscript from Madame Chiang, which Doubleday planned on publishing. Quentin broke off from Eleanor and set out on his own to Lijiang to collect more examples of the rare scrolls, which depicted "the hells, tortures and paradises through which dead tribesmen must pass."[9]

The period of domesticity, publishing work, and New York socializing that marked Ted and Eleanor's marriage in the late 1930s was one of the happiest of their lives. Like a pair of newlyweds, they decided to build a home of their own. For years, Ted had anticipated inheriting Sagamore Hill, which made buying a home an afterthought. Yet as he and Eleanor reached middle age, and with Edith in no rush to leave the only family home she'd ever known, they elected to build on land that had held an apple orchard in Oyster Bay. Son-in-law Bill McMillan, an architect, designed a redbrick country house with a mansard roof and sentineled by four chimneys—solid and conservative, which suited the tastes of both Eleanor and Ted. They moved in in the spring of 1938—and would have just three years together at the home they named Old Orchard.[10]

Politics was never completely forgotten in the Roosevelt family. While Ted and Eleanor settled back into life in New York, the 1936 presidential election loomed. It represented the first real opportunity for the Oyster Bay Roosevelts to challenge cousin Franklin's leadership in Washington. Ted's role as head of the National Republican Club gave him a platform from which he set out on long campaign tours and speaking engagements on behalf of Governor Alf Landon of Kansas, the GOP nominee for president. The party was grateful for Ted's willingness to be the counter Roosevelt to Franklin, once again, out on the stump—even as it continued to hold the idea of Ted's candidacy at arm's length.

But Ted's slide toward political irrelevancy, at least as an office seeker, continued as FDR trounced Landon that fall. Increasingly Ted was seen as a fading figure on the American political scene, a man whose time had simply never come. Though he remained relatively young as far as a political life was concerned, he was on no one's list as a top candidate. Neither Ted nor Alice was going to shrink away from political squabbles, however. Unfortunately for Ted, the next fight that he picked with the president would place him firmly on the wrong side of history.

TWENTY-FOUR

AMERICA FIRST

As war neared once again, Ted believed that the United States should remain neutral, and he soon joined sister Alice on the America First Committee, a group that advocated against American involvement in the European conflict. Speaking often and passionately against what he called "the stampede" toward war, he rebuked FDR for bringing the United States ever nearer to hostilities across the Atlantic. In a 1939 speech, he asserted that "our frontiers are not in France—our frontiers are on the shores of our hemisphere. I do not believe in wars of benevolent meddling," he added, "or in benevolent meddling of any kind." In Cincinnati, he asked an audience, "Why should we fly to the defense of London or Paris? Who in Europe would fly to the defense of Cincinnati or Chicago?"[1]

In a January 1940 speech in Topeka, Ted recalled the service of Great War vets like himself: "It doesn't look today as though the victory we won was effective in ending war. With two-thirds of the European countries under the rule of dictators, it doesn't look as though the victory we won was very effective in making the world safe for democracy. We not only failed to end war or to make the world safe for democracy, but we damaged ourselves."[2]

As the GOP presidential primary race heated up, Ted threw his support behind Thomas Dewey, the district attorney from New York who had achieved fame by ending the career of mobster Dutch Schultz. Ted helped Dewey, whose clout didn't reach much farther west than the Hudson, to meet the "right people" in national Republican circles, including a long list of newspaper editors.

When Dewey's campaign faltered at the Republican National Convention in Philadelphia that summer, Roosevelt quickly offered his support to GOP candidate Wendell Willkie, despite a personal dislike for the man. Always the good Republican soldier, Ted once more hit the trail to campaign against his cousin.

Despite his public protests against intervention, Ted was never a dyed-in-the-wool isolationist, and hardly a pacifist. He continually stated his support for the Allies, particularly Great Britain. But he was greatly concerned about what war would do to the United States. Again and again, he worried over the state of democracy in the country, suggesting that the last war had taken the nation to the brink of revolutionary change. Now he fretted over Franklin seeming to usurp more and more powers for the presidency.

Ted held no esteem for the fascists or for the Soviet Union, and unlike fellow antiwar advocate Charles Lindbergh, he had no admiration whatsoever for Hitler's Germany. Though whispers of anti-Semitism dogged him, Ted was proud to remind all who cared to listen that he was part of the National Conference of Christians and Jews and had long supported Jewish causes in New York, including serving as a member of the committee of Rabbi Stephen Wise's Zionist Organization of America. For his America First stance, however, Ted was attacked as a Nazi sympathizer and coward—a particularly galling charge for the twice-wounded veteran. Even as he opposed FDR, Ted agreed with the president that the country needed to prepare for conflict and began to promote the same sort of officer training camps that had been established before the Great War. The old Plattsburgh, New York, camp was once again opened, and Ted spent a month there in training in the late summer of 1940. But he remained an adamant foe of the New Deal and his cousin's political style.

In a campaign speech on behalf of Willkie just before the election, he railed against FDR's ambitions for a third term: "When a man believes he is indispensable to a country that man is, in his own mind, a dictator, for obviously one who is indispensable must at the same time be infallible." Despite a need for preparedness, Ted still opposed the course toward war in which he felt FDR was steering the nation. "We are told that the foundations of our liberty are in Europe. That is trash. The foundations of our liberty are here in America. As they are here, this is the place we should defend them."[3]

Of course there was one other reason for his hesitation in supporting the coming war, one that he could not very well talk about and never did: the horrible personal toll brought to the family by World War I. The Roosevelts had already served their nation at a dear cost. As much as Ted might have been willing to give to a war effort now, he could hardly do so with the innocence that he and his brothers had brought to the last war. He had lost his youngest brother, after all, and he and Archie had been gravely wounded. Now Ted himself had three sons who were of service age; Kermit had three more; and Archie had one. Could he and his brothers in good conscience send another generation of Roosevelts off to war?

Then again, what else could he do? He was the son and namesake of the man who had essentially invented the idea of Americanism—the notion that a virile service to the nation was at the root of all citizenship; that to be an American was to be willing to fight for your country when fighting was needed—here remained the most animating political and personal philosophy of Ted's life. This is what the family had preached to the nation in 1898 and again during the First World War. This was the lesson that the brothers had learned at the knees of their mother and father. Ted could no more shirk his duty than he could deny his last name.

If the concept of Americanism seemed a little dusty, a little dated, a little long in the tooth in the modern era—how would a group of Ivy Leaguers trained at Camp Plattsburgh, and how would a Rough Rider, for that matter, stand against a German blitzkrieg in this new war?—then so be it. The Roosevelts would still be there.

Witness brother Kermit, who in an attempt to right the floundering ship of his personal life had decided that his best chance for redemption lay in service. Though Kermit had spent most of the past few years communing in Manhattan hotels with bottles of bourbon and a mistress, he cleaned himself up, tried to make amends with Belle, got her blessing, and made contact with some of his former well-heeled connections, including his cousin Franklin and Winston Churchill, who finagled a commission for Kermit in the British army.

Now, at the age of fifty and hardly in fighting trim, Kermit sobered up, shipped to England, and was placed with a special-forces mission in Norway. Despite his age and condition, Kermit served heroically, hauling wounded comrades to safety; but the assignment ended badly for the Brits. By the fall of 1940, just before the presidential elections in the United States, Kermit was out of the fighting, serving with the British in North Africa. Accounts suggest that boredom quickly set in, and he once again started drinking.[4]

For most, Kermit's circumstances might have been a cautionary tale of an aging man trying to resurrect his youth in a battle where he ought not to have been. For Ted, it was one more nudge toward service.

Ted continued to make his political arguments against intervention, though by now Germany had swept through Czechoslovakia, through Poland, through France, was pounding England in the Blitz, and shoving the British from the Continent at Dunkirk. On the other side of the world, Japan was sweeping through Asia. All while FDR was defeating Willkie and winning his third term as president.

In January 1941, Ted and Eleanor dined with Charles Lindbergh and his wife, Anne. Afterward Ted remained confident enough in the America First cause to write his son Cornelius that he felt "the big group of the people [in the country] do not want war." But the headliners, he wrote— including Willkie, who had just returned from a tour of Europe "a quivering mass of sentiment"—"are embarking on plans that I believe [will] lead to war."[5]

In fact, Ted was hedging his bets as well. The previous summer, Ted had written his old friend General George Marshall, now chief of staff of the army, volunteering to return to active duty. Marshall agreed to order

Roosevelt into the service for a brief twenty-eight-day enlistment. Now Ted was hoping for a full-time appointment from Marshall, but was concerned that he would be denied that chance for "political" reasons. He suspected that Franklin might not want him to serve in the army after his many months of battling against the notion of intervention in the war.[6]

As the winter of 1941 progressed, so did developments leading toward America's entry into the war. In March the Lend-Lease Act was passed, committing the nation to even closer ties to Great Britain. Ted commented, in another note to Cornelius, that "In the days when old procedure governed we undoubtedly would have been considered at war with Germany and Italy now."[7]

But he still held out hope that the America First movement might prevail. To aid the cause, he and Eleanor even financed the printing and distribution of a hundred thousand copies of "A Letter to Americans," an antiwar essay written by Lindbergh that had originally appeared in *Collier's* that March. This while Ted was still lobbying General Marshall to be recalled to the military. To Ted, there was nothing inconsistent about his position, though he confessed to brother Archie's son Archie Jr., "I am continually getting on the horns of a dilemma. Being as strong as I am against entering the war, I have to be exceptionally careful that I don't get myself yoked up with people whose views I do not share." At a recent meeting of the directing board of America First, for instance, "I found that three out of four with whom I was sitting at table were all for everyone refusing to cooperate, enlist or fight in case we did get into war." In no way did they represent Ted's sentiments. "I have fought and will fight our entrance, but if and when we are committed," he wrote, "I will do all I can to bring the war to a successful conclusion."[8]

The horns of this particular dilemma were not going to go away anytime soon. Ted could not continue to be both an America Firster and a warrior in his cousin's army. In the end, he was glad to have his mind made up for him when in April Ted finally got the call to active duty from George Marshall. It turned out that the chief of staff had been waiting for the commander of Ted's old infantry regiment to be promoted to brigadier general so that Roosevelt could immediately be appointed and assume charge of his beloved 26th Infantry. Ted was to report to Fort Devens in Massachusetts before April was through. Joining him at camp would be his youngest son, Lieutenant Quentin Roosevelt.

Eleanor had thought Ted was growing increasingly depressed about his circumstances and the circumstances of the country prior to the call-up. Now there was an instant improvement in his demeanor. He was invigorated, if not quite enthused. He had something purposeful to do in the coming crisis, even if it was precisely the position he'd left after the end of the Great War.

Eleanor, always looking out for her husband's publicity, was a little disappointed that the press didn't make a bigger deal of his appointment to command his old infantry regiment. She told Cornelius in a letter that "Gen. Marshall had wanted a big story to come out, as it would have been good for the army and nice for father." A bigger splash would also have allowed her the "small consolation of . . . mak[ing] a snoot at my friends who have been shrieking for war, and who would never have fought."[9]

She was somewhat mollified late in April when the *New York Times* ran a story with the announcement of Ted's command and followed it with a photograph of Ted and Quentin looking sharp in dress khakis at Camp Devens beneath a caption that read, "The Colonel Welcomes a New Officer."[10]

TWENTY-FIVE

OUR COUNTRY, OUR CAUSE, OUR PRESIDENT

Just shy of fifty-four years old, Ted Roosevelt Jr. was back in the army. Back in the world of barracks and training, drills and commands. Back among unpolished recruits, stiff salutes, and mistimed marches over dusty camp streets to the shouted cadences of exasperated sergeants. He found that in the twenty-two years since he had last donned the uniform, the army hadn't changed much. Equipment was always in short supply, the infantry still carried out-of-date weapons, and, incredibly, the cavalry still rode horses. In contrast, Ted had been around the world several times since then; served in Washington, D.C.; run for governor of New York; climbed the Himalayas and hunted in China; lived in palaces in San Juan and Manila; fished for bass with Harpo Marx in Vermont; and traded quips with Alexander Woollcott and Dorothy Parker at the Algonquin Hotel in Manhattan. Now he was back sleeping in military quarters, dressing in khakis, helping to train the young officers of the 1st Division command in the traditions of the unit he'd been proud to be a part of in the previous war.

As with every position he ever assumed, he took it seriously and did his job well. He was a living reminder of the great traditions of the 1st Division: the first infantry division to arrive in France in the Great War, the first to fire on the enemy, the first to lose one of their own to combat, and the first to supply American troops in the trenches against the Germans. It had won the Big Red One nickname from its distinctive combat service patch, which indeed had a red "1" in the center of a five-sided badge. It would end the war one of the most renowned combat divisions in the history of the U.S. Army, but it had plenty of fame already stemming from its experiences in the First World War. And there was every expectation that should the United States enter the new world war in Europe—a possibility growing stronger and stronger every day—the 1st would once again be among the earliest combat units thrown into the fighting.

The fact that in the Great War, U.S. troops arrived so late and so ill trained to the fighting was not a thing that Theodore Roosevelt Jr. could easily forget. The inexcusable delays had been a constant refrain within the family for the first year of that earlier war. Now once again, infantry divisions were behind where they needed to be when Ted arrived at Fort Devens. It was only a few months earlier, in the fall of 1940, that the army had begun its expansion for war. At that time, only eight regular army infantry divisions existed (there would ultimately be more than one hundred, including National Guard units). There were one armored division, one cavalry division, no airborne divisions, and one battalion of paratroopers. By the spring of 1941, the army was fast filling with draftees, and training camps were springing up all through the States. Far better than training in France, as had happened twenty-four years earlier.

The 1st Division was closer to ready than most army units. It consisted largely of veterans and volunteers in the summer of 1941—just a handful of draftees in its numbers. The majority of its combat soldiers were drawn from the Eastern Seaboard, and many of the officers were West Pointers. When more draftees began to arrive that fall, friction inevitably arose between the veteran troops and the newcomers, but for the most part the blend seemed to be coalescing.[1]

Fort Devens was just west of Boston and not far from Ted's old prep school, Groton. To be close to Ted and Quentin that summer, Eleanor took a room in the Groton Inn—a fact that she and her husband considered ironic; Ted had come full circle back to the stomping grounds of his youth.

Aside from being a training camp, Devens was designated a reception center for all New England draftees, so it teemed with fresh-faced recruits. Beginning with the 1940 army buildup, the camp also bustled with construction to accommodate the ever-growing number of young soldiers (eventually twelve hundred buildings and an airfield would rise on the site). For all the work, Ted, Eleanor, and Quentin found time to take a number of day trips around Massachusetts, and Eleanor, who was becoming an accomplished photographer, snapped a photo essay of Massachusetts country homes that appeared in *Life* magazine that fall.

The 1st Division was split into three different infantry regiments; along with Roosevelt's 26th, there were the 16th and the 18th. The largely New York and Massachusetts population of the outfits was opened up to a wider geographic mix of soldiers when the draftees started to bulk up the size of the regiments from August and September onward.

Their stay in Massachusetts was relatively brief. In October, Ted, Quentin, and the 1st Division were moved to North Carolina to practice field maneuvers, and Eleanor followed, staying at Pinehurst for a few weeks. Each morning she would load up her car with Coca-Cola and raisin cookies and drive out in the North Carolina dunes, looking for the 26th Regiment. When she found it, she would wave to Ted and Quentin, maybe catch lunch with them, and then head back to Pinehurst, picking up hitchhiking soldiers on the way back into town. She wouldn't identify herself until the end of the rides, the better to catch unguarded assessments of their commander. "When I left them I would tell them I was the Colonel's wife and watch their grins as they waved me out of sight."[2]

At the end of the first week of December 1941, the 1st Division had finished its exercises in North Carolina and was taking trains back to Devens in Massachusetts when the first wave of Japanese bombers swooped down on Pearl Harbor. For the nation as a whole, that Sunday was a haze of anger, fear, and nervous anticipation. From coast to coast, citizens held their breath, wondering what treachery might follow and if they had the mettle as a people to respond to a call to war.

Neither Ted nor Eleanor recorded an immediate response to the attack, but a few days later Ted wrote to his mother as if the tumult were already settling into a kind of routine: "Well, a week of war has passed and I think the country has settled down. All leaves were cancelled for this [the 1st] Division but I think that a few days may be given as soon as the higher command gets its feet under it." He let her know that the 1st Division would be busy. The division "was the only one in this area [the Northeast] that had its leaves cancelled." He thought it likely that the 1st would be sent ultimately to the Asian mainland, but "we definitely have to gain control of the Pacific" before that could happen.

He gave Edith a rundown on what his boys would be doing: Teddy III was going to go into the Marines; Quentin was with his dad, of course, in the 1st Division; and Cornelius would probably enlist in the engineering corps any day now.

As for himself, Ted let his mother know that he had just learned from Washington that he was being promoted to brigadier general. "I never expected it," he wrote. "Indeed in some ways I'm sorry . . . I care deeply for the 26th Inf.—In a way it's an enlarged family. On the other hand it probably will do something to make people feel that in this war the hatchet [between him and Franklin] is buried which is very important now."[3]

Marshall had finagled the promotion for Ted, but did so with the full blessing of General Frank McNair, who headed U.S. Army training and preparation for overseas service. Ted had done well with the 1st Division, and he was so advised by the chief of staff. "I have been absolutely cold-blooded in this business," Marshall wrote Ted regarding the promotion, "but when your name was brought up in high commendation for the leadership you displayed, it was a great pleasure for me to confirm my opinion of the old days in France."[4, 5]

A few days after getting word of the promotion, Ted went to Washington to receive his general's star. While there, he asked for and got a few minutes with the president—a meeting he knew would draw the attention of the press and offer an opportunity to publically indicate to the nation what he had just written to his mother, that the hatchet was indeed buried.

No one bothered to record what was actually said between the two cousins at the White House, but it was no doubt cordial, sober, and brief. It was a remarkably busy and chaotic time for Franklin; he had just a few minutes for Ted. But they were both gracious men. For all their disagreements with one another, the cousins evidently maintained a good humor in their personal connections. The most recent correspondence between the two, prior to this meeting, pertained to "a mystery portrait" that had arrived at the White House from a shirttail relative in Basel, Switzerland. Franklin passed it on to Ted, wondering to which branch of the family he might belong. Ted wrote back, "I don't believe the gentleman, who looks like he swallowed a watermelon, is an ancestor of mine." Franklin was unwilling to claim the portly "baronial-looking" man in the painting for his clan either.[6]

At any rate, Ted emerged from the White House after their meeting to tell a throng of reporters that any feuding between him and Franklin was over. "This is our country, our cause, and our president," he said.[7]

Ted headed back to Massachusetts for more training, and presumably a shipment overseas with the 1st Division. A few weeks later, in the spring of 1942, George Marshall promoted a commander with a reputation as a profane, tough-as-nails soldier's soldier named Terry de la Mesa Allen to the position of major general of the 1st Division, with Ted Roosevelt as his assistant commander. In the process, Marshall made one of the most legendary pairings in World War II history. He did so with a warning to Allen:

"One comment I would make: Theodore Roosevelt and you are very much of the same type as to enthusiasm, initiative and a restless desire to get into things. I am a little fearful that two people so much of the same type will probably not get along too well, in other words, that he will probably get in your hair. I hope this doesn't develop, for he has had a long history with the First Division, is an A No. 1 fighting man with rare courage, and what is rarer, an unlimited fortitude."[8]

Terry Allen was the son of a West Point graduate and career officer in the U.S. Army named Sam Allen. Allen's peculiar middle name, de la

Mesa, came by way of his mother, who was the daughter of a Spanish officer who served for the Union in the American Civil War. The name gave Allen a whiff of the romantic, though he grew up a rather humble army brat on posts throughout the United States, including West Point, where his father taught philosophy for four years. When Terry reached college age, he started an undergraduate career at the Academy as well, but washed out after just two years. He was a beautiful rider and physically gifted, but he failed to apply himself academically. He also had a propensity for undisciplined behavior and was afflicted with a serious stutter.

Allen went off to American University in Washington, D.C., where he earned an undergraduate degree, but still harbored a desire to join the military. Soon after his graduation, he won a competitive army exam that allowed him entrance into the service, where he wound up commissioned as a second lieutenant. He was stationed on the Mexican border, using his graceful riding skills to round up smugglers on the dusty desert plains.

By the time the First World War broke out, Allen was a captain in the army cavalry, and known as one of the best polo players in the service. He'd also achieved some renown as a handsome bachelor and spirited carouser. Neither his horsemanship nor his carousing was of much use when he arrived in France; Allen was shunted off to headquarters duty. To get a combat assignment he simply showed up with a group of potential officers at a graduation ceremony for a class in infantry command, somehow convinced the commander that he'd been a student through the duration of the session, and walked away as a major in a battalion of the 90th Division. He subsequently served with distinction at Saint-Mihiel and Aincreville, winning a Silver Star and catching a bullet in the mouth. Curiously, the wound seemed to cure his stutter, but put a hole in his cheek that subsequently caused him to make a sucking noise for the rest of his life when he was talking or smoking a cigarette.

Home from the war, he spent the next twenty-one years back in the cavalry, with mixed progress. He finished 221st out of 241 officers at the Command and General Staff School at Fort Leavenworth (Dwight Eisenhower was at the top of the class), but he made a reputation as a soldier's officer among the men who served under him. He also caught the eye of

George Marshall at the Infantry School in Fort Benning, Georgia, and got his name committed to Marshall's famed Little Black Book—a source the general used frequently during the war to tap talented officers for positions in command.

In 1940, a year after Marshall became chief of staff, Allen got his first general's star, and two years later, he got the 1st Division, joining Ted Roosevelt in Fort Devens. Marshall's warning to Allen, upon giving him the assignment, was no doubt necessary. The two, Allen and Roosevelt, were much alike: both were too lax in their command, and too undisciplined for their own good. Both had displayed remarkable personal bravery during the Great War and a devotion to the welfare of the soldiers in their command.

Allen and Roosevelt had other similarities: each had a taste for whiskey at the end of a hard day, each smoked heavily, and each was notoriously casual in their dress, flouting military spit and polish. In fact, Roosevelt's own aide, Lieutenant Marcus Stevenson ("Stevie"), who would join Ted soon after the 1st entered combat that fall, called his boss "the most disreputable-looking general I have ever met." Allen's language was blue and Roosevelt's was frequently interjected with quotes from obscure poets. Each was colorful in his own way and popular with the press, a fact in Allen's case that led to resentment from his superior officers. The fact that Roosevelt and Allen were from distant ends of the social spectrum never seemed to bother either man; they got along famously from the beginning.

Their introduction was a whirlwind affair. By the time Allen joined the 1st, it was already being prepared to sail for England, and Roosevelt was scheduled to ship with the first contingent to go, the 16th Regiment, from New York Harbor in July. Allen would subsequently sail with the rest of the division, packed on the *Queen Mary* in early August.

Even as the 16th sailed for the British Isles, the American high command—including Marshall, Harry Hopkins, Chief of Naval Operations Ernest King, and General Dwight David Eisenhower—was meeting with its British counterparts at Whitehall in London, hashing out a strategy for how the Allies ought to attack Axis forces in the opening gambit of the war in Europe.

The American contingent to the Whitehall meeting was considering the idea of a direct assault against the Germans in France as late as July 1942, though the British thought this notion was suicidal. They argued for other possibilities, including a roundabout invasion that would begin with an action against Norway, or an invasion of Vichy French North Africa, which was considered a far more accessible point of entry into the war for the green American army.

As a consequence, Ted Roosevelt knew nothing of his troops' ultimate destination as he sailed with his part of the 1st Division toward Liverpool that July on the *Leonard Wood*, a well-used transport, named interestingly for Ted's father's old Spanish American War comrade and Ted's commander at Plattsburgh. The *Wood* was a rusty old bucket, and the only way to spruce it up, according to some wag traveling with Roosevelt (quoted approvingly by Ted), was to find a boom large enough to lift the ship and sail a new one underneath it.

In the first of many wartime letters to Eleanor, whom he addressed invariably as Bunny (they would never be so distant from one another for so long in their married life as they would be now), Ted described the packing of the transport, his last good-byes in New York (including a trip to the office at Doubleday), and ship life on the crowded transport to England. Ted organized deck drills and entertainment, as well as a Fourth of July celebration, which included music from the regiment band, the singing of "God Bless America," and a speech from Ted in which he told the men how he had sailed to France on this day twenty-five years earlier, with this same division to fight for the same cause of battling European authoritarianism with American democracy. Then he recited the Gettysburg Address as a restatement of that cause.[9]

Some nurses also sailed with the 16th Regiment, and Ted was generally thankful for the diversions they supplied to his troops, though his Puritan side was offended when, in the midst of a song-and-dance show put on by the women, one of the nurses "appeared in nothing but a suit of flannel underwear," Ted wrote to Eleanor. "Cheap stuff. I'd have stopped it had I known."[10]

He was much more forgiving when he discovered that F Company had smuggled a fox terrier on board in a barracks bag. The dog, known as Whitey, had been a pet of the company for a couple of years at Fort Devens prior to their departure. The men decided they couldn't part with him when they set sail, and Ted would ultimately help them avoid quarantine laws to smuggle Whitey into England.[11]

Son Quentin arrived with Terry Allen and the rest of the 1st Division on the *Queen Mary* with the second wave of division troops as Ted nervously waited in Tidworth in south central England, where the 16th Regiment was stationed before heading off to training in Scotland. Ted was seriously concerned over German submarine attacks. Catching a huge transport ship with nearly a full American division on board would have been a devastating blow to the Allied cause and a boon to the Germans. Ted was also nervous because Eleanor was coming to England as well, flying in on a Pan Am Clipper. As she had done during the first war, Eleanor planned on spending this world war serving with the Red Cross, this time in England. After she arrived in August, Eleanor immediately started work setting up a servicemen's club in Tidworth.

By the time they both arrived safe and sound, Ted and the 16th had entrained for Scotland, where the regiment began practicing amphibious landings with British commando teams as they awaited assignment. These landings were exacting and physically demanding exercises for the men, as well as for commanders such as Ted. Which is to say nothing of the extraordinary demands they made on a man of his age. But this was to be a war where amphibious assaults would be common. And Ted would participate in more of them than any general in the American army before the war was through. All of the practice was necessary, which made it no less exhausting.

Other aged Roosevelt men continued to serve. Ted's brother Archie had also petitioned the president for some role in the service, despite the fact that his Great War wounds had left him so severely handicapped that the army ruled him disabled. Nonetheless, Archie begged to enlist, and his cousin Franklin found him a place, serving as a lieutenant colonel in a division sent to the Pacific. Once there, Archie, in typical Roosevelt fashion, volunteered for hazardous duty and served with distinction.

Among other assignments, he served as a spotter with a small reconnaissance unit on a South Pacific island, sighting Japanese artillery units for
Allied guns. He later suffered yet another war wound while fighting with
the Australians, which would eventually lead to his being mustered out
of the service once again. Archie was the only army soldier in the two
wars to be twice declared 100 percent disabled.

Kermit's life was fast growing tragic. After his stint with the British
army in North Africa in 1941, he returned home, but quickly stumbled
back to the bottle and his mistress. Belle, his forgiving wife, appealed once
again to the president: Could Franklin use his office to help locate her
husband, who had disappeared with his girlfriend? She, too, thought he
might be able to once again get his circumstances in order if he were back
in the service, this time with the U.S. Army.

Franklin, uncertain of whether his cousin was beyond redemption,
wanted to see Kermit at the White House before he made any decisions.
Kermit agreed to a meeting, but instead skipped it and disappeared with
his girlfriend on a bender. FDR actually had to enlist the FBI to find
Kermit, who was finally corralled in California and shipped off to a sana-
torium to get dry. The president and George Marshall ultimately placed
Kermit with the army air force in Alaska, where he wound up in the fall
of 1942, just as Ted was preparing to leave Great Britain for the first great
Allied invasion of the war.

TWENTY-SIX

TORCH

Operation Torch, as the upcoming attack on Axis forces had been dubbed by Allied command, began in late October 1942, with three large convoys sailing toward North Africa. Two of these fleets came from Great Britain and carried the 1st Division, the 1st Armored Division, and the 34th Division, along with a large contingent of British forces. These troops would carry out an amphibious assault on French Vichy forces along the Algerian shores of the Mediterranean, sweeping in an arc from Oran, on the western edge of the attack zone, to Algiers in the east, where the Brits would lead the invasion.

The last convoy would sail directly from the United States across the Atlantic to attack French forces in Morocco, on the northwestern side of the African continent. The U.S. Army units attached to this mission were the 3rd and 9th Divisions, under the command of General George Patton. Their assault would be centered on the city of Casablanca, on the Atlantic shore.

When the grand leaders of the Allied cause had finished their deliberations at Whitehall back in August, they finally settled on North Africa as the best point of invasion for this opening salvo of the war in Europe. Letting American troops acclimate themselves to the fighting with an assault against the Vichy troops of France seemed like a more sensible introduction to war than any sort of cross-channel invasion against the forces of Nazi Germany. A subsequent linkup with the British army of Viscount Bernard Montgomery, already in North Africa, suited the British command as well.

For the men of Terry Allen's 1st Division, however, the mystery of their ultimate destination remained when they embarked from the same Scottish port at which they'd arrived almost three months earlier. For the first few days, the troops lingered in British waters, awaiting the go-ahead for passage to a continent that would be unknown for several days more.

Quentin and Ted had the good luck to ship together on H.M.S. *Monarch of Bermuda*, which gave them ample opportunity for talks in Ted's cabin on several evenings over the course of the voyage. Now twenty-three years old, Quentin had grown into a talented young man with a promising future. He'd always been a fine student and had musical and artistic gifts as well as the Roosevelt instinct for adventure and exploration. As a student at Groton, he and a classmate had spent a summer in the Southwest on a ranch—a typical Rooseveltian rite of passage. While out exploring one day, the pair entered a cave, began digging around, and found a prehistoric bone in the rubble. It turned out to be that of a previously unknown Pleistocene Epoch antelope prized by the American Natural History Museum. Scientists there named the newly discovered animal in Quentin's honor. While he was still an undergrad, he had journeyed with his mother to China to study Chinese art in Szechuan, the same province his father and uncle had explored in their hunt for the giant panda. Upon his return to Harvard, Quentin graduated cum laude, writing his senior thesis on the artwork of the Nakhi people prior to entering the service.

Now, just out of school and off to war, Quentin was brimming with excitement and trepidation. He told his father that he thought they'd look back on these days "as full of romance." They talked about home: clamming on Oyster Bay, the family dogs, getting yelled at by the longtime housekeeper, Signorina, for bringing "treasures" into her kitchen at Old Orchard—the same sort of slimy creatures that Quentin's father had brought home to Sagamore Hill as a boy. They also chatted about how to arrange things at Old Orchard after the war. Gaining no points for their interior decoration skills, father and son envisioned "a war corner" in the library with medals and citations hung on the north wall of the room on a black velvet background.[1]

On October 27, the transport ships were given leave to set off down the coast of western Europe toward their ultimate destination, which they soon learned was North Africa. "Here I am off again on the great adventure at fifty-five," Ted wrote to Eleanor as they headed south.[2]

The men settled into the voyage. They tried to keep busy with calisthenics and bunk entertainment, but there was little room on board for exercise, and what room existed was littered with ship fixtures, cables, and coils of rope. Ted wrote to Eleanor about his growing fondness for tea, of a medieval history that he was reading, of writing to all of his children. He also told her she should check in with cousin Eleanor, who was in England at the time. Ted told his Eleanor to get Franklin's Eleanor to come down to the club that Ted's Eleanor had opened for American troops in Tidworth—there'd been a lot of press about all British women were doing for the war effort, and Ted thought his own wife deserved credit for her efforts.

The sea got a little rough, and seasickness visited the infantry. Roosevelt went belowdecks to cheer the men up by telling them that if they thought their transport was rolling, they ought to look at Allen's headquarters ship nearby, which was twice as rocky. When they entered German submarine waters off the coast of Spain, the journey got tense—a state that only increased on November 2, when Ted got his assignment for the invasion.

He was to command the western portion of the assault, leading the 26th Regiment onto the beach designated as Y, just west of Oran in North Africa. Once on the beach, his men were to turn east and move along the coast toward Oran, serving as the lower part of the jaw in a pincer move against the Algerian city.

Allen was to command most of the remainder of the 1st Division in an attack against the village of Arzew, on Beach Z, about twenty miles east of Oran. His assault would open with a contingent of five hundred specially trained Army Rangers, commanded by William O. Darby, arriving first at Oran Harbor. Not yet the famed Darby's Rangers that would become a legendary special forces unit during the next months, they were now part of an army experiment styled after and trained by British special forces in Scotland the previous summer. They would spearhead the initial assault to the east of Oran, after which Allen's 16th and 18th Regiments and 1st Armored units would move against Oran as the upper jaw of the pincer.

On Beach X, thirty miles west of Oran, another contingent of the 1st Armored would land to support Roosevelt's assault on Oran from the west.[3]

As the convoy sailed passed Gibraltar and toward its destination in Algeria, word came of Montgomery's victory over the Germans at the Second Battle of El Alamein, news that cheered everyone in the convoy. Ted was also excited by a conversation he had with Quentin in the wake of election news just coming from the States. The GOP had done well in the congressional elections that week, and Quentin, as a consequence, had expressed an enthusiasm for politics and a plan for getting into the profession after the war. His postwar strategy was to find some solid work, perhaps in newspapers in a Western state, and work his way into the political realm as a sideline until an office presented itself back in New York.

To Ted, this talk of a political future for Quentin, on the brink of one of the most dramatic moments in their lives, felt like a satisfying passing of the torch. It offered the opportunity of a graceful exit from the same life for him. "That would be nice, wouldn't it?" Ted wrote Eleanor of Quentin's decision to enter politics. Then he added a melancholy footnote about his own future political prospects. "Q. thinks we go back into politics—Poor lamb! He does not realize as we do that we are done. This war effort will finish us. When it's through, if we survive, we will be considered too old. All we will want anyhow is a chance to be a little quiet and sit in the sun."[4]

In truth, few expected a fierce fight from the French forces in the invasion. In fact, there was some question as to whether they would fight at all: it was generally understood that there was little heart in the Vichy military defense of North Africa. Last-minute secret negotiations between Allied general Mark Clark and senior officers in the French army in Algeria in late October had failed to negotiate a way out of battle.

If there was fight in the Vichy, it would most likely come from Oran, not Algiers, went the Allied thinking. The French navy was based in Oran, and it had endured a bitter attack from the British earlier in the war and harbored serious resentments against the Royal Navy. Coastal batteries around Oran, along with fourteen destroyers and a battleship, were expected to offer stiff resistance to the invasion.

Oran itself was a city of about two hundred thousand people, a cosmopolitan mix of French, Africans, Arabs, and Spaniards. Beyond its harbor, the coast was extremely rocky and unsuitable for landing except for the three beaches designated X, Y, and Z by the 1st Division. The best of these sites was at Arzew, where Terry Allen was heading with the bulk of the division.

West of Oran, toward the Atlantic Ocean, where Ted Roosevelt and the 26th Infantry Regiment were landing, the landscape rose up into mountainous hills; the highest, Djebel Murdjadjo, peaked at about two thousand feet and overlooked the city from its western suburbs. This was the goal of the 26th for D-Day plus one.

There was a third assault planned, aimed directly at Oran Harbor, in the heart of the city. A battalion of American infantry from the 6th Armored Infantry Regiment placed on two transport cutters that had sailed all the way from the Great Lakes to this Mediterranean destination was to lead the attack into the city. While the Brits insisted on commanding the operation, it was surmised that having American soldiers in this assault would somehow dampen the French navy's enthusiasm for the fight. The battalion's large intent was to land quickly to prevent the French from scuttling its fleet in Oran Harbor, causing chaos and a general mess in a port that the Allies intended for heavy use in the weeks and months to come.

The cutters, with face-blackened infantry aboard and armed with weapons and grappling hooks, prepared to board French ships in the harbor. They didn't get the chance. Instead French destroyers raked the decks of the Great Lakes transports, ripping holes in the ships and killing sailors and infantrymen alike. The two cutters were sunk before the sun rose on the morning of November 8, and were soon joined by twenty-seven French ships put to the bottom of the harbor by the Vichy navy to prevent Allied use and to clutter the passage. They joined three hundred Allied dead either in the deep of Oran Harbor, or floating lifeless on its surface.[5] It was an inauspicious beginning to the battle in North Africa. Undeterred by the troubles in the harbor, however, the rest of the convoy carrying the 1st Division sailed east and west of Oran into Algerian waters, and continued the assault. At one o'clock the next morning, five thousand troops of Ted Roosevelt's 26th Regiment were lowered into landing craft about five miles offshore in the dark, pounding surf. Their destination was a seaside resort called Les Andalouses, about a dozen miles west of Oran. The difficulties of climbing down the rope nets into the rocking landing craft were quickly compounded by the seasickness that followed once the GIs were aboard. The bottoms of the craft were soon covered with heaving soldiers sitting in misery in sloshing water as the boats bounced and slammed on the waves toward the beaches.

As with all amphibious landings, this one was chaotic and full of dread. When the craft slammed into the beach, some soldiers stepped into water five feet deep and dragged themselves forward to a shore weirdly dotted with shadowy cabanas, as if just vacated by sunning tourists. Others plunked combat boots onto soft Mediterranean sand and tried to sprint forward. The landing craft, too, found a mixture of smooth landings and water-covered sandbars, which caused a number of vehicles and guns to be deposited in several feet of rough water. One gun crew was left at the beach to extricate a particularly badly stuck cannon.[6]

The major blessing for all involved was that there was no sound of firing from the shore. Ted had come ashore with the first wave at Les Andalouses and had immediately begun encouraging his men forward. Many of them, simply relieved at surviving their first amphibious landing, clung to the beach as if it were the only goal of the invasion.

The 26th soon gained the beachhead, and was quick to establish a headquarters near the resort. Oddly enough, a man in a British officer's jacket stood in front of a one-story rock house at the top of the sand, like some abandoned sailor looking for rescue from the Americans. He turned out to be the beach master and offered directions to the blacktop road leading east toward Oran. Using the password "Hi-Yo Silver," troops of the 2nd and 3rd Battalions of the 26th were quick to turn their attention down the coastline toward the hills guarding Oran from the south and east. They finally hit French opposition at about eight that morning, when the leading edge of the 26th bumped into and engaged three French armored vehicles heading out from Oran to see what was coming toward the city. They were destroyed by mortar and antitank fire from the 2nd Battalion.

Soon after, French batteries from Djebel Murdjadjo opened fire, aiming primarily at the convoy, five miles offshore. One of the landing craft, still ferrying soldiers ashore, caught a direct hit and was destroyed. Also hit was the *Monarch of Bermuda*, the transport that had brought Ted and most of the 2nd Battalion from Scotland. The shore fire caught the attention of the British battleship H.M.S. *Rodney*, which soon sailed a few miles down the coast and began answering the French shore batteries with quieting fire.

The 26th came to a halt about half a dozen miles west of Oran at the end of D-Day. All in all it had been a fairly smooth landing for the five thousand infantrymen who came ashore from Ted's unit. He wrote Eleanor later that initial contact with the French "was neither a tough fight or a walkover."[7]

On the other side of the city, Terry Allen's forces had likewise met little opposition at the beach, but were slowed advancing west toward Oran. William Darby's Rangers were able to scale cliffs above Arzew to set up mortar teams to protect troops coming onto the beach. But soon after the first-day assault, elements of his units got bogged down in heavy fighting by the French Foreign Legion outside the city of Saint-Cloud, between Arzew and Oran. In a move that immediately endeared him to his own soldiers and made perfect tactical sense as well, Allen chose simply to bypass Saint-Cloud, rather than risk unnecessary bloodshed, both civilian and military, in a frontal assault of the city. After leaving a regiment outside the obstacle to continue pressuring the French, the rest of the 1st simply skirted Saint-Cloud and continued on to Oran. With Roosevelt's 26th coming from the west and Allen attacking Oran from the east, the rest of the 1st had more than enough firepower to overcome French opposition and take the city.

On D-Day plus one, Roosevelt's 26th bumped into French shelling on its way up the hills south and west of Oran. A line of tanks, accompanied by about six hundred Moroccan Zouaves, also joined the fray. Quentin's battery was among the group of artillerymen who made quick work of these "ancient Renaults," but the infantry remained to spar with the 26th.[8, 9]

Roosevelt joined the battalion forcing its way up toward the summit of the Djebel Murdjadjo at Mers El-Kébir, the town where the French battery was centered. The toughest fighting of the invasion followed, and Ted Roosevelt was in the thick of it. He and a jeep driver were reconnoitering with a small squad beyond the advance battalion's lead guard when they began to encounter small-arms fire from a ten-man patrol of horse cavalry. Exposed to the fire in his open jeep, Roosevelt grabbed his rifle, stooped behind the windshield and started to return fire, as if he were riding in a true shotgun position in some Hollywood stagecoach Western. The patrol was driven off, and Ted was ultimately awarded a Bronze Star for the action. Or as Ted put it in a letter to Eleanor, "The old man went in with the assault wave . . . to the final objective. Also he got him a French cavalryman with his carbine when they came in on the left flank."[10]

The old man also got his first prisoners in the exchange, and was able to take the fortress that topped Mers El-Kébir above Oran. A price was paid: Ted lost his aide, Bob Emery, in the assault, along with a number of other good men. The heights above Oran were taken, however, by the end of the day, November 9.

Allen, whose bypass of Saint-Cloud had hastened the advance toward Oran, joined forces with the 26th to bring the city into Allied hands by ten thirty the next morning, on the third day of the invasion. Saint-Cloud would surrender a few hours later. Just under 90 officers and enlisted men from the 1st were killed in the Oran portion of the invasion, while another 250 were wounded.[11]

George Patton's invasion of Morocco to the southeast took a few hours longer to wind up, but by the time Casablanca and the airport at Port Lyautey were taken on November 10, Operation Torch was complete. With the exception of the disaster in Oran Harbor, it had proved a success for U.S. troops. Solid ground in North Africa had been won at fairly minimal cost.

Now would come the hard struggle against a far more formidable foe. The Germans were just to the east, in Tunisia, getting shoved there by Montgomery and the British Eighth Army. The newly arrived invaders, British and American, would now be asked to pinch German general Erwin Rommel from the west.

TWENTY-SEVEN

DESERT

The Algeria that the 1st Division settled in was a country that looked to many Americans seeing North Africa for the first time like a Southwest U.S. desert. Ted Roosevelt described it as "brown, brown, and more brown (just before rains in late December turned it green, green, and more green)."[1]

American troops were followed "in almost comic fashion by hordes of Arab children" according to journalist Ernie Pyle, who was part of a small but highly visible contingent of war correspondents in Algeria. The kids mimicked the GIs' password, Hi-Yo Silver, as if it were a peculiar American greeting.[2]

Out in the countryside, Ted saw wheat fields, olive groves, and orange trees contrasting with a rougher landscape. "The hills are rugged with low desert scrub and occasionally rather scrubby pine woods." The presence of the great desert, he wrote Eleanor, "unseen but felt" was "as strong an undercurrent as the backwoods were in the early history of our country." The mix of ancient history and modern influences struck him, too. "Here we have automobiles running down a road on which travel little donkeys loaded with fagots and Arabs sitting on top. Modernistic apartments and four miles away men and women living in caves. Life unchanged since the days of Carthage [mixed with] films from Hollywood."[3]

The 1st Division was given a few weeks of rest after the invasion, affording Ted the time to write to his children, Cornelius, Teddy, and Grace, as well as his sister Ethel. He also got a new aide, "[Marcus] Stevenson from San Antonio," who, according to Ted, "led his platoon gallantly [at Oran] and is a very nice boy." Stevenson, a tall, rangy young man with a Texas accent and, in time, a dashing mustache, would become a fixture in Roosevelt's orbit through the rest of the war.

For the first few weeks in Algeria, Ted had Quentin for company, too. Ted and his son went off to visit a Foreign Legion post, climbing a tower and touring a legion barracks, where they were shown a trophy room full of "tattered flags from long-ago battles—uniforms and weapons used since the legion's inception more than a hundred years ago."[4]

The French were largely satisfied with the change in their circumstances and not only welcomed American forces, but for the most part opted to join them in the fighting against Germany. For the American GIs, the dry air and cool winter weather in the desert was a happy change from the damp of Great Britain, and there was a sense of accomplishment following their first taste of action. Unfortunately, their satisfaction quickly evaporated when Eisenhower decided to give overall command of the Allied forces in Algeria and Tunisia to British lieutenant general Sir Kenneth Anderson.

Though Eisenhower and army corps commander Lloyd Fredendall had been pleased with the quick progress of American forces, the British, it turned out, were less impressed. They whispered about the botched assault on Oran Harbor, discreetly criticizing the Americans for the debacle; most Yanks agreed, on the other hand, that if botching had occurred, it had been carried out by the Brits. Regardless of these opinions, the Allied command ultimately agreed that the newly arrived Americans were too inexperienced and untrained to play first chair in the coming campaign against Rommel and his Panzers.

One of British lieutenant general Kenneth Anderson's first actions as the new commander of Tunisian forces was to divide the 1st Division, assigning sections of the 18th Regiment to a British corps. They went off on an offensive to Tunisia, trying to reach the port city of Tunis before German reinforcements from Sicily could arrive there to secure its harbor for Axis supply lines. Meanwhile, the 16th Regiment and two battalions stayed with Allen in Oran. Ted Roosevelt would soon be assigned one of the joint Allied command units, a mix of 1st Division infantry and French troops. The 33rd Field Artillery, with Quentin attached, was ordered, along with much of the 26th, to join a unit of Free French fighters and the II Army Corps in southern Tunisia. In other words, the 1st Division was spread out all over Tunisia in a potpourri of Allied units.

Quentin left his father's command, much to Ted's chagrin. He had loved having his son close to him during the months of training, the voyage down the European coast to Africa, and through the invasion and the stay in Algiers.

Ted was told by Quentin's battalion commander and others in the 1st that his son was becoming a fine young officer, but Ted had intense and conflicting desires: as much as he wanted Quentin to shine in service and win the sort of combat acclaim that he himself had won in the Great War, Ted was far more cognizant of the very real dangers modern war presented than his father had been when Theodore sent his sons off to France in 1917. In fact, Ted had encouraged his other two sons, Teddy III and Cornelius, to avoid the army and the possibility of combat duty. He was frankly full of worries about Quentin and felt somehow that by keeping him near he could help keep his youngest out of harm's way.

The horrible dangers of the theater were soon realized when word arrived from northern Tunisia that one of the battalions from the 18th, assigned to the British offensive there, had been badly mauled trying to relieve a British unit at a place called Longstop Hill. There had been much confusion between the two allies during the process of relief, and not only was the American battalion ultimately driven from the hill with heavy casualties; they were once again blamed by the British for botching the operation.

Terry Allen was not pleased when word of the criticism reached him. He assigned his own 1st Division intelligence officer to do a follow-up report on Longstop, which suggested that the American battalion had been badly handled by British command. Allen marched over to the office of the chief of that offensive, General Charles Allfrey, and presented him with the intel report from his own division.[5] The pissing match that followed typified the strained relationship that colored the first few months of the new Allied command in North Africa.

Few members of the 1st Division were happy with their circumstances, including Ted Roosevelt. Along with Quentin's absence, the splitting up of the American force, and the general lack of activity of the 1st Division, another matter rankled Ted. Just after the invasion an order was sent to top commanders by the British Ministry of Information at the behest of unidentified "U.S. advisors." The communiqué was sent as a guide to press censors working under their command. It stated that no mention or photographs of certain U.S. officers could be made without permission of these unnamed U.S. advisors. There was a list of sixty exceptions to this rule that included top commanders for Operation Torch such as Eisenhower, Mark Clark, George Patton, and others. Also included in the order, however, were the names of three people who were singled out as not to be mentioned in any press. They were Brigadier General Theodore Roosevelt Jr., his son Lieutenant Quentin Roosevelt, and Henry Wallace Jr., the son of the vice president.[6]

In the most understanding scenario, there might have been good safety-of-the-family reasons for the ban. The Roosevelts were cousins of the president, after all, along with being the son and grandson of a famed former president; if knowledge of their presence on the front became common and known to the enemy, it might unduly jeopardize their service.

Then again, the scenario seemed a little far-fetched. Within the U.S. Army, Ted's presence was already widely known, and Quentin was just one of many sons of well-known and important figures serving with the Allies. Ted and Eleanor couldn't help but believe that this order came from his political enemies, meaning Franklin, who simply wanted to deny Ted and his family publicity for their service. For a family that thrived on acknowledgment of their wartime accomplishments, it was a cruel blow—not just for Ted, but even more important for their ambitions for son Quentin.

With simmering anger the family noted that newspaper reporting on the invasion of Oran was extremely curious: one account of the invasion fighting named twenty-eight officers involved. One general's actions were described in detail, and sounded much like Ted's duty, right down to the jeep ride in which the man was taking shots at the enemy with his rifle from the front passenger seat, but no name was given in the article.[7]

All of this put Ted in a pretty sour mood at the beginning of the New Year. He was made no happier when he received a copy of a *New York Times* article that came out in late December, an article written by one of his cousin Eleanor's "pet correspondents" (the phrase was Ted's—the president's wife was known to have many friends on the staff of the *Times*). The story was intended to describe in complimentary fashion Mrs. Ted Roosevelt's work in England during the war. But there was no mention of Ted, his role in the war, or the roles of any of their children.[8]

The Allied battle for North Africa began with the broad strategy of pinching Rommel's forces between the incoming Allied troops pouring onto the continent at Oran and Algiers and Field Marshal Montgomery's forces, which had recently whipped the Germans at El Alamein and were now nudging Rommel west into Tunisia. The new Allied troops were to create a line running north and south down the eastern edge of the Atlas Mountains in central Tunisia. The idea was for Montgomery to push the Germans toward this line, leaving Rommel no place to go but north. The ultimate goal was to squeeze Rommel up and out of North Africa at Tunis on the Mediterranean.

Unfortunately the line proved too thin to pressure the veteran Panzer divisions attacking it, and Allied command was not initially up to the task of countering the well-executed assaults of the experienced Germans. Montgomery was slow applying pressure from the east, and everywhere the Germans felt pinched, they simply powered their way forward past Allied lines. There was no squeeze being exerted on the German forces.

General Anderson's decision to divvy up American troops across the Allied armies benefited none of the forces, and General Fredendall was proving to be a timid and indecisive general. At every step, the Allies were being outgeneraled and outfought by the Germans.

By the middle of January, Roosevelt had moved to Constantine, where he was briefly rejoined by Quentin. It was an old North African town that had been both a Numidian stronghold and a Roman city, with a triumphal arch and aqueducts.

Allen and Fredendall soon arrived to discuss plans. The American 1st Armored Division was advancing on Rommel's 21st Panzers just to the south in what was intended to be the first concentrated use of an American division against the Germans. Roosevelt's troops were to head in that direction, too.

This latest move, to Pichon in central Tunisia, put Roosevelt and his unit just north of the heavy fighting. First Division troops with Ted remained mixed with British and Free French forces so that only about 40 percent was a cohesive American entity. Ted complained to Eleanor about the difficulties of going into battle with such a unit. Command was confused, communications were difficult, cohesiveness was lost.

Ted's troops included French and Arab infantry battalions and artillery units that combined British, French, and American troops from the 26th. He had arrived in the sector on the heels of some losses and found a dispirited collection of soldiers. Allen later commended Roosevelt's work at Pichon to Eisenhower, lauding Ted's executive ability, his initiative, and his practical combat knowledge in boosting the morale and defensive capabilities of his troops.[9] But Ted himself sounded dispirited writing to Eleanor in early February as he was preparing for an attack from the Germans. He said that he was writing by the light of a candle, that he hadn't had a change of underwear for twelve days, that it was bitterly cold, and that the army apparently had not realized that the North African desert might be cold in the dead of winter.[10] "I'm so glad I packed my woolies," he wrote.[11] He also reassured her, as he would throughout the war, that he was in good health: "If anything I've put on a few pounds."

The French units under his command were even more woefully under-supplied than the Americans. According to Ted, they had "no modern equipment, poor clothes, poor food and heavy casualties." Even so, Roosevelt was preparing to send the French troops back into the line under a different command to the south in support of Allied actions there. And all he could offer them before they left were some medals to help build their morale.[12]

The Allies' north-south line in central Tunisia in the foothills of the Atlas Mountains was bisected by a series of passes and valleys—Faïd, Ousseltia, Kasserine—that would serve as the highways for attack and retreat over the next month and a half. On February 14, south of Roosevelt's command, two German Panzer divisions came sweeping around the mountains above the Faïd Pass, surprising the Americans' 1st Armored Division and the 168th Infantry. Tanks, artillery, infantry, and dive-bombing planes raked an area about ten miles long. American tanks fought valiantly, but they'd been caught unawares, and the U.S. Sherman tanks lacked the firepower of the German Mark IVs. Panzers rolled through the valleys with a cocky sense of superiority, pausing above infantry trenches to give their treads a slight turn and dip to crush and grind the GIs trapped beneath.

The Allies, including the French troops from Roosevelt's combat group, were pounded at Faïd, pounded on a plain just west of the pass called Sidi Bou Zid, and pounded once again at Sbeitla. They were soon in full-fledged retreat, heading toward Ousseltia to the north, near where Ted waited.

They were also pushed west toward Kasserine Pass, a mile-wide gap in the Atlas hills in west-central Tunisia, which, despite being an ideal position, was underdefended by the Allies, with just a battalion of engineers and the 26th Battalion of Terry Allen's 1st Infantry, which was rushed into the breach at the last moment.

Fighting on rocky, scrubby desert terrain—a mix of plateaus, rocks, and dusty hills with winds whipping up sandy grit everywhere—German forces soon had the Allies in retreat wherever they met. Artillery pounded the Allied defense all day and at night; Messerschmitts made killing swoops down on the battlefield; and enemy patrols sliced through them in the dark. In the morning, Rommel's tanks came rolling down the pass to finish off the job. The roads were soon full of vehicles leaving the battle or abandoned in the flight. Infantry used any means possible to exit the killing fields. Even Allied hospitals were evacuated and so were command unit headquarters.

Over the course of a week from mid-February onward, a variety of Allied units met the enemy on battlefields that stretched fifty miles east to west across the Tunisian hills and the passes. Units of the 1st Division, from the 16th, 18th, and 26th Regiments, fought Rommel's Panzers at Sbiba, at Kasserine, at Djebel el Hamra on the western edge of Tunisia, but they never fought as a single unit. Even Fredendall's headquarters, seventy miles from the initial front (a distance that prompted much snickering criticism, as did the air raid tunnel he spent many weeks digging there before the attack), felt enough jeopardy by the time Rommel's divisions crashed through Kasserine that it began to pack for a move northeast of its current position.

The German advance petered out only when Rommel's troops became stretched too thin by the rapidity of their movement. The leading edge of their offensive was slowed at Djebel el Hamra by the 16th Infantry Regiment, along with the 1st Armored Division, and British and American artillery units. Rommel decided to call off the dogs and head back toward the German starting point in eastern Tunisia.

Among the Allied troops left in the wake of the attack was Lieutenant Quentin Roosevelt, gravely wounded by a strafing Messerschmitt near Kasserine. A bullet had passed through his lung and lodged between his liver and kidneys. He was taken to a field hospital soon after, but now the station was about to be overrun and needed quick evacuation, however dangerous that might be to his condition. Sixty miles away and in the dead of night, Ted Roosevelt heard the news of his son's wounds and rushed to find a jeep. He took off in the dark, racing against the tide of the chaotic retreat, trying to find Quentin, not knowing if he would arrive to find his son dead or alive.

Quentin was sleeping on a cot in the same field hospital to which he'd been initially taken when his father found him. Quentin had improved since arriving, but he still had a temperature of 104 degrees and still needed to be evacuated. Ted told the nurses not to wake him, but they told the general that his son had been asking for him all day. Ted bent to kiss Quentin's forehead, thinking that his brave soldier son looked like a little boy again. He woke him in the process. "I did feel he was our little boy," Ted wrote Eleanor. "Lying there dirty and unshaved. He was a little muzzy from drugs and that made him younger still." But Ted was beyond glad to see Quentin alive and hopefully on the mend. Some finagling was needed, but with the help of hospital staff, Roosevelt made arrangements for his son to be flown to care back in Algeria.[13]

He tried to reassure Eleanor about Quentin's condition and prognosis. The doctors thought it would take six weeks for their son to heal, by which time, Ted wrote Eleanor, "the hard fighting here should be over." After that, he said, "I'm going to get him in a little safer place."[14]

At the headquarters of the U.S. Army II Corps, moved now to Djebel Kouif, northwest of Kasserine, despondency reigned. Confidence had been drained both from the troops and command by their failures in the Tunisian hills and plains. Fredendall's timidity in the fight was noticeable to all. This was the first real battle between American troops and Rommel's Panzers, and it had been an embarrassing rout. Several divisional commanders complained to Eisenhower, as did the British. The last straw came when Eisenhower's eyes and ears on the ground, Major General Omar Bradley, put his two cents in; it was time for new command in Tunisia, Bradley told Ike, so Fredendall would be heading home. Coming in his place was the man who'd led American forces in the invasion of Morocco in November and was now in the midst of outlining the next invasion down the line after North Africa, in Sicily. That planning would have to be put on hold, Eisenhower told "Georgie" Patton; he was needed at the II Corps.

Patton already had one of the most vivid reputations in the army. Some considered him a brilliant and aggressive commander, and just the man to whip the Second Army into shape; others thought he was an arrogant blowhard full of himself and a healthy measure of bull. He had been a chest-out, shoulders-back army man for more than thirty years, ever since his days at West Point. A Californian with family ties that stretched in two directions, to the Old South of antebellum Virginia and the days of Old Mexico in California, Patton had participated as a heptathlete in the 1912 Olympics and served with General John J. Pershing in Mexico before World War I and again in the Great War, where he served with distinction and became one of the U.S. Army's pioneer proponents of tank warfare. Between the wars he served under army chief of staff Douglas MacArthur and became a close, if overbearing, friend to Dwight Eisenhower. At the outset of World War II, Patton commanded the 2nd Armored Division, training in the deserts of Southern California, until he was tapped to lead the Moroccan component of Operation Torch in August 1942.

Now, after his successes there, he arrived at Djebel Kouif in a style befitting his ego. Sirens wailed, soldiers stopped and gawked, some casually saluting, much to the general's displeasure, as Patton led a contingent of armored cars into the city square, "standing like a charioteer" in the lead vehicle.[15] He took little time kicking the despondency out of the army corps. A man who not only relished spit-and-polish soldiering, but who also felt that one of the biggest problems in the Second Army was its lack of discipline, Patton quickly made his presence felt by fining almost every soldier who greeted him for crimes ranging from missing ties to unpolished boots. He was particularly put off by the wool caps that were popular among 1st Division soldiers. Patton filled his jeep with confiscated caps, pulled from the heads of soldiers, as he patrolled his new command.

When he came to review Allen and Roosevelt's 1st Division headquarters early one morning, with Bradley in tow, he found Allen and Roosevelt just waking up—Ted, in fact, was still in his robe. Allen and

Patton had a long history together in the army, stretching back to joint service in Mexico before the Great War and afterward, serving together in the cavalry. They had gotten along well enough, according to most accounts, but Patton was the sort of commander who always felt obliged, on occasions when he felt onstage, to show some dramatic side of his character. Here at his introduction to the 1st Division, perhaps the most heralded unit in the U.S. Army, he felt obliged to be insulting.

The 1st Division command—Allen and Roosevelt—had created a row of slit trenches to guard against Luftwaffe attacks at Djebel Kouif. To show his contempt for this bit of caution, Patton asked Allen which trench was his. When it was indicated, Patton proceeded to unzip and relieve himself in the trench, while Allen's extremely loyal 1st Division soldiers looked on with barely contained furor. Allen was a man they'd served loyally and with deep respect through many weeks of fighting; George Patton was the newly arrived peacock swiping their perfectly good caps. It was claimed that there was an audible click of safeties being removed from their weapons by the bodyguards of Allen and Roosevelt when they witnessed this act of contempt.[16]

Despite this remarkably offensive start, Patton actually offered something to Allen that the division commander had been clamoring for since Oran: Patton's first order was to unify the 1st Division; Allen would now have full command of his old unit.

"Big news," Ted wrote Eleanor, "F[redendall] goes—& a man I like comes in & that makes all the difference in the world." He gave a thumbs-up as well to Omar Bradley's arrival as Eisenhower's second-in-command in North Africa. All the changes in the II Corps command meant that "We are going to have real soldier men who have lived with troops, led them and fought with them in charge."[17]

One of Ted's chief new duties under Allen was to serve as a liaison between command and the many and disparate units that made up the 1st Division. As the 1st recovered from the German offensive and the disaster at Kasserine, Ted spent time traveling to and encouraging the various battalions and companies scattered in the area. "This war is not like the last," he wrote Eleanor. "We are all over the place . . . I'm full of admiration for the men. They've had a very long spell of fighting and hardship but their spirits are not broken. They are not even slightly bent. I have a good time inspecting them & talking to them. We have solemn little jokes that would amuse no one else.[18]

"Today I spent going around the units to buck them up. I don't believe in pep talks. I'm sure it's much better to walk among the men and just say what seems appropriate—Find out about rations even if you can do nothing—Let them see you have a personal interest in them."[19]

Ted was fast growing into an unforgettable character to the men he commanded. He spent more time with the frontline troops than Allen and visited soldiers daily. His disheveled dress and casual style, continued even after Patton's arrival, underscored his approach to the GIs he commanded. His concerns were their concerns, and they appreciated him for it. Ted walked with what one journalist described as a "gamecock" gait, quick staccato steps, sometimes aided by a walking stick that he carried folded in his field jacket. His salute was casual and quick, an angular swipe from forehead all the way down to his sternum, and he made a point of using it often—not for discipline's sake, but to acknowledge everyone in his command who might remember and note the return salute of a man who was a Roosevelt. On his visits to each and every battalion or company, he made a point of checking with the unit cook to make sure the men were getting the best food available. He was thinking of the Joes, and they knew it and appreciated the effort. He had no trouble emphasizing the fact that he was, by comparison to these kids, an elderly gentleman who had seen this movie before, in France, way back in 1918. When he returned from these visits back to regimental headquarters, the band would strike up an old tune, "Old Soldiers Never Die, They Just Fade Away" as he pulled in with aide Marcus Stevenson in his jeep.[20]

Bradley, who would turn out to be no great friend of Ted's, told a story in his autobiography. Roosevelt, Bradley wrote, was "a brave, gamy, undersized man who trudged about the front with a walking stick . . . hold[ing] the division together by personal charm. His cheery bullfrog voice had echoed reassuringly among the troops in every Tunisian wadi in which riflemen fought the Germans."[21]

One night, when Bradley was with Roosevelt watching a blacked-out 1st Division convoy pass slowly up the road, Ted shouted with his distinctly hoarse voice at some shadowy soldier passing, "Hey, what outfit is that?"

"Company C of the 18th Infantry, General Roosevelt," came back the anonymous voice. None of the soldiers in the 1st Division had to see Ted to know who was calling.

TWENTY-EIGHT

A BATTLE PLAYED AT MY FEET

Three weeks after Kasserine, the II Army Corps, led by the 1st Division, was ready to turn the tables on Rommel. With Montgomery's British set to attack German forces from the east in southeastern Tunisia, and Alexander's British army fighting Germans to the north, Patton's II Corps was ordered to push in the center, with Allen's 1st Division directed at Gafsa.

Gafsa was a dusty town of about ten thousand people, fifty miles southeast of Allen's troops in west-central Tunisia. It had been passed back and forth between the enemies three times already and had not fared well in the exchanges. On March 16, the 1st set off in a tightly organized advance of nearly fifteen thousand men in vehicles and marching over dangerous turf laid thick with mines.

The Americans were a regrouped and reorganized army. As much as they might have griped about Patton's peremptory ways and his confiscation of their wool caps, he had in fact revitalized the unit. The II Corps, "long an orphan of the British First Army," was now an entirely American force, and the 1st Division, which hadn't been united since the landing at Oran, was once again a fighting team.[1]

Carefully guided by military police serving as traffic cops, the 1st reached their jumping-off spot at four the next morning. Infantry surprised a unit of Italians with their advance. As sunrise came, the American force swept around the Italian left flank and by 10:00 a.m. had forced the surrender of most of the Italian troops. "By dawn the show was on," Ted wrote Eleanor, "machine guns spluttered, artillery rumbled. We caught the Italians unprepared. On the north we came down on them from the mountains—a devilish climb. On the south we swept around their right flank. By then the original objectives were taken and crowds of prisoners were being marched to the rear."[2]

They found the Italian soldiers half starved and grateful to be out of the fight. The POWs fell on the canned rations offered to them by the GIs like they were receiving full plates at a banquet. A thousand Italians were taken in the opening battle, with not a single German among the lot. In fact, the only evidence that the Germans were supporting their allies was the terrifying sweep of dive-bombers lacing the field with machine-gun fire that kicked up rapid puffs of dust when the bullets were not hitting men and machines.

And, of course, the bombs themselves. As Ted described one bad moment, "They came down on us constantly. Once I was caught in a valley by a raid. A bomb hit within twelve paces of where I was lying. My helmet was struck by a fragment and knocked galley-west, but I was unhurt though a couple of men were killed. By the way, don't wear your helmet strap hooked. If I had my head would have gone rolling off inside the helmet." A warning that Eleanor, reading the letter in London, doubtless had little use for.

After securing Gafsa, the 1st Division was ordered to continue on to the oasis of El Guettar, about twenty miles southeast, where it was anticipated that the Italians who had not surrendered would now be regrouping in order to attack. Some intelligence units thought the Italians had moved completely out of the area, and probing for the enemy was the principal component of the nighttime maneuvers.

Just beyond the oasis, two ridges of hills formed an arc overlooking a valley that spread wide, forming a natural amphitheater with a dusty expanse beneath. A highway ran in the gap between the two ridges, making it a good place to defend an attack, but the question remained, was this where the rest of the Italians had settled after Gafsa?

Allen sent the 18th Infantry, with Ted Roosevelt attached, south of the road to probe the southern ridge, while the 26th Infantry climbed the ridge to the north of the highway. The 16th Infantry was kept in reserve back toward Gafsa. William Darby's 1st Ranger Battalion, supported by division artillery and the 1st Engineers, was to lead the advance on the far left flank, climbing to the highest positions on the line of the ridge overlooking the plain at a hill called Djebel Orbata.

The far tips of the two ridgelines arced in toward the plain. If the Italians were in the area, they would be found somewhere within the semicircle. The 18th and 26th found their destinations and began to curl inward and soon enough met resistance—the Italians were there, nicely trapped between the pincers of the 1st Division, which held the heights on the battlefield, with American artillery now moving forward and tucking beneath the ridges. Allen set up his command post in the same vicinity.

During the night, with "the bright moon of Africa lighting the arid country," rumors of tank movements on the plain filtered up to the hills from American reconnaissance units below. Confirmation of the rumblings came in the form of spitting machine-gun fire emanating from somewhere on the dark plain. At dawn on the morning of March 23, it wasn't the Italians that appeared like a nightmare vision to the Big Red One, but a column of Panzer tanks, creaking and rolling across the plain in a slow-motion vision, accompanied by infantry already warming their guns. "There is no mistaking the German m.g. [machine gun]," wrote Ted. "It's shots are fired so rapidly the sound is like tearing cloth."[3] For the first time in North Africa, the unified 1st Division would face the forces of Erwin Rommel.

Ted rolled out of his blankets with his boots still on from the night before. He drove in the pale desert moonlight to a forward observation post with the 18th, on the ridge to the south, and saw clouds of dust and flashes of light from artillery fire across the plain. Finding a good position from a trench in the first ridge, he had an awe-inspiring view that morning: "At dawn the battlefield lay at my feet on a circular plain about seven miles in diameter. I could see it all," he wrote Eleanor.[4]

Ted counted twenty-four German tanks heading toward them from the south (there were actually more like thirty-five). They moved slowly, deliberately, clinging for shelter to the edge of the high ground at the foot of the ridges that the Americans held. Their intent was obvious; tanks are not elusive machines. They were trying to turn Roosevelt's position on the right flank, in the hopes of getting beyond the 18th and between the 1st Division and Gafsa behind. Enemy shells whizzed above them and hit behind; some struck the ridge itself. American artillery opened up and Roosevelt sent tank destroyer battalions forward. The German Stukas came swooping out of the sky once again, flying so low to the ridges that officers emptied their pistols as they streaked by.[5] The tanks kept coming and got in close to the 18th's right flank when two Panzers were hit simultaneously. The rest, Roosevelt wrote, "hesitated, milled around and withdrew, leaving two destroyed tanks nearly in our line to mark the high tide of their advance." The men near to Roosevelt cheered "as if it were a football game," he recalled, "and it did seem as if it were."[6]

The tanks had been turned, but the day was far from over. German artillery and dive-bombing planes kept the American positions hot. And on the American left flank, two U.S. artillery battalions were in grave danger after being placed too far forward. The battalions were forced to retreat by Panzer units, as were two infantry units, which likewise got caught out on the plain. The tanks, which Roosevelt described as milling around, actually stayed active and the field was lively until the afternoon. As A. J. Liebling wrote for the *New Yorker*, "All day long . . . the German tanks fiddled about the field . . . while field artillery shot at them and a battalion of eighteen American tank destroyers, waddling into action like bull pups, drew their fire and returned it."[7] Ted put it to Eleanor a little more plainly: "The Plain became a smoky, dusty dream . . . dotted with destroyed tanks and vehicles."[8]

The final German assault opened just before 5:00 p.m. with yet more dive-bombers, flying so low to the ridge that Ted told Eleanor, "I felt I could reach up my hand and grasp them."[9] These were followed by armored infantry units—Panzer grenadiers intent on climbing directly through the American infantry up on the ridges. Roosevelt called the artillery and ordered them to use time fuses—shells that burst in the air above the ground and then fell and rolled at their targets. The effect was catastrophic to the Panzer infantry. "Just in front of me were about 400 men—a German unit," Ted wrote to Eleanor. "We took them under fire and they went to ground behind some sand dunes. The artillery went after them with time shells, air bursts. In no time they were up running to the rear. Black bursts over their head. Khaki figures, realing [*sic*] and falling."

Patton arrived on the ridge at Ted's slit trench, which Ted was sharing with Allen at the time, to witness the final attack, crowding Ted out of the trench in the process. They watched as the 1st Division gunners sprayed the valley below, back and forth, zeroing in on the grenadiers until they were flushed out and racing from the battlefield. They were mowed down as they ran.

"I knew it was their last big effort," Ted wrote. He and the rest of the division could hardly contain their pride: they'd broken the 10th Panzers, a division that had never known defeat.[10]

Ted's work that day was described in a citation awarded several weeks after El Guettar. On March 23 the German 10th Panzer Division had counterattacked the 1st Infantry with two direct assaults employing fifty tanks, infantry, dive-bombers, and artillery against the 1st Division's line of defense. Throughout the entire day and the following night General Roosevelt and the 18th Infantry remained on the front lines. From there, he personally supervised the forward elements of the division, and his observations assisted in the coordination of the defense of the entire divisional sector. Ted was on the highest point on the ridge and constantly subjected to enemy fire of all types. The only natural protection afforded Ted's position was a slit trench, which he wound up offering to Patton. Roosevelt's decisions to call for artillery fire on advancing enemy infantry resulted in "virtual annihilation of these troops," said the citation. And he exposed himself to enemy fire time and again, to shout words of encouragement to his men and officers, along with showing "great fortitude and courage in remaining at his post where he could personally direct the action of the elements."[11]

At Terry Allen's headquarters that evening, about fifty correspondents gathered for an update on the battle. They had been waiting miles away from the action before being jeeped to the front, knowing only that the 1st was engaged in some heavy action. Beneath a blossoming almond tree, the sounds of guns and reconnaissance planes echoing around the tent, Allen took questions. "He tried to look grave and modest," wrote Liebling, "but the corners of his eyes and mouth occasionally betrayed him. 'I think the division has done fairly well today,' he said."[12]

Ted closed his letter to Eleanor about the day with a hint of calm and a touch of incredulity: "Nightfall brought us rest. We'd thrown back a Panzer division with heavy losses. I never expect to see anything like this again."[13]

TWENTY-NINE

THE TINE

The 18th Infantry was pulled off the line on March 25, while the 26th and 16th continued to take the battle to the Germans, joined by other elements of the II Corps. They moved among the rough hills that marked the area, continuing to engage the Panzer forces, pushing them east. After a brief rest of two days, the 18th was thrust back into the action in support of the 16th Infantry toward another of the numbered hills along the highway leading toward eastern Tunisia.

During the height of the battle of El Guettar, Ted had spent two days without sleep, washing, or brushing his teeth. He caught his breath on the twenty-fifth, but soon was back with fighting units from the 1st, where he served until the end of the month, when word came that Montgomery had broken through the German line at Mareth. Contact was made between the II Corps and Montgomery's Eighth Army on April 7, and on April 10, the Allies, now fighting as a combined force, took the city of Sfax on the Mediterranean, giving them control of all of southern Tunisia. The Germans were boxed into the northeastern part of the country with their backs to the exits in Tunis and Bizerte. The beginning of the end of the battle for North Africa was nigh.

Patton was given leave to continue his planning for the invasion of

Sicily. The II Corps would be commanded by General Omar Bradley for the final push in North Africa. The American army was to sweep around behind the British First Army of Harold Alexander in preparation for the final assault against the Germans. The 150-mile maneuver put the II Corps on the left flank, to the north side of the British, pointed toward Bizerte on the Mediterranean. Alexander's forces were to push the Germans out of North Africa at Tunis, southeast of Bizerte.

Once they circled past the British, the 1st and 34th Divisions were expected to move abreast of one another up the Tine River. The valley of the Tine was narrow and the region heavily mined. The assignment of the 1st Infantry Division was to clear out the hills on the northwestern side of the valley, while a combat team from the 34th protected the road that ran through the valley beside the river. After the infantry cleared out the valley of German infantry, the 1st Armored Division was given the job of sweeping up the southeastern side of the river for the further advance of the division.[1]

As they first moved north and into position for the attack, Ted had a period of relative calm between the action in central Tunisia and the movement up the Tine. He was able to catch up on his correspondence with family, including Quentin, who, it turned out, needed more time for convalescence than had been anticipated—in fact, he was scheduled to sail to a hospital on Long Island by the end of April. Ted wrote to his mother to inform her of Quentin's circumstances, that he was heading home and would be hospitalized near her: please take a peek in and look after him, as Eleanor was still in England.

He also took a moment to worry over his brother Archie. In her last letter, Edith had written of Archie's dangerous service in the Pacific, and Ted, perhaps forgetting the circumstances of his own duty, took a moment to tell his mother that Archie should go home, that this war was not meant for men of Archie's age. "Conditions are so bad even for the young men," he wrote.[2]

Ted wrote to Eleanor in England, too, thanking her for lately sending him a new cigarette lighter. He added another request: could she please send a new copy of *Pilgrim's Progress*? His old one was getting battered.[3]

A few days later, Ted wrote Eleanor about a feeling of pending relief he was having on the eve of the attack in the Tine valley that the "Germans are breaking before us. If they do then Tunis will fall & then only Bizerte & the peninsula will remain—we may get a breather! I may get a bath & sleep in a bed—perhaps nights on end—just think sheets!"[4]

As if recognizing that he might be sounding a little too exhausted to a worried wife, Ted reassured Eleanor with some bravado: "Don't worry about my health—the old iron man is still bumping along—like the one-horse shay—'running as usual much the same'—It's the careful life I've led!"[5]

The ultimate capture of Bizerte two and a half weeks later did not include the Big Red One. Of all the brave and tough fighting done by the 1st Division in the North Africa campaign, the operation up the Tine River valley turned out to be the most controversial. From the last week of April through the first week of May, the 1st moved just ten miles up the Tine valley, past a series of mostly barren hills, occasionally covered by knee-high wheat fields that provided what cover was available against the well-defended fortresses established by the Germans in the area. It was tough fighting; battalion combat teams from the 18th, 26th, and 16th Regiments had to battle for almost every significant lump of North African hill that rose above the valley.

The most trying of these actions began early on the morning on May 6, when the 18th Regiment forded the river, west to east, to get a toehold on that side of the Tine. It was a battlefield maneuver, a simple path-of-least-resistance decision, but in the process of its undertaking, the 18th got caught out in the open in a searing cross fire of mortars and machine guns from German positions to the northeast. Two companies of the regiment were bloodied badly and begged for aid from the 26th, which had remained on the left flank, to the west of the river. But the 26th couldn't help without themselves being caught out in the open, so the pounding continued until Allen got permission from the II Corps to bring the 18th back to the west side of the river.

Omar Bradley could be a prickly commander and had a rather deep streak of moral righteousness that predisposed him to tsk-tsk at Terry Allen's reputation as a gun-slinging commander. Even before he took over command of the North African forces, Bradley felt he needed to keep a close eye on Allen. Here at the Tine, he felt he had evidence of Allen's willingness to skirt orders. He excoriated Allen for "order[ing] his division into a completely unauthorized attack"—that battlefield crossing of the Tine by the 18th. Allen in Bradley's mind had proved himself an undisciplined glory hound far too eager to take risks with his forces. Ted Roosevelt got lumped into the same category. Of the action on the Tine, Bradley wrote later, "Had we not been on the threshold of the first important U.S. Army victory in Africa, I would have relieved him [Allen]—and Teddy Roosevelt—on the spot."[6]

There was a dispute, however, over just who ordered the regiment over the river that morning. Allen pointed to a communiqué that he said he'd received from the II Corps command on the eve of the river crossing. It ordered the Big Red One to "contain or destroy enemy forces" on the eastern side of the Tine River. Which is just what he ordered his troops to do.[7]

In the grand scheme of things, it was a small matter: the 1st Division had been fighting too long anyway and needed to be pulled out of the action for a rest. The battle that remained in North Africa—the taking of Bizerte by the II Corps and the taking of Tunis by Alexander's British forces—was ably handled, and the Germans were driven from North Africa in a matter of days by Allied forces.

But lingering resentments and dissatisfaction among Bradley, Allen, and Roosevelt remained. The problems extended back to the moment when Patton had assumed command of the II Corps and arrived at division headquarters loaded for bear, ready to tighten the loose ship supposedly run by Allen and Roosevelt. Allen and Bradley had a ready-made personality conflict: Bradley was a teetotaling, straitlaced officer, while Allen was an alleged wild-hair, a drinker, a maverick, whose nickname "Terrible Terry" suggested why they wouldn't get along. Years later, in his autobiography, Bradley recalled with fond admiration all of the straightened ties and the confiscated caps demanded by Patton as a necessary corrective to instill discipline in the unit. To some extent, Bradley's attitude was shared by the high command as a whole. Even the 1st's colorful nickname—Big Red One—suggested that the division was one that had read too much about itself. It had grown cocky and undisciplined was the assessment of Bradley, Eisenhower, and Patton.

It didn't help that Allen likewise made great copy in newspapers and magazines. The same week he ordered the 18th Regiment to the eastern side of the Tine River, the *New Yorker* published the second of two stories profiling Allen and Roosevelt as they stood against Rommel's tanks at El Guettar. Ernie Pyle had written extensively about Allen, as well, and *Time* would soon put him on the cover of its magazine. The 1st Division had already had a reputation in the army for arrogance before the war began. Bradley and the other commanders weren't the only generals in the military who felt that they might need to be taken down a peg or two. All that was needed was a good reason—which the men of the outfit were about to provide.

The 1st Division arrived in Oran for a leave from action almost straight from the battlefields in the Tine valley. They were war-grimy and exhausted, ready to paint Oran some color other than sandy brown. They came into town from a bivouac an hour away and arrived late in the day, just before the wine bars in Oran were set to close.

The weather had turned desert hot in the city, and many of the 1st Division GIs, still wearing their woolen olive drab winter-issue uniforms— the only garb they'd been given during their stint in North Africa—were surprised to find the service and supply soldiers back in Oran wearing comfortable khakis. Many were also dismayed to find most of the rear-echelon soldiers wearing campaign ribbons—medals that had not yet been issued to the guys who'd been doing the actual fighting at Gafsa and El Guettar.

Trouble ensued. The Big Red One troops started challenging the supply soldiers about their ribbons. Where had they been acquired? Had any of these guys been at Kasserine? At Gafsa? At the Tine? The MPs who arrived to cool things down themselves came under attack. The 1st Division troops went on a tear, ripping ribbons from shirts and picking fights with service supply troops and the MPs who came to intercept the brawlers. Though the fighting turned out to be far short of a riot, it was bad enough to be an embarrassment.[8]

High command—Bradley, Eisenhower, and Walter Bedell Smith—was furious with this wilding. It was hardly the sort of image the II Army Corps wanted to project, and they immediately pointed fingers at Allen and Roosevelt. Ted was not only lumped together with Allen; he was also seen as possibly a worse example of a general refusing to instill discipline in his men. His popularity was seen as proof of the problem. His command wouldn't be so enamored of him, went the thinking, if he cracked the whip every once in a while. Bradley later suggested that Roosevelt directly encouraged the behavior in Oran while out in the field in North Africa. "To lighten the lot of his troops in the Tunisian djebels Roosevelt liked to tease them on the pleasures that awaited their return to Oran. 'Once we've licked the Boche,' he would say in his rough voice, 'we'll go back to Oran and beat up every MP in town.' This was one of the few admonitions the 1st Division took literally," Bradley wrote.[9]

There is no proof beyond Bradley's somewhat speculative assertion that Ted actually encouraged any of his soldiers to make trouble in Oran. Nonetheless, he and Allen became more deeply ensconced in Bradley's doghouse. Bradley was ready to pull the 1st Division from the next campaign, when an interesting champion insisted he needed the fighting capabilities of the 1st. For all his initial criticism of the division, George Patton had grown to appreciate what it could do on the battlefield. As the man chosen to lead the upcoming invasion of Sicily, he could pretty much pick and choose whom he wanted to lead the head of his assault. And he wanted the Big Red One. High command's problems with Allen and Roosevelt went on the back burner. They would lead the 1st in the invasion of Sicily.

THIRTY

KERMIT

With the Germans finally pushed out of Tunisia, Ted found himself wait-ing for the next action in a suddenly calm North Africa of Mediterranean beaches and desert tours. He visited Carthage, spent time with an old friend, future British prime minister Harold Macmillan, and was surprised to be awarded a Croix de Guerre by the French army for his service dur-ing the just finished campaign.

In a letter to Eleanor, he wrote about sightseeing in Carthage, telling her the area was rather pleasant but there was "almost nothing left of the once great mistress of the Mediterranean." Not surprisingly, as he stood overlooking these ruins while serving in the midst of yet another great war, Roosevelt's thoughts turned to classical history. "That's what these countless ruins make you think," he wrote. "Carthage, Rome, the Vandals, Byzantium—gone."[1]

Quentin, like his father, received the Croix de Guerre from the French, as well as a Silver Star from his own army. Ted was happy to learn that the publicity ban against Quentin had been lifted so that his wounding and med-als could be reported to the press, and the *New Yorker* had reported on Ted's role in the fighting at El Guettar, but John Lardner of the *New York Herald* published a story about traveling in a jeep through Tunisia with a general who recited poetry through most of the sojourn. For those in the know, it was easy to recognize Ted, but Lardner was not allowed to identify him by name.

Ted also ran into FDR's son Franklin Jr., a lieutenant commander in the navy, who was passing through Tunisia; they had a pleasant dinner. "Just as nice as possible," Ted wrote Eleanor. "An attractive boy—well-known Roosevelt charm and all that."[2]

In early June he noted to Eleanor that he had now served longer in the Second World War than he had in the First. He hadn't seen her in going on nine months and counting. As for Eleanor, she was leaving England soon, heading home to watch over Quentin, still recuperating in a Long Island hospital.

The hardest moment of this interlude came in June, when word arrived of his brother Kermit's fate. Kermit's decline had been long, but had become particularly precipitous in the past couple of years. Sent off to Alaska in 1942, he helped to form an Inuit militia, which was to serve as an insurgent Allied unit against the Japanese should they invade. The assignment kept Kermit out of trouble for several months.

But Kermit's health was bad and getting worse. His liver was shot from years of drinking and from malaria, which he'd first contracted on the River of Doubt with his father years before. He was sent to a hospital in Vancouver to recover, but once there, hooked up again with his mistress. Soon he escaped from the infirmary and went on a booze-filled journey that ended back in New York, where family once again cleaned him up and shipped him back to service in Alaska in early 1943.[3]

On June 3, exhausted by the futilities and the failures of his life, miserably sick and tired, Kermit put the barrel of his service revolver beneath his chin and pulled the trigger.

Ted got the news just a few days later. "Of course I have no details," he wrote Eleanor. "Just a message to say that he had died in Alaska—nothing more. I don't know if it was sickness or war." He recalled to her his travels with Kermit, the good times they had had as a couple with Belle and Kermit, Ted and Kermit's childhood together; but thinking of Kermit's decline and the depths of his estrangement from the family, Ted wrote the harsh assessment of one brother hurt by the other's dissipation: "He really died five years ago."

THIRTY-ONE

SICILY

In early July, the 1st Division sailed for its newest mission. As with the invasion of North Africa nine months earlier, the GIs were kept in the dark about their destination until they were all boarded and well under way. But there was no great mystery about where they were sailing. Guesses were confirmed when troops were handed booklets titled *A Soldier's Guide to Sicily*.

Lectures on the island's terrain soon followed, as well as familiar boat drills—practice loading and unloading the landing vessels strapped to the sides of the transports. Supply troops distributed mosquito and sunburn lotion, water-purifying and salt tablets, as well as lice powders.

More than three thousand vessels sailed in the armada to the largest of the Mediterranean islands; it was the single biggest collection of ships yet assembled for an amphibious assault. The men on board were assured that the army air force controlled the skies above them, just as the sheer size of their fleet assured them that the navy controlled the sea. No Axis planes troubled the convoy as it steamed toward Sicily; the bombardment their airfields on the island were receiving from Allied planes and naval gunfire was a powerful deterrent.

As they had in North Africa, British and American Allies faced a combined force of Italians and Germans. Fissures in the Axis alliance, however, were already evident. The resolve of the Italian people in this fight was beginning to waver, a fact sensed by their German allies, who tried to bolster local fighting spirit by letting Sicilians know that they would stay on the island to the bitter end. Beaches were mined, roads inland were blocked, bridges destroyed. To further prod Italian fortitude, the Germans made reading any of the propaganda literature dropped by Allied planes punishable by death.

If the 1st Division soldiers weren't completely rested by the few weeks off they'd been given since they'd driven the Germans out of North Africa, they were at least somewhat revived. "The old man is feeling positively gay," Ted wrote Eleanor on July 7 as he sailed toward Sicily on the U.S.S. *Barton.* "I'm fit as can be and think we've done everything possible to make the show a success."

He and his men were getting to be old hands at this. Many of the soldiers on board were the same who had traveled with the 1st Division to Oran from Scotland in November, but there was a difference: "There is no tension, no excitement and they know they are up against the toughest kind of proposition. That must come from being veterans. . . . They're not the fresh, smooth-cheeked boys you saw at dances more than two years ago at Devens," he wrote to Eleanor. "They've got a hard bitter look."[1]

As they sailed on to Sicily, however, the anxiety returned as the miles to the beach city of Gela neared. "This will be the last [letter] for the present," Ted wrote Eleanor. "The ship is dark, the men are going to their assembly stations. Before going out on deck they sit in darkened corridors to adjust their eyes. Soon the boats will be lowered away. Then we'll be off."

Six miles off the coast of Gela, Terry Allen sent a simple message to all units of the 1st Division. It read: "Good luck, gang! Do it again!"

Paratroopers led the way into Sicily. Dropped in wave after wave late on the night of July 9, they landed inland, shooting up airfields and enemy headquarters in a successful mission to soften shore defenses in preparation for the main body of the invasion. Boats were lowered at 12:30 a.m.

on the tenth. A special unit of sea scouts was the first to land, setting up color-coded electric lanterns, yellow and blue, which marked landing areas on the beach. Enemy searchlights began to scan the beach and the sand dunes beyond.

Out in the surf, the 1st and 2nd Battalions of the 26th felt the scan of the searchlights, too, about one hundred yards from shore. Machine-gun fire started to pepper the water from left and right. Artillery from the hills back of Gela suddenly opened up and crashed down on the beaches, disrupting the landscape and pounding holes in Axis beach defenses, which the experienced American infantry ran toward, looking for avenues up off the beach. Tracers lit the sky as the American boats hit the sand and the infantry spilled out and flattened themselves against the enemy fire.

U.S. Navy guns began blasting at the enemy's arcing searchlights mounted on homes in Gela, in the process smashing the houses to rubble. They aimed for the artillery with similar success, and as a first wave of Italians from the machine-gun emplacements started to call out in surrender, Italian-American interpreters came forward to aid interrogations.

Ted and his faithful aide Stevie came in at 5:00 a.m. and headed for the regimental command post to get a progress report. About a hundred mostly Italian prisoners were already in hand. Ted sent the 1st Battalion northwest toward Gela, where U.S. Rangers had already entered. The town was beyond the sand dunes of the beach, in the surrounding hills. The majority of Axis gunfire was coming from here, but resistance wasn't particularly heavy.[2]

As first light began to rise above the Mediterranean, the 1st Battalion reported that it had taken a railroad junction just east of Gela, while the 2nd Battalion radioed that it was in control of a group of hills to the side of the village. From the command post near the beach, Roosevelt wanted to know if anything was being done to silence the artillery, still causing havoc in the landing area where the 3rd Battalion was now coming ashore. As if in answer the navy bombardment intensified, and Gela itself took the brunt of the consequences. Ted soon drove off with Stevie to check the front lines.

As the 3rd Battalion came ashore and joined the fray, the hills between the 1st and 2nd Battalions quickly got cleared, and the 1st Battalion swung around behind Gela to trap any defenders left in the village. The surrender of these Italian troops was delayed when five tanks came from north of town to challenge Darby's Rangers on Main Street. Darby's men stood their ground and brought the lead tank to a standstill with a 77mm gun. A second tank was soon halted as well, and eventually all five were placed out of action as they wandered into and got trapped in various culs-de-sac in Gela.

By 7:30 p.m., the 26th had captured the village, and the 1st Battalion had advanced a thousand yards beyond where they dug in for the night and set up defensive posts. The 2nd Battalion was to the northeast of the 1st at a similar distance. The 3rd had advanced all the way beyond the outskirts of Gela until it ran smack into a heavy concentration of cross fire from Axis mortars, machine guns, and artillery, an indication that there was still plenty of fight in the shore defense of the enemy.

Early the next morning, the 3rd Battalion radioed the command post back near Gela that it needed ambulances and aid men; their losses were getting heavy, and the shelling continued. To Roosevelt and the rest of the command, it had been a successful day, but the position of the 1st Division was a bit precarious. Not enough heavy equipment made it to shore during the hours after the landings. Now they were vulnerable to counterattack, and rumor had it that out there in the Sicilian darkness, ready to lead the next day's charge, hoping to punish the invaders for their audacity, was the Hermann Goering Panzer Division.[3]

At dawn enemy air attacks began over Gela Bay; Axis planes would continue to pound the battlefield all day long. Concerns at the 26th command post, however, were concentrated on the 3rd Battalion, the most vulnerable unit in the regiment, stretched out north of Gela. It remained the focus of Axis ground attacks and looked that morning at 6:00 a.m. as if Panzer tanks were hoping to swamp the 3rd, with the prospect then of turning south and directly assaulting the defenses around Gela. These consisted of the Rangers, the 1st Battalion, and the 2nd Battalion, arrayed in a semicircle north to northeast around the outskirts of the village.

There were no reserve troops yet onshore, and only a single platoon from an antitank unit. Almost all of the divisional antitank companies deployed on Sicily had been called to duty the day before to stanch a tank attack against the 16th Regiment farther west in the fighting.

The army air force and the navy supplied solid covering fire, but at 8:00 a.m., when thirteen Panzer tanks appeared out of the hills to the northeast, swung past the 3rd Battalion, and pointed directly at the 1st and 2nd Battalions directly outside of Gela, it looked like the intent of the Axis enemy was not simply to destroy a battalion, but also to push the invaders all the way back to North Africa.

The tanks massed outside of Gela and struck. The 2nd Battalion held firm, but all its riflemen had in defense were armor-piercing ammunition, rifles, and hand grenades, plus a heavy weapons section with machine guns and mortars. That one antitank platoon had two 47mm guns, which weren't nearly enough firepower to turn a baker's dozen Panzers. General Roosevelt got on the horn to Terry Allen to inform him of the dire circumstances. "The 26th has had tank attacks," he yelled. "Don't know how bad yet. What I want to know is when are they going to get the medium tanks ashore. The situation here is not very comfortable." The 3rd Battalion had already been hit by tanks, Ted informed Allen; the 2nd Battalion was still holding but had minimum antitank support. Was there any possibility of getting those medium tanks soon?[4]

Navy gunners began to increase their support of the 3rd Battalion, but with so many vehicles and troops, enemy and American, locked now in a tight battle space, exact coordinates were needed for effective fire. Word came from division that amphibious jeeps were heading for shore, carrying guns for antitank units, but just as they were arriving, the Rangers and the 1st Battalion up on the northern side of Gela faced a new threat from an Italian tank unit: ten French-made tanks backed by a battalion of Italian infantry had arrived on the scene. Meanwhile, the 3rd Battalion was forced to pull back from its position north of Gela to hook up with the 1st, closer to the village.

His patience gone, Roosevelt called the 16th Regiment to ask again about the medium tanks. "Goddamn it," he yelled when told of further delays, "I'll come and pull those tanks out myself. We don't want them tomorrow!"[5]

The situation around Gela grew so tense that every available man on the beach was called into action to form a firing line below the village, among the sand dunes. This included supply officers, intelligence, carpenters, and electricians, who moments before had been frantically trying to organize the unloading of supplies and equipment from the landing craft, still streaming into shore from the hundreds of vessels bobbing out in the Mediterranean.

Out of the chaos suddenly appeared two medium tanks finally delivered from the 16th Infantry to the beach at Gela. Field artillery arrived onshore soon after from the convoy and quickly set up to support the 1st and the 2nd. Navy fire homed in on the enemy tanks as well, and by 10:30, the progress of the Panzer advance was halted and Axis infantry, coming on the heels of the tanks, decided to back off, too.

By midday, the three battalions of the 26th were resting in place, the battle receding before them. Word soon reached command that seven friendly tanks were now ashore, ready to back up the 26th in case the enemy resumed the attack. It was a close call indeed. A review of the situation found that all of the 26th Regiment battalions were dangerously low on ammunition. And interrogation of the German tank crews involved in the battle revealed that they were indeed part of the famed Hermann Goering Panzer Division—the best of the best in the Axis fighting army.

Even Omar Bradley was impressed by what the 1st Division had done at Gela. "Three months before, on April 23, Patton had prevailed on Eisenhower to substitute the veteran 1st Division for the 36th on this invasion. In doing so he may have saved II Corps from a major disaster," Bradley subsequently wrote. "As we had anticipated, the burly Hermann Goering Panzer Division lunged down the Gela road with its tanks in a bold effort to throw Allen's division back into the sea. I question whether any other U.S. division could have repelled that charge in time to save the beach from tank penetration. Only the perverse Big Red One with its no less perverse commander was both hard and experienced enough to take that assault in stride. A greener division might easily have panicked and seriously embarrassed the landing."[6]

Less than a month after this high praise, Bradley would have yet another opinion of the "perverse" commanders leading the Big Red One.

On D-Day plus 3, northeast of Gela, the 1st Division took the Ponte Olivo Airport, the source of German air attacks in the first days of the invasion. Now began the full-fledged Allied push to drive Axis forces out of Sicily.

The 1st Division would take the center in a three-pronged attack to the north side of the island. On the right flank of the 1st, the British Eighth Army, led by Field Marshal Bernard Montgomery, moved up the eastern coast of the island, while on the left, George Patton, with the 82nd Airborne and the 3rd Infantry Divisions, raced toward Palermo on the northwestern side of Sicily. All three forces would move ultimately toward Messina, in the northeastern corner of the island, with the 1st Infantry assigned to slog through the mountainous center of Sicily.

At Mazzarino, the division encountered its first substantial number of Italian civilians. There was some uncertainty about how the Americans would be greeted, but as the 2nd Battalion of the 26th Regiment entered the town they were stupefied by the cordiality of the reception they received. Their jeeps could barely get through the streets, and all the Italians were waving white handkerchiefs or homemade American flags and shouting *"Viva Americani!"*[7]

Meanwhile, the 16th and 18th Regiments, out on the left flank of the 1st Division's advance and hooked up with units of the 3rd Division, had a different greeting from the Sicilians in a trio of villages. Pockets of resistance temporarily slowed their advance but overall progress was good on all fronts. Roosevelt arrived at the 26th command post in Mazzarino to report just that to Allen.

But at Barrafranca, north of Mazzarino, the 26th ran headlong into the Hermann Goering Panzer Division once again. Barrafranca was a clump of stone houses that rested at the end of a narrow valley surrounded by a trio of gray hills. The Germans were well concealed within this setting.

According to Ted, the "village was older than time and filthier than the Augean stables." He commanded a group of tanks and infantry in a nighttime action to secure the ground. "The moon was full as we wound over the countryside," he wrote Eleanor. "Leading such an effort has a particular thrill—no one knows what the next heart beat may have in store. Then comes the first flush of morning, the rattle of the tanks, the walking troops loom clearer and clearer. Suddenly there comes the rattle of small arms and the fight is on. By light it seems as if a week had passed."[8]

The 26th was once again successful and continued north toward Messina. Roosevelt had had only three hours of sleep in the past forty-eight. Nonetheless, he was feeling well enough to brag to Eleanor about the action, writing, "The old man still can fight." But there was also a sense of hopeful exhaustion in his note. He closed it by writing, "I feel it's almost the last effort of the campaign."[9]

Messina rested on the tip of a peninsula on the northeastern edge of the island. Across a narrow channel from the city were mainland Italy and the rest of the continent of Europe. Famed Mount Etna rose above the landscape just down the eastern seaboard from Messina and formed the eastern pillar of the stout defensive line the Germans had built in a semicircle at the landward entrance to the peninsula. Montgomery's Eighth Army remained headed in this direction. Patton continued from Palermo toward Messina with the 3rd Division on the northern coast of Sicily. Troina was the center post of the German line, and it was here that Roosevelt, Allen, and the 1st Division arrived in the last week of July to begin an assault against the city that was considered the gateway to Messina.

Built on a mountainous ridge with barren countryside surrounding it, Troina was a natural stronghold well guarded by German defenders who had had weeks to position and strengthen their fortifications in anticipation of this moment. From the day the Allies landed on the beaches of Sicily three weeks earlier, Panzer troops were essentially backpedaling toward this peninsula and Messina, with the ultimate goal of getting as many troops as possible across the narrow strait to safety in mainland Italy before Allied troops penned them in. Conversely, the Allied goal was to keep to a minimum the number of Germans who could hop to mainland Italy to fight another day.

Already exhausted from three weeks of hard fighting through the heart of the island defenses, the 1st Division walked headlong into another hard brawl. They were joined outside of Troina by elements of the 9th Division, by an infantry battalion of French Moroccan Goums, and by more than 150 artillery pieces and air support.

It was not enough to force the German lines. A full week of artillery pounding and infantry probing dented, but did not smash, German defenses. A nighttime effort by the 26th Regiment to outflank the village to the north and cut off German escape to Messina to the east was stymied by well-sited artillery in the hills around the village. In the process of trying to block an exit of German troops, the 26th Infantry itself was cut off from the rest of the 1st Division. Allied attacks and Axis counterattacks ensued. Hilltop positions were swapped between American and Axis forces. For days, the division rammed against the defenses of Troina, but could only count their progress in yards rather than miles. Though running short of food and ammunition, the 26th held on.

Meanwhile, on the northern end of the German line, the 3rd Division had been slowed as well at San Fratello, where a Panzer division had ensconced itself on a ridge above the narrow coastal highway. The commander of the 3rd, General Lucian Truscott, finally ordered an amphibious flanking maneuver, which sent 3rd Division troops to a village beyond San Fratello, where they successfully landed and turned back toward the German-occupied ridge. It was a dangerous and surprising maneuver well executed by Truscott's troops, except all the Germans were gone by the time they arrived back at San Fratello.

German defenders were escaping Troina and the whole island of Sicily as well. The 9th Infantry Division moved into the Troina area to relieve the exhausted troops of the 1st. Two days later, after more American pounding, the German defenders abandoned the city. They had done their duty: thousands of German Panzers had escaped to the Italian mainland.

The reaction of the Allied command to this perceived failure to contain the enemy in Sicily was swift. Despite having fought well through most of the Sicily campaign, Bradley and Patton were rankled by what happened at Troina. The loss of forces in the 1st Division and the aggressiveness of that nighttime assault by the 26th showed Allen, once again, to be a reckless commander. To Bradley's mind, the actions of the 1st at Troina were an extension of what had happened in the Tine valley back in the spring, and the rampage at Oran after that. It was the same old story: a lack of discipline in command was evident to him. He decided to relieve both Allen and Roosevelt, using the excuse that he was simply rotating the command; Terry and Ted had been in combat now for more than nine months. It was time for them to go somewhere else. "After 24 days of campaigning the 1st Division was painfully reduced in strength," Bradley later wrote. "I passed Eddy's 9th Division through the 1st Division and halted the latter in place at Troina. Here it had waged its last battle of the Mediterranean war."[10]

Bradley went further in his critique: "Under Allen the 1st Division had become increasingly temperamental, disdainful of both regulations and senior commands. It thought itself exempted from the need for discipline by virtue of its months on the line. And it believed itself to be the only division carrying its fair share of the war."

The reason he let Allen go, Bradley said, was because he "had become too much of an individual to submerge himself without friction in the group undertakings of war. The 1st Division, under Allen's command, had become too full of self-pity and pride. To save Allen from both himself and from his brilliant record and to save the division from the heady effects of too much success," Allen had to go.[11]

As to why Ted Roosevelt had to go, too, Bradley's rationale becomes even more convoluted. "Roosevelt's claim to the affections of the 1st Division would present any new commander with an impossible situation from the start. Any successor of Allen's would find himself in an untenable spot unless I allowed him to pick his own assistant commander. Roosevelt had to go with Allen for he, too, sinned by loving the division too much."[12]

Curiously enough, in his personal diary, George Patton also took credit for dismissing Allen and Roosevelt. In his version of events, the idea of getting rid of Ted and Terry emerged before Troina when General Clarence Huebner became available for reassignment. Patton and Bradley conferred, and in Patton's telling, it was he who called Eisenhower to ask that Allen and Roosevelt be relieved "without prejudice on the ground that their experience will be of great value at home and that they are now battle weary." The plan was to have Huebner replace Allen, and General Norm Cota replace Ted—both were favorites of Patton's. "I got Ike's permission to relieve both Allen and Roosevelt," Patton later told his diary, a thing he knew would cause complaints due to Ted's popularity. "There will be a kick over Teddy," he wrote, "but he has to go: brave, but otherwise no soldier."[13]

The kick began almost immediately. When word spread that Allen and Roosevelt were being relieved, a palpable anger was felt among the troops of the 1st. The journal of the 26th Regiment's action report at Sicily gave a sense of the unit's appreciation for Ted: "Beginning at Oran, where Teddy had followed his old outfit on the beach of Les Andalouses up to the slopes of Djebel Murdjadjo, and had stayed the three days until Armistice was signed . . . [he was] the leader, who turned up whenever gun powder began burning furiously in any sector, the man with the strutting walk and the unmistakable bullfrog voice, who was apt to show up either at two in the afternoon or two in the morning; the General who was often out in front of the main element in an advance or in a battle. [He] was the General who had rallied the wavering ranks on Gela Beach and had turned them around to face the tanks that were within a few hundred yards of the beach. He could be counted upon to show up where the fighting was fiercest, the struggle in the balance, showing that golden-toothed grin of his, and walking along as though sauntering on a quiet street instead of an area whizzing with bullets. This was the General who could take what the battle had to dish out, and face up to it."[14]

On August 6, Ted and Stevie drove up to the division command post in Troina for the last time to personally let the men know what had transpired. There was no ceremony, no handing over of the divisional reins from old commander to new. Terry Allen was elsewhere, as were Generals Huebner and Cota. Ted pulled a good-bye letter from his jacket but broke down as he tried to read it to the men of the 1st Division standing silently around him. All the years with this outfit, all the battles, all the jeep drives from unit to unit, young face to young face, in the dark

Mediterranean nights, laughing, telling lame jokes, leaning on tank treads and wheel wells, sharing cigarettes, soothing fears, and making sure they were fed decently.

His personal good-bye was left unfinished. He just couldn't get the words out and later sent his letter to command headquarters, where it was placed on a board for all to read:

6 August 1943

TO THE OFFICERS AND MEN OF THE 1st DIVISION

More than 26 years ago the 1st Division was formed, and I joined it at that time. I have served with it in two wars and have served with no other unit.

We have been together in combat; we know each other as men do only when they have been battle comrades. I do not have to tell you what I think of you, for you know. You will always be in my heart.

I have been ordered away. It is a great grief to me, and my hope is that some time I may return, for it is with you that I feel that I belong.

Your record is splendid. You are known as assault troops the world over. You will add in the future new honors to our history. May luck go with your battle worn colors as glory always has.[15]

Brigadier General Theodore Roosevelt, Jr.

THIRTY-TWO

EXILE

Ted would remain deeply hurt and confused by his relief for some time to come. Before he left Sicily he went to see Bradley and Patton, asking for a reason. Both generals stuck to the line that Allen and Ted were simply being "rotated out" by the War Department. Ted asked Patton if there would be any blot on his professional record and was assured that no, that wouldn't happen. They'd fought valiantly and well. It was just time to go.

Patton later described Ted as "all perturbed" during their encounter (as if Patton were surprised by the reaction), and, in fact, Roosevelt's hard feelings about his relief would ultimately be directed far more at Patton than at Bradley. Ted would later write bitterly to Eleanor, describing the moment in combat at El Guettar when Patton arrived at the front lines while Terry and Ted were sharing a slit trench dug just for two. The Luftwaffe began dive-bombing their ridge, and Ted offered his spot in the trench to the commander. Without hesitation, the "fearless" Patton dove in.[1]

Lingering was not encouraged in this man's army, and Ted was quickly ordered to Algiers to report to General Mark Clark, commander of the Fifth Army, who was preparing to lead the upcoming invasion of Italy.

Clark needed someone to serve as a liaison to the French army of Marshal Alphonse Juin, which was to be part of that assault. Ted had worked well with the French in North Africa and seemed a natural for this assignment. His duties were to begin at once.

In Algiers, Ted met with Walter Bedell "Beetle" Smith, Eisenhower's chief of staff, who told Roosevelt frankly that he was not considered qualified to be a division commander—that was why he hadn't replaced Terry. The high command thought Ted "one of the most gallant officers in Africa," Smith told him, but he lacked the regular army experience, as opposed to his unassailable combat background, necessary to command a division. This was probably just another way of saying that he lacked the qualities of a disciplinarian, but it really didn't matter much one way or another. Ted would not win a fight with command.[2]

In Algiers, Ted was comforted by a reunion with Quentin. Fully mended and back for action, his son was on his way to report to duty with his old artillery unit in the 1st Division. Ted mentioned the possibility of getting him reassigned to the China-Burma-India theater with Joe Stilwell. They agreed, however, that it would be a good idea for Quentin to spend a few months back with his unit before his father tried to work channels to get him reassigned. It would look better on his résumé if it didn't appear that Quentin was eager to escape the 1st Division.

Ted's spirits were a little better after reporting to Juin and his assignment with the French troops training in North Africa. Still assuming that he would get back to combat leadership soon, he told Eleanor in a letter written near the end of August that he was "going to use the future months to get into prime physical condition—Oddly war does not do it," he wrote.[3]

Algeria was a far more relaxed and comfortable existence than it had been just a few months before. Ted liked the young French officers on Juin's staff, and the dining was excellent. Al Jolson was playing for the USO in Oran, and after a little *commedia bouffon*, in which Jolson was running down one street, searching for Ted, and Ted was running on a street one block over, looking for Jolson, the two old friends hooked up and had a pleasant evening together.

Ted grew fond of Juin, and his French improved somewhat. He got a letter from Quentin, who was back with his old unit in the 1st. Quentin told his father that he was missed in his old division. The phrase most often heard when discussing Ted was "the most gallant man I've ever seen on the battlefield."[4]

In late September, Ted went back into action, now with the French, at the invasion of Corsica—his third amphibious landing of the war—and then on to Italy, where he took part in the mountainous campaign around Monte Cassino, beginning in the winter of 1943. By the end of the year, someone calculated for Ted that he now had more days on the front line than any other American general in the army.

Aide Marcus Stevenson remained with Roosevelt throughout the fall and winter. The two made a unique pair. Stevie's facial hair had grown into a thick handlebar mustache, and according to the next man he would drive for in the war—Ernest Hemingway—he looked like a long, lean Texas Ranger. Throughout their time with Juin's troops, Stevie refused to learn a word of French. Beside the short, wrinkled Roosevelt—hobbling on a cane, dressed as if he'd just stepped from a morning nap, spouting poetry, and dutifully working on his prep school French—the two men made a memorable odd couple. They had been together now for more than a year and had grown very close. To add to their distinctive Mutt and Jeff appearance, Stevie had stenciled the words *Rough Rider* just below the windshield on Ted's jeep, which made it perhaps the most recognizable vehicle in the Fifth Army. As the two drove around the Italian countryside, GIs took to mimicking Roosevelt's bellowing voice, calling "Stevie!" in a good-natured imitation of the general as the two-man combat team passed.

Ted continued to long for a combat command and action outside of Italy. He began to cultivate Mark Clark, who Ted felt "liked him" and thought he "was a good soldier" and might want to take him north in Italy "because it will build up morale [for the troops] to see you around."[5] The fact of the matter, however, was that Ted knew the Big Show would be in France in the coming year, and that's where he wanted to be.

In January, he wrote to Bradley, pleading his case: "I want very much to be with you," he wrote. "As far as I'm concerned I'm not worried about promotion. What I want is to get into action leading American troops again. That's where I can do best and render the greatest service. Also I've had more amphibious experience with more echelons than any other American general."[6]

Bradley responded from England as if he didn't understand a word Ted was writing. "I have been down to your old division only once and then only for a short time. I am sure glad to have them up here with me. . . . I understand you have been fighting under difficult conditions down there [in Italy], and that in Tunisia and Sicily we didn't see 'nothing' as far as terrain is concerned. . . . I don't know of any vacancy here now and I doubt if there will be any as long as we are just fighting a paper war. . . . It is nice to have 'Ike' with us and to be under his command again. Congratulations on the fine job you did on Sardinia."[7]

Dejected and angry, Ted passed the contents of the note on to Eleanor, calling it "the letter of a man saying no but doing his best . . . to retain my friendship."[8]

As the fighting in Italy grew increasingly bitter and prospects for moving to the French theater were growing dim, Ted sent Eleanor to lobby old friend George Marshall at his office in Washington for reassignment. In Ted's own opinion currying this sort of preference was a very "un-Roosevelt" thing to do, but as he explained to Eleanor, "it was all right to try to pull strings and ask favors if what you wanted was a more dangerous job than the one you had."[9]

If there was a single thing that everyone knew about Ted Roosevelt, it was that heading toward a dangerous job was second nature. Whether Marshall had a role in the decision or not is unknown, but toward the end of February, Ted let Eleanor in on the news he'd just received: he was on his way to the Big Show after all, once again as an assistant divisional commander, this time to the 4th Division, which was currently training in England.

In a rush, he said heartfelt good-byes to Juin and his other French colleagues, and to Mark Clark, who awarded Ted another Legion of Merit for his service in the Italian campaign. Then he headed for the airport on February 28 for his flight to North Africa and on to England. A happy man.

Roosevelt had been sick with the flu earlier that winter, and the moment he climbed on board the flight to Algiers, flu-like symptoms returned. By the time he landed, he was feverish and went quickly to bed at the hotel. He woke up at 3:00 a.m. bathed in sweat, but his fever had broken. He felt well enough to get breakfast that morning and head back to the airport to catch his next flight, to Gibraltar, on the way back toward England.

By the time he got on the plane, the fever had not only returned with a vengeance, but also his flight was forced to land in Oran due to bad weather. He spent the night trapped in the city where he'd first arrived in North Africa.

Feeling the pressure of his circumstances, needing and wanting to get to England, he chose to avoid the infirmary and stayed with a friend. The weather remained bad, however, and he spent nine hours at the airport in Oran the next day, waiting for a flight out, until he was finally told that nothing was getting out. Once more he went back to his friend's house, and this time he let his hosts send for a doctor, who found Roosevelt had a temperature of 103. The doctor diagnosed pneumonia. Alarmingly, Ted was also experiencing dull pains in his chest. He was urged to go to the hospital for a proper diagnosis, at which point Ted "got rid of him," as he told Eleanor in a letter.[10]

The fever broke once again and Ted caught a flight to Casablanca to bypass the bad weather over Spain. There he landed at the airport, where by coincidence he ran into "nice, silent" Melvin Purvis, the FBI agent who had shot John Dillinger. By the time Ted caught a plane, he was sick once again and had to fly all night to northern England, where he landed. Finally, he caught a train to London, where, despite his condition, he felt obliged to report to Beetle Smith at command headquarters. Smith told him that his letter to Bradley had prompted a conference among Eisenhower, Smith, and Bradley, where the three decided that "the thing to do was to get [Ted] here."

Stevie was once again on the job in England. After the meeting with Smith, he got Roosevelt to a hospital, where Ted was tended to by a doctor from Alabama "whose entire family for the first time in their history will vote republican if F runs [again]," Ted was pleased to note to Eleanor.[11]

When politics runs in the blood, it runs deep.

THIRTY-THREE

NOWHERE ELSE TO BE

Ted spent the next three weeks in a London hospital, being treated for a particularly virulent case of pneumonia. His illness was accompanied by the same sort of minor chest pains he'd felt in North Africa, attributed to the condition of his fluid-filled lungs. He got some much-needed rest during his stay but continued to welcome a host of visitors while he recovered, including 1st Division officers, other military acquaintances, and old friends from his endless circles of cosmopolitan associates. Quentin, stationed with the 1st in England in anticipation of the European invasion, stopped by, too, with some very big news: he had fallen in love with an American nurse from Kansas City named Frances Webb, and they were planning to be married, here in England, before he sailed on D-Day.

Ted passed the news on to Eleanor, who was upset for a host of motherly reasons: first because Ted failed to cable the news from the hospital the instant he heard it; second, and more important, because she would miss the wedding; and last, because she knew nothing of this Frances Webb other than Ted's assurance that she was a very nice young woman.[1]

Eleanor decided that she must immediately contact Frances's parents in Kansas City to introduce herself, except it turned out that Frances had neglected to tell her folks about her engagement. It was Eleanor who spilled the beans when she made what she thought would be a polite introductory phone call to the Webbs. Both mother and father of the bride were taken aback and upset by the news. After a long explanation of who she was, who Quentin was, and what sort of life he'd led prior to this, Eleanor was able to assuage the parents.

Meanwhile, Ted was not only out of the hospital by the last week of March; he had also reported to his new assignment with the 4th Division, where he took an immediate shine to its commander, General Raymond "Tubby" Barton. As Barton drove Ted around to introduce him to the troops, he stopped before a group of men, pointed at Roosevelt, and asked if they knew who he was. Ted was pleased when a corporal immediately said, "'Yes, sir, that's General Roosevelt of the 1st Division.' General Barton said, 'Right except for one detail. He's of the 4th Division now.'"[2]

The division had shipped from North Carolina to England in January. Though new to the war, the 4th had a solid World War I record and looked to Ted like it was ready for the war. Ted needed to acquaint himself with his new outfit, however, and so toured the 4th Division camps in a new *Rough Rider* jeep—once again stenciled by Stevie, who took the wheel for Roosevelt. The jeep's nickname was a vanity that Ted publically claimed embarrassed him; to his wife, Eleanor, however, he expressed pleasure at the fact that he, Stevie, and the jeep got to be quickly known among the Allied troops readying for the invasion.

Driving around southern England in *Rough Rider*, Ted saw the green landscape teeming with green-uniformed Allied troops, milling around green tents, alongside their green equipment. To the south, east, west, and north of London, the gear and manpower of the largest invasion in the history of mankind mounded like a vast open-air warehouse on acre after acre of countryside. Military vehicles were massed near the ports along with mountains of supplies and provisions, from field rations to medical supplies to tons and tons of munitions. Shipping of every description clogged the harbors.

There were soldiers in encampment, soldiers strolling on country lanes, soldiers flirting with English girls in town squares and on city streets, much to the chagrin of the Tommies, who aside from facing greater competition for eligible young women were also resentful of the fact that they were paid far less than American GIs. But anticipation of the coming action in France was far and away the greatest source of tension.

For ten miles inland from the coast, a restricted zone ringed southern England. Those living within the area could not leave; those living without could not enter. Everyone, friend and foe alike, knew the invasion of Europe was coming, but the question was where on the Continent it would arrive.

As a newcomer to the region, Ted himself was just learning details of the invasion as it neared. He found himself sitting through one strategy session after another, which he enjoyed far less than the simple give-and-take of talking with the boys. He got plenty of that, too, however: a tank battalion was added to his command, and it turned out to be the same one that had served with him in Sicily. Roosevelt walked down a line of Shermans, chatting up the crews, listening to the memories of that time as if it were long ago. "Sir, does the general remember the time ..."

He met British field marshal Bernard Montgomery when Montgomery came to address the 4th Division. One of Monty's aides asked Ted what relation he was to the General Roosevelt of the 1st Division in North Africa. Very close, Ted informed the man. Exceptionally tight, in fact.

There was even time to make a habit of fishing for trout in a stream that ran near the 4th Division encampment and time for a bit of socializing with English "country folk." He also got into the city to dine with a few well-heeled friends, including, one evening, when he dined with a tableful of the British gentry at Beetle Smith's apartment.

Ted was able to serve as best man at son Quentin's hastily arranged wedding to Frances Webb, who was working with the Red Cross in London. The nuptials were held in a little church in Blandford, England, and attended by a host of Quentin's comrades from the 33rd Field Artillery.[3]

Eisenhower and the Supreme Allied Command had recently moved from near Whitehall in the heart of London to a western suburb called Bushy Park. Here the leaders of Operation Overlord finalized plans and specified locations for the coming invasion as they intently studied maps, tides, and weather.

Ted got invited to a dinner hosted by Ike in May, which celebrated the anniversary of the German defeat in Tunisia—a nice occasion, according to Roosevelt, "because there were no long speeches." Eisenhower gave a simple talk to the effect that the reason for the gathering was that he thought everyone involved in that first expedition ought to get together before this next one. Ted wholeheartedly endorsed the sentiments.[4]

An amphibious exercise a few days earlier, on April 28, had been a disaster. Eight LSTs (Landing Ship, Tank) filled with GIs sailed off the coast of Devon and were sunk by German E-boats, which had been alerted to the Allied convoy by heavy radio traffic. The E-boat was a speedy hundred-foot vessel designed to prey on Allied ships in the English Channel. A squadron of these torpedo boats, which could thrum at speeds of up to forty knots, worked out of Cherbourg and stumbled on the Allied exercise early in the morning.

The troops were practicing in Lyme Bay, in the southwestern corner of England off a beach called Slapton Sands. The E-boats struck the group of American LSTs in an instant and were gone just as quickly. Eight hundred American servicemen were lost, and fears that invasion plans had been revealed worried Allied planners intensely. So mortified by the disaster were commanders that they ordered a complete blackout on information regarding the exercise.[5]

Roosevelt obeyed the order. To Eleanor, he described the practice as though nothing untoward had happened, focusing instead on the "familiar feeling of being in landing boats again." "The men slowly feeling their way to their positions on pitch black decks." "No one speaking; the shapes of the troops dimly visible against the sky"; the equipment on their backs "giving them the grotesque shadows of goblins."[6]

Of the training exercise, Ted had seen so many now that he could actually wax poetic about the operation. The boats filled up surprisingly quickly, he wrote, "the hawsers whine through the pulleys as they lower [the landing craft] to the sea." "The craft slips out into the night and all around are other small craft and the black shapes of the transports. In some fashion, still mysterious to me, the assault craft sort themselves into waves and circle until the time comes to start for the line of departure."

Through all of his training, all of his camaraderie with his troops, all of the tactical briefings, Ted had an ulterior motive. Almost from the minute he arrived at the division, Ted lobbied to be part of the first wave. Even before the 4th's final assignment was fully known, Ted was whispering in Tubby Barton's ear: he wanted to go ashore in the invasion as soon as he could.

Numerous reasons could be offered why Roosevelt was not a good candidate to storm the beaches of Normandy. Chief among them was that he was fifty-six years old and had just recovered from a serious case of pneumonia, which had laid him up for three weeks. Periodic chest pains had plagued him for weeks, though of course he kept that to himself. What's more, due to severe arthritis in his ankles and knees, which exacerbated his ancient football injuries and his World War I wound, he walked with a cane. He couldn't see very well, either. In addition, his son Quentin, newly married, would be going ashore at Omaha Beach in the first wave, one beach over from his father's 4th Division's Utah Beach; the War Department would likely frown on the deaths of two Roosevelts in a single battle.

Yet for all these negatives, Ted Roosevelt was his own strongest, and most relentless, advocate for going in with the first troops. He was, incontrovertibly, a cool character and marvelous battlefield leader—assessments that everyone around him, from other commanders to the men who served under him, agreed upon. He was utterly fearless and would no doubt be a steadying influence to the hundreds of soldiers who would follow him to the beach. He was also more experienced than any other commander in Europe, having participated in three amphibious landings already.

These were the arguments Roosevelt presented to Tubby Barton. Yet there were other, far more personal reasons why Ted wished to be part of the invasion. Ingrained within him was a sense that he needed to be part of this great historic enterprise. He was a Roosevelt, after all, his famous father's eldest son. This was the invasion that was going to finally rid Europe and the world of the scourge of Nazism; this was the moment when the Allies would strike back. Just as his father had felt compelled to be part of the charge up San Juan Hill forty-six years earlier to prove his mettle, so too would Ted create for himself the same sort of "crowded hour" that Theodore had considered an essential rite of passage. Never mind that Ted, in World War II alone, had already created such a superior war record compared to his father's that the whole conflict might be considered one long "crowded hour." Indeed, perhaps that's what it was for Ted, an extended proof of his character and worthiness. But he needed the final act, his participation in the seminal moment of the Big Show. He needed to go in the first wave with the troops on D-Day.

As of mid-May, however, Ted Roosevelt had yet to receive confirmation from General Barton. Ted stewed and fretted and badgered while he awaited orders, continuing his duties as assistant commander of the 4th. These included more participation in amphibious training sessions, more inspections of the troops, watching field maneuvers, and attending more meetings with his fellow commanders, going over again and again the plans for H-hour on D-Day.

On May 26, Ted Roosevelt wrote a last request to General Barton. He listed six "facts" that he hoped the general would consider before making a final decision. The force and skill with which the first elements hit the beach would determine the ultimate outcome, he wrote. Rapid advance inland was vital to keeping the beaches clear for subsequent waves. The behavior of the first wave would predict the behavior of subsequent waves, and accurate information from the first elements would be crucial for subsequent waves. When Barton himself arrived on the beaches, he should have someone there who could give him the best assessment possible of the circumstances.

To these, Roosevelt added the last and, to him, most important fact: "I believe I can contribute materially to all of the above by going with the assault companies."

Raymond Barton was a year younger than Ted Roosevelt, a West Point grad and career army officer. Roosevelt liked him from the moment they met and wrote Eleanor that he was "a fine character of a real American type." Not only was Barton sound on military tactics, Ted felt, but he was a true leader as well. "I've seen so much of generals who were neither that it's a joy to be with him."

For Barton's part, the feelings were mutual. Simply put, he liked Ted and respected him. But he also did not want to be the general who sent Theodore Roosevelt's son to his death on the beaches of Normandy.

This would be unlike any other amphibious landing in World War II. Along the Normandy coast loomed mile after mile of defenses as formidable as any that had ever been built. Bristling with razor wire, mines, underwater booms and chains, man-made obstacles called hedgehogs that looked like giant jacks scattered in the sands, impenetrable concrete pillboxes, and an army that had spent much of the past four years arraying these defenses in the most strategic locations available on the Normandy coast—this is what the Allied forces were sailing pell-mell into. This is what Tubby Barton would be sending Ted Roosevelt into if he agreed to the request. On a cane.

Nonetheless, he finally conceded to Ted's pleas, though not without deep misgivings. Later, he would recall, "When I said goodbye to Ted in England, I never expected to see him alive again."

A few days later, on May 30, Roosevelt wrote Eleanor, "Well, Bunny, I'm where I would be—going with the front lines in the assault. It's nice—they don't think of me as going anywhere else."[7]

THIRTY-FOUR
THE DELECTABLE MOUNTAINS

After months, even years, of anticipation, the great assault on Hitler's Reich was set to begin in June 1944. Its precise timing had been boiled down to coincide with the tide on the beaches of Normandy between the city of Le Havre to the east and the Cotentin Peninsula to the west. On the early morning of June 5, British and Canadian troops were to take the lead on the easternmost beaches, code-named Juno and Swordfish; American soldiers would be landing at the two most western beaches along the Normandy coast: Omaha and Utah.

In late May, General Eisenhower ordered all troops involved in Operation Overlord to head to marshaling areas on the British coast. The 4th Division had been camped in locations in Devon, and they dutifully loaded up their gear and marched, or trucked, once more, through the green English countryside toward the sea. It was a mass movement of vehicles and columns of men huffing and chugging past the downs and hedgerows. Citizens waved as they passed, but the coastline was oddly bereft of civilians; most had been evacuated a few weeks earlier in anticipation of this movement. There were twelve slow-moving convoys from the 4th Division alone heading to the same staging areas along the coast that they'd visited in late April for their disastrous exercise off Slapton Sands: Torquay, Brixham,

Plymouth, and Dartmouth, all names steeped in English history; ports and harbors that had watched the comings and goings of vessels and fleets, sailors, soldiers, and adventurers for hundreds of years, leaving the coast of Great Britain to carry out the trades of the nation and to defend its empire. Here was a force, however, that time had never witnessed.[1]

Eisenhower and his command had narrowed the options for the invasion down to three days, June 5, 6, or 7, but the uncertainty of D-Day led to a brief period of intense anticipation and expectation as thousands of troops squeezed into quarters abandoned by the good folk of southern England or, more likely, encamped in tents. All contact with the outside world was shut off, meaning no outgoing mail was allowed, no conversations with any of the locals who might still be lingering in the area. Briefings of field officers began, and maps, photographs, and sand tables of the Cotentin Peninsula were distributed. Like their commanders, the field officers sat and watched the weather, the moon, the tides, waiting for nature to offer its most propitious moment for the invasion of France.

To meet the first of the three dates that offered a window of opportunity for invasion, June 5, troops needed to be loaded onto their transports by the end of the day on the third, a Saturday. But having spent a week of fretful anticipation in their coastal staging areas already, most soldiers were eager to get moving. On June 1, command opened the harbor gates and allowed the GIs to begin embarkation.[2]

When the task at hand was biding time, Ted was hardly an exemplary figure. But he did his best. On the third, he gathered with over a thousand officers at a giant aircraft hangar to hear a final briefing from command on the upcoming invasion. General Omar Bradley opened a pep talk by saying, "Gentlemen, this is going to be the greatest show on earth. You are honored by having grandstand seats."

With his loud, raspy voice amplified by the acoustics of the hangar, Roosevelt tried unsuccessfully to whisper, "Hell, goddamn! We're not in the grandstand! We're down on the gridiron."[3] Nervous laughter echoed beneath the rounded tin of the ceiling.

With 2,727 ships carefully coordinated to carry out the assault, the ongoing loading seemed to take forever. Soldiers laden with gear trudged up the gangplanks of the troop transports in well-rehearsed fashion, and soon sat down for navy-cooked meals, which were always a treat for the infantry. The 4th Division was divided between the transports U.S.S. *Bayfield* and U.S.S. *Barnett*. Barton and the command were crammed aboard the *Bayfield*, while Ted was on the *Barnett*, attached to the 8th Infantry Regiment, the unit heading in with the first wave. A pounding storm forced both transports to button up and batten down when the loading was done late on Saturday. When rain continued to fall in sheets all the next day, Eisenhower postponed the attack from the fifth to the sixth. There was no time to let Tubby Barton's division off the transport, so the 4th Division stayed crammed aboard their ships all day on Sunday.

Waiting in nervous anticipation, everyone went through their assignments again and again. The 4th Division was heading for Utah Beach on the Cotentin Peninsula, an outcrop of land that ran roughly perpendicular to the east-to-west line of the Normandy coast, jutting out to the north. Utah was the westernmost landing area of Operation Overlord, but the beach itself was on the eastern side of the peninsula, which meant that landing craft would actually be sailing to the west from transport group staging areas in the English Channel.

In anticipation of an Allied invasion, the Germans had flooded the land just in from the Cotentin coastline in an effort to slow any progress of a force coming in from the Normandy beaches. American troops, having struggled to come ashore, would be greeted by a watery barrier just in from the sand. The Allied command knew this and planned to drop two paratroop divisions in the interior of the peninsula in the early-morning hours before the infantry landed. Their mission was to secure the half dozen causeways that ran through these flooded lowlands from the landward side of the invasion in order to support the 4th Division's seaside assault.

On the *Barnett*, waiting for the action to commence, Ted began to pen a long letter to Eleanor that he would add to over the next two days. He was well aware of the significance of the moment. "We are starting on the great venture of this war and by the time you get this letter, for better or for worse, it will be history. We are attacking in daylight the most heavily

fortified shore in history, a shore held by excellent troops. We are throwing against it excellent troops, well armed and backed by excellent air and
good naval support."[4]

Ever conscious of his soldiers, he described men overburdened with
supplies, complaining that headquarters staff who decided what a soldier
would carry into battle had rarely experienced combat: "they have not
slogged through sand or mud with fire falling around, they have not slept
fitfully in the cold."[5] Yet the soldiers he encountered on deck were not dwell-
ing on the fighting to come, he wrote, except "to wisecrack" about their
circumstances. Among the officers, it was all sober business—endless reviews
of what they were to do once they landed.

The miserable rain kept the ships buttoned up both Sunday and Monday, adding to the tension and anxiety on board. How many more card
games could the guys play? How many more sweethearts needed writing
to? In his ongoing letter to Eleanor, Ted waxed philosophical about modern warfare, just how massive and complex it had become, how many
moving parts were involved. He was happy to be on the *Barnett*—the same
ship that had transported him to Sicily. It helped simplify his own tasks:
"I know where the quarters are, I'm in the same cabin I used [before]."

Finally, he came to some hard news that he had to deliver. He had yet
to give Eleanor specifics about his role in the attack, telling her simply
that he was "where I would be." Now he was direct: "I go with the assault
wave, hit the beach at H hour. I'm doing it because it's the way I can contribute most. It steadies the young men to know I'm with them, to see me
plodding along with my trench cane."

There was more: not only was he going into France on the first wave
at Utah Beach, but also Quentin would be one beach over, at Omaha, an
hour later. "It could even be worse for him," Ted wrote frankly, knowing
that the Germans, having received the initial hit from the Allied invasion,
would be pouring troops into their defenses just as Quentin's wave was
hitting the beaches an hour after the first assault. What could be done
about any of this now? By the time Eleanor received his letter, his fate and
Quentin's would most likely be decided.

In preparation for his landing, he was once again rereading *Pilgrim's*

Progress, contemplating the Delectable Mountains. The mountains rested just beyond the Valley of Death and offered a glimpse of the Celestial City, the beautiful goal of the journey. The reference prompted Ted to recall for Eleanor all the pleasures of their wedding day, thirty-four years earlier and just a couple of weeks from this day. He remembered their happiness in the first few years of their marriage, living in San Francisco.

"Bunny," he wrote, "together we have seen and done much. We've seen the world—every continent not as tourist but meeting and knowing the people. We've played our part in government, and taken part in the two greatest wars of history. We've seen the whole world changing. Above all we've seen not only our children grow to men and women but we've seen their children."

He set the letter aside, knowing that Eleanor would understand what he was trying to say. "It is very difficult to write anything which really tells what one feels" is how he'd phrased this problem in writing to his father years before, trying to explain his love for Eleanor when they had just become engaged. It was a difficulty he would always have.

Just after mess on June 5, the commanders of the 8th Infantry gathered in Ted's quarters for a final meeting. They found the general with his unfinished letter at his side, now reading a Western. The gathering lasted almost to midnight. There were hugs and a few choked-up good-byes among the men when it broke up.[6]

Before he left his cabin that morning, Ted added a few final words to Eleanor: "Our life has been very full—our feet were placed in a large room—and we did not bury our talent in a napkin. We're under way and the time is short now. What the future holds for our armies or us as individuals no man knows."[7]

THIRTY-FIVE

"SEE YOU ON THE BEACH"

Belowdecks on the *Barnett*, Ted Roosevelt noted a pretense of casualness among the soldiers of the 8th Regiment. Maybe even some bravado. There was desultory card playing, some chatter, some quiet corners and long stares as young men considered—or avoided considering—the circumstances they would face come morning. Roosevelt moved among the soldiers calmly, speaking softly and soothingly, offering reassurances from a man who had done this same sort of landing two times before, three if Corsica were counted.[1]

About midnight, over the ship's loudspeakers, a few declarations were read from General Eisenhower about the mission, about liberty, about "rescuing the oppressed." Then Roosevelt himself was asked to come on the ship's intercom and offer a few brief words of encouragement. He ended with the simple promise: "I'll see you tomorrow morning, 6:30, on the beach."[2]

The 8th Infantry was mainly Southern boys from Florida, Alabama, and Georgia, about six hundred men strong, commanded by Colonel James Van Fleet, with Roosevelt attached. Van Fleet was a distinguished leader, a West Point grad who had served as a battalion commander in the First World War and would eventually win promotion to major general in this conflict. The 8th had yet to face fire in the war, but Van Fleet had faith in their fighting ability. He characterized them as "squirrel-shooters" and "country boys who weren't afraid of the dark and could find their way forward in the woods and feel at home." Their assignment was to hit the beach running and get as quickly as they could to the causeways that led off the sand and into the interior of the peninsula. Roosevelt would be performing the very same duties he'd outlined just ten days earlier in his memo to General Barton asking for this assignment: providing calm and steady leadership on the beach and to subsequent tasks at hand.[3]

It was near 1:30 on the sixth of June when the order was given to climb aboard the collection of landing craft that dangled from the *Barnett*'s side above the English Channel. The transports were floating east of the Cotentin Peninsula, as were the accompanying landing craft and support vessels that hovered around her, the *Bayfield*, and the *Joseph T. Dickman*. A half dozen boats, both starboard and port, hung from two stacked decks, waiting to be loaded and lowered into the Channel, where they would motor south and slightly west toward Utah Beach. Meanwhile, more landing craft arrived at the *Barnett*'s side in the waters below, and troops of the 4th Infantry started to climb down the slippery, water-soaked rope webbing into the heaving craft. It was a well-practiced routine made immeasurably more difficult by tension, darkness, and the choppy sea, not to mention the overloaded packs carried by the soldiers. One man slipped and found himself dangling upside down, saved from falling into the dark sea by a single foot stuck in the rope net. A pair of his buddies managed to grab his shoulders from the boat below, unhook his boot, and pull him into the landing craft.

Back in his cabin, Ted was informed that his boat was about to be loaded. Now he began to feel the nervousness of all those around him. "Where is my life belt?" he demanded of Stevie. Informed by his aide that he'd been given three already, Roosevelt snapped, "Damn it, I don't care how many you've given me. I don't have one now." Stevie found another belt, and then, after making sure Roosevelt had his pistol and cane, they proceeded up to the deck.[4]

Tucked in an inner pocket of Roosevelt's field jacket was a little book of poems by an obscure nineteenth-century English writer named Winthrop Praed. There was nothing special about the poetry—Roosevelt simply knew that if he wasn't killed in the first wave, eventually moments would come when he could take comfort in reading. He'd learned to take books along on his amphibious assaults.

Controlled chaos reigned deckside. The landing craft already in the channel down below were filling or filled, and now it was time to load the railside boats. Roosevelt would not have to climb down the rope ladder to dive into a craft rocking and rolling in the choppy sea. His boat was at the ship's rail, which still required that Ted make a five-foot jump into the craft. When a soldier reached out to help, Roosevelt swatted the hand with his walking stick. "Get the hell out of my way," he said. "I can very well jump in there myself." He hopped aboard, caught his balance in the rocking boat, and then looked around at the tense faces surrounding him. He grinned as the boat was lowered to the ocean and so did they. This is what he was here for; this is why he had lobbied Barton to let him be in this first wave.[5]

Spray burst over the side of the landing craft the moment it hit the water, soaking the men to the skin. In the English Channel surrounding them, a dozen more landing craft circled around their rendezvous points for what seemed like an eternity. When all boats were accounted for, the craft coalesced into a convoy, each bound for a specific target on the coast of Normandy. The throttles were opened, the engines picked up speed, and the boats thrust toward land.

Below the sides of the gunnels, the men huddled tight, their heads tucked, their shoulders hunched, protecting themselves from the salty ocean spray. Despite having practiced for hours in these tubs, the men grew sick from the undulating sea, and the stench of vomit soon permeated the boats. As they steamed ahead, the navy coxswain, perched above the heads of his load of GIs in the back of the tub, measured the pace of the craft to the line extending on either side. Each craft jockeyed ahead or fell back, fighting the waves, as all kept bounding toward shore for what would be a tense and uncomfortable three-hour journey.

Out in the darkness of the Cotentin Peninsula ahead, legions of paratroopers of the 82nd and 101st Divisions initiated the assault that would ulti-

HIS FATHER'S SON
291

mately lead them toward the same beaches to which the 4th Division was headed. The grand plan had the airborne troops sealing the exits from the beaches as the seaborne infantry pushed the Germans inland.

Trouble started hours earlier, under the cover of night, as the airborne armada neared the French coast. A cloud bank over the Cotentin rattled pilots of the nearly four hundred C-47s carrying their cargo of paratroopers. Then a hail of flak suddenly shot up from German coastal batteries. Up in the planes, the jumpers watched as fragments arced toward them, illuminated by brightly colored tracers that ascended like fireworks into the path of the aircraft. Some planes avoided the clouds and fire by heading up, while some took a low route. Some slowed down, while others sped ahead. Some planes took hits and slowly banked back toward safety in England. Those too badly damaged began the fatal plummet down. In any case, the actions wreaked havoc with the drop zones below. When the "sticks" of paratroopers were hooked in and ready to jump, not only were the men terrified of floating to earth in a sky full of flak and brilliantly colored tracers, marking their descent for gunners below, but they already knew, or could easily guess, that the evasive maneuvers meant they were being dropped in locations that were nowhere near their intended targets.

The paratroopers had planned to land in fields just beyond the inundated lowlands behind the beach. Instead they found themselves dropped in widely scattered territories from the village of Ste.-Mère-Église, about ten kilometers from the sea, all the way to Pont l'Abbé, another ten kilometers farther to the west of Ste.-Mère-Église.

Many fell in terrifying isolation; some dropped in fields purposely flooded by the Germans, the weight of their equipment and entangling chutes trapping them underwater; at least one dropped in a large pile of manure; and some dropped famously in the heart of Ste.-Mère-Église. It was there that a brass bell in the church tower rang the alarm as a hay barn burned on the edge of the town square. Into the madness floated jumpers from the 505th and 506th Regiments of the 82nd. Private John Steele's chute hooked on the church steeple, and there he hung for what seemed an eternity as down below townspeople raced to put out a fire. German soldiers from the local garrison encountered American paratroopers below, and the church bell continued to ring just feet from where he was trapped.[6]

Meanwhile, throughout the lower third of the peninsula, a scattering of individual paratroopers from a variety of regiments and divisions gathered in ad hoc units. Armed with little chirping handheld crickets that were supposed to signal other paratroopers to friendly comrades in the dark, officers and enlisted men gradually began to head east toward their intended assignment: the causeways leading off of Utah Beach.

Destroyers guarded the flanks of the flotilla delivering the 8th Infantry to Utah Beach while rocket ships and guide boats sailed in its midst. The majority of the long and endless stretch of vessels were landing craft, however. The stench of oil fumes from the countless ships and boats filled the air, adding a chemical irritant to the GIs' sea-tossed stomachs and inducing more vomiting. The first sounds of battle cracked behind them in the form of the thunderous guns of the U.S. Navy. The rushes, whistles, and shattering booms of the cannons offered no real comfort to the soldiers in the landing launches, despite their understanding that these weapons were employed on their own behalf.

Now a few German batteries opened up onshore in response, occasionally landing their shells near the launches, sending up spray, but hitting no one. The flashes of the guns onshore blended with the explosion of navy shells landing among them to offer a brief color show that was quickly subsumed by the drone of Allied planes arriving overhead.

Silhouetted in the early-dawn light the bombers swept above, wave after wave after wave, filling the sky. Allied air superiority would turn out to be one of the crucial factors in the success of the invasion, but of the two American beaches attacked, Omaha and Utah, the precision of the U.S. Ninth Air Force over Utah would prove an aid to American ground forces storming the beaches below. Using smaller, medium-range B-26 Marauders rather than the higher-altitude, bigger-bombed B-24 Liberator planes employed at Omaha gave an accuracy to the strikes that was lacking on the beach to the east. Attacking from four thousand feet, about ten thousand feet lower than the Liberators, the Marauders could pinpoint German targets below, from bridges to railroads to frontline positions.[7]

Nearing the shore, Roosevelt saw "blazes of light" followed by clouds of dust rising above the shoreline and obscuring the landscape as the Marauder weaponry began to rain down on the German emplacements at Utah Beach. To the GIs jostling in the landing craft, heading for the sand, any effort to pound the defenses waiting to greet them was a good thing.

One Allied plane was hit on its return from dumping its payload and arced into the sea "like a meteor" not far from where Ted watched. A lone German fighter plane swept down toward the first wave of craft, intent on destruction, but a British Spitfire appeared instantly on its tail and brought it down with three staccato bursts of fire. On and on went the landing craft: they passed a capsized guide vessel with a man clinging to its bottom, and another sailor, who looked wounded, hanging on to him. The man clinging to the ship waved for help, but of course there was no stopping for rescues at this moment.[8]

The landing boats picked up speed as the shoreline neared, passing the slower-moving tank landing craft (LSTs) that were supposed to arrive on Utah simultaneously with the infantry. The LSTs, hardly smooth-sailing vessels in the best of circumstances, were having a hard time negotiating the choppy seas.

For all the mass of men and machinery they'd left behind in England and out in the Channel, the role of the 8th Infantry in this undertaking had been whittled down quickly and dramatically. Every man in the first wave knew he was part of a massive invasion that stretched for miles along the Normandy coast and included soldiers from the United States, Canada, and all of Great Britain, but here, as they neared the sandy beach, matters were boiled down to their small flotilla of landing craft motoring toward shore, carrying a little more than six hundred GIs from the 8th Regiment. Would they or would they not survive the onslaught?

Beneath gray skies in the early-dawn light, peering over the gunnels of the craft as his troops ducked and huddled beside him, Roosevelt tried to make out familiar landmarks as shore details began to emerge in the gloaming. Through smoke and dust kicked up by the bombardment, the beach appeared, a long stretch studded with wire and obstacles that looked like overgrown jacks tossed by a giant hand.

Land was close, but reaching the beach was still difficult. Currents off the peninsula were notoriously unpredictable, flowing both north and south in uncanny fashion, particularly during peaks of low tide. Making matters worse, navy coxswains looking through the haze of early-morning light and dense smoke were alarmed to note that their landmarks were missing, presumably smashed by naval or aerial bombardment.

At 6:30, Roosevelt's craft finally brushed sand and the boat ramp dropped, sending the American warriors out into battle. A string of craft beside them likewise deposited other soldiers in waist-deep—and some-times deeper—water. The shock of the landing, the sudden openness revealed with the gate coming down, the push of men clambering out of the craft, and the surge of adrenaline combined to make a collective rush, like a football team bursting onto a field.

Except the push was immediately dampened by a slogging wetness. Amid German shelling and bullets that ripped through the water and ricocheted off the landing craft, the men waded toward the sand dunes that marked the shore ahead of them, dragged down by the weight of water and their own equipment. They were facing artillery, mined beaches, and a thick hail of small-arms fire from well-sited emplacements up and down the dune. Men dropped near Roosevelt—"some silent, some screaming." A scout for E Company was the first to reach the sand dunes and was wel-comed with a bullet that instantly killed him. Waddling with heavy, water-logged backpacks, the troops pushed on till they hit the sand and then scrambled across some four hundred yards of beach. Among them was "Grandpa" Roosevelt—as he described himself later to Eleanor—"puffing," hobbling on his cane, aided by fifty-six-year-old adrenaline. He finally made it to the seawall, his heart pounding while he was sucking for air.[9]

The moment he had time to appraise the circumstances surrounding him, Ted Roosevelt knew something wasn't right. On the seawall was a house that according to all the photos and maps he'd seen was simply not supposed to be there. There was supposed to be an earthen square—a mysterious structure they'd nicknamed the "Mud Fort" back in England—

that was nowhere to be found. And where was the windmill that should have been right in front of them?[10]

They were in the wrong place, a potentially disastrous circumstance, given the 8th Infantry's status as the first ashore. The continued landing of the 4th Division was predicated on the preparations of the 8th. Inland, the paratroopers were expecting to greet the invasion force on the other side of specific causeways leading from Utah Beach. An error on these plumb lines could skew the architecture of the whole attack.

Gunfire continued on the beach and out in the water. Shells rained down. Roosevelt had arrived at the seawall in the company of the ever-present Stevie, who carried a tommy gun and a radio. They were attached to E Company of the 8th Infantry, commanded by Captain Howard Lees, "a great tower of a man," according to Roosevelt. There at the house where the "Mud Fort" was supposed to be, they set up a Command Post (CP), and all scrambled up the dunes beyond the wall to get a better look at just where they were. From higher ground, Roosevelt was able to spy the windmill far to the north and determined that the regiment was about a mile south of where it ought to have been. They needed a new plan post-haste, and Roosevelt decided to seek counsel.[11]

Ted headed back down to the beach and began to "hotfoot" back and forth between the beach and the CP, looking for officers to consult with. Just coming ashore was the 2nd Battalion of the 4th Division, headed by Lieutenant Colonel Carlton MacNeely, which had landed at 7:00 a.m. and was immediately thrust into the attack on the German positions. The third wave of infantry arrived soon after, commanded by Colonel Van Fleet. His 1st Battalion was immediately pounded by German 88s, but got some assistance and protection from two U.S. tanks that had arrived at Utah and were setting up in the sand.

It was at the tanks that Roosevelt, MacNeely, and Van Fleet huddled in the lee side of the armor. Maps came out, fingers pointed here and there, and the clock kept ticking on the landing. All agreed with Roosevelt that they were well south of where they were supposed to be and despite any confusion that might follow with the paratroopers coming from the peninsula, the best option available to them was to push straight ahead.

Many would later record that it was Ted Roosevelt who then made the most famous pronouncement to come from Utah Beach on D-Day: "Gentlemen, we'll start the war from right here." Later Van Fleet claimed that the words and decision were actually his. In any case, the phrase become famous and described exactly what happened next: the 8th Infantry pushed straight forward from the misplaced landing.[12]

It was no casual decision. The complexities of a landing like this went far beyond the movements of the first wave. Each successive unit for days to come would be influenced by where the attack inland would be undertaken, including the many engineering units that had been planning for weeks to follow prescribed pathways into the interior of the peninsula. The 1st Engineer Brigade, tasked with ensuring that supplies and equipment could get from the beachhead to the advancing infantry, would, in particular, feel the burden of the change. They would need to steer U.S. Navy landing vessels toward this new location at the same time as they constructed paths out from the beach to causeways that they were not even certain existed.

Meanwhile, the 8th Infantry had to reassess what it knew about the German defenses in this particular stretch of beach. They had known coming ashore that five enemy strongpoints were constructed just beyond the beach, each centered on at least one concrete pillbox. Numerous German machine-gun nests were snuggled among the dunes and densely packed minefields guarding the causeways. But luckily the 8th soon learned that German defenses weren't nearly as intense at Utah as they were at Omaha Beach to the east. It seemed that by landing south of their intended target, U.S. forces had sidestepped a number of German coastal installations and more withering fire.

Which was not to say the difficulties of Utah Beach weren't intense. From the seawall Captain Lees's E Company attacked snipers holed up in two houses in the dunes and took them out with BARs. Captain George Mabry of the 2nd Battalion, 8th Infantry crossed the dunes with his G Company and was near the entrance to Causeway 1, to the far left on Utah Beach. He and his men halted at the realization that they'd stepped into the middle of a minefield. Mabry had already lost three men to the devices on the way in.

Now he could go no farther without continuing through the same dangerous field, nor could he go back without risking the prospect of losing more men to what they'd just gone through. There was really no choice: he ordered his unit to charge straight ahead toward an enemy foxhole. G Company killed several Germans and captured more, taking the nest with ease.[13, 14]

Meanwhile, troops kept coming ashore. Amid continuing rifle fire and shells, Roosevelt stayed down on the beach to help guide the succeeding waves of incoming troops to the revised position. He directed those who halted on the sand to move inland, and steered those heading north of the new positions back to the south. He called for a medic to help a soldier with a blackened face who had been caught in a shell burst just seconds after hitting the water. In years to come, scores of veterans would remember seeing him directing traffic on the beach with his .45-caliber pistol in one hand and his walking stick in the other. In fact, he never pulled the pistol from its holster during the course of D-Day, but the image was settled in the minds of his men.

A sergeant from the 8th encountered Roosevelt on the beach "with a cane in one hand, a map in the other, walking around as if he was looking over some real estate."[15]

A medic from Iowa ran into him at the beach wall and asked the general, "How do things look, sir?"

"I think the Krauts know we're here!" Roosevelt answered.[16]

A team of 4th Division engineers, sent to blow up obstacles on the beach, saw him walking near the seawall in the midst of a field they were just about to explode. A sergeant yelled, "Go knock that bastard down—he's going to get killed!"

Roosevelt's presence quickly became legendary. Over the years, countless GIs would claim they heard him say, "The war starts here"—far more than could have fit behind that tank in the Utah Beach surf. A kid from Boca Raton recalled seeing him in his jeep (which he didn't yet have), waving his cane, and exhorting the troops to "move on, move on," up the beach. But Ted Roosevelt was doing precisely what he said he would do: providing calm and experienced leadership on an extremely hazardous battlefield.[17]

Colonel Arthur Teague, CO of the 3rd Battalion, 22nd Infantry, came ashore in the midst of a German shelling that destroyed a couple of landing craft in his group. Teague made it to the seawall and was greeted by Roosevelt and advised that they were south of their intended position but making progress inland. "He wanted action from my men immediately after landing and asked me to get them down the beach as soon as I could. This was about 0930 hours."[18]

Hustling to the sand dunes, Teague lost two men to mines, but once there, he was able to get his bearings. He ran to a firing trench marked by barbed wire and sandy beach grass. There he bumped into one of his lieutenants wounded by sniper fire. Farther on he found the lieutenant's platoon engaged in a firefight. The platoon was able to root the Germans from their positions and ultimately gathered seventeen prisoners. Teague quizzed them about the numbers of defenders at the beach and the locations of land mines, but was told that they'd only arrived at their positions in the night and knew nothing of its circumstances.

Up near the old French fort north of their revised position, a tough fight was under way. Aided by U.S. tanks coming ashore, elements of the 8th managed to capture a hundred more German troops. Nearby, one of the tanks scored a direct hit on a gun turret mounted on a pillbox.

Still directing traffic on the beach, Roosevelt was in his element. His hand was slightly wounded by shrapnel from German fire at some point, but it was an injury he proudly displayed to Van Fleet. The old man, standing there with his walking stick, hobbling back and forth along the beach, was his old self, greeting incoming GIs with encouraging words and "cracking the same sort of corny jokes he told us in Africa."[19]

Despite the gun battles and shelling, resistance was lighter than expected through the morning, with groups of German troops continuing to surrender from their various strongholds as the attack ensued. It was as if they had been stunned by both the initial bombardment and now the invasion. And the mistake of landing to the south was turning out to be fortuitous. German defenses were ill prepared at Utah Beach; there simply wasn't much fight in them.

Just after 11:00 a.m., Captain Mabry's unit came upon the pillbox guarding Causeway 1. A German machine gun opened up, and Mabry sent someone down to the beach to locate a tank for assistance. The man came back with two. One of them came forward and put its gun muzzle directly into the pillbox vent and started blasting. In no time, a white flag appeared and thirty-six Germans surrendered. The entrance to the causeway was open wide.

Mabry sent scouts cautiously out toward its western edge, through the wetlands, to look for the paratroopers. He warned his men that the jumpers may or may not have arrived, and to be careful to identify them before shooting. The scouts inched forward. Suddenly an orange flare shot up from the far end of the causeway and a pair of paratroopers stood up. Mabry's scouts recognized American flag patches on their shoulders, and the two groups merged.

"Fourth Division?" one of the paratroopers asked the scouts.

"Fourth Division," he heard in response.

The link between paratroopers and infantry was made at Utah Beach.

A little more than four hours after the first American forces had landed on Utah Beach, it was cleared and the only Germans left were either dead or prisoners.

Of course, the day was not even half over and—as Roosevelt and Van Fleet well knew—the war was just starting. But the invasion had gone remarkably well. Reinforcements were already streaming onto the beach along with mortar, armor, artillery, and engineering units, and thanks to the work of the paratroopers on the other side of the causeways, no German forces were coming to shore up Axis defenses. At Utah Beach at least, Hitler's "impregnable" Normandy defenses had been breached just hours into the invasion that would ultimately put an end to his Reich.

When General Barton arrived at Utah Beach shortly after 11:00 a.m., he found Ted Roosevelt bursting with information. Their reunion was happy and emotional, with hugs and wet eyes. The man whom Barton had sent ashore doubtful that he would see again was here fully alive "with a perfect picture of the entire situation. I loved Ted," Barton would later write with simple frankness. "You can imagine the emotion with which I greeted him when he came out to meet me. I embraced him and he me."[20]

As the day wore on, Roosevelt once again directed traffic, now back by the causeways. It was no small task: both Roosevelt and Barton knew that any traffic jams bringing troops into the beach would invite enemy counterattacks. Getting off Utah Beach and into the interior remained the central mission of the invaders. It was how many 4th Division troops remembered the brigadier general, waving them into the interior over Causeway 2. An executive officer from the 12th Infantry Regiment recalled Roosevelt "stomping up and down a dusty road . . . leaning on his cane and smoking his pipe as unperturbed as though he were in the middle of Times Square." He was enjoying himself now, calling to the passing troops, "'It's a great day for hunting. Glad you made it.'"[21]

In all, he wrote Eleanor, he'd probably walked twenty miles that day on the beaches and causeways. Late in the afternoon, his *Rough Rider* jeep was brought ashore, and he and Stevie once again, and blessedly, had wheels.[22]

THIRTY-SIX

OLD SOLDIERS NEVER DIE

In the days that followed, the 4th Division marched inland, first toward Ste.-Mère-Église, and then north, toward Cherbourg. Its assignment was to capture the whole Cotentin Peninsula to secure the port at its very northern tip for continued Allied use in the invasion.

Almost immediately, the U.S. Army ran smack-dab into a Norman agricultural landscape absolutely antithetical to quick advance. Ancient hedgerows separating one farm from the next now intervened between Allied and German forces, blocking tanks and troops. It was hoped that Cherbourg would be taken in a week's time, but not only was the battle for the peninsula more difficult than expected; Omar Bradley decided to cut off all possible escape routes for the Germans on the Cotentin before assaulting Cherbourg itself. A wide swath of territory needed to be cleaned out first, much of it intersected by those dense hedges that made fighting extremely difficult.

Just a week after D-Day, Ted was sitting in a regimental headquarters, "a little gray stone Normandie Chateau—square courtyard & tower complete," as he described it to Eleanor, wanting to give her a feel for this new battle he was fighting. "I'm here because the reg[iment] is in trouble and a German attack is expected. We've just been strafed by German planes."

Ted was doing what he had done for almost two years, stepping in to lead young men in battle, showing them the cool and resolve necessary to continue. "In the room where I am there is a mélange of all—officers, NCOs, privates—some sitting on chairs, some on boxes, some [on] the floor. Of course, it's filthy dirty and there's a litter of rifles, tommy guns, belts, ration tins and maps. The men are bearded, dirty and their faces are drawn. I don't suppose there's a man here who's thirty but they look old." Ted was replacing a colonel "whose reg[iment] adored him." The man "has just been hit by h[igh] e[xplosives] and evacuated—."

In the past twenty-four hours, Ted had sent three battalions on three different attacks, he wrote Eleanor; each of the missions had been "hot at the line of departure." Bullets flew through the hedges, and shells thumped in the fields. "Sometimes it is hard to get the men up and on—I don't blame them," he wrote. "My job among other things is to keep up morale. Sometimes it's hard . . . I'm doing it right now. I stopped writing for a moment to 'bitch' on K rations & reports—."

Of course, as was always the case with Ted Roosevelt Jr., he was not just any old man at war, but the son of a former president, one whose face was now on a mountain in South Dakota. Ted was a man of whom these young soldiers could say for the rest of their lives, *I once shared a château in Normandy with Ted Roosevelt*. A character. A gruff old guy with a booming voice, a quick laugh and a gold-toothed grin, a cane and an old knit cap. *Think of it, me, elbow to elbow with Ted Roosevelt Jr.*

There were successes. "At times in our advance the infantry has gone forward with tanks—when we do this we sweep the Germans before us. The tanks flush them from the hedgerows and the GIs shoot them like rabbits." But the price for these advances was evident in a backward glance. There lay "a hard fought field. It's not pretty. Battlefields are not. They're strewn with debris, helmets, haversacks, weapons and in huddled heaps the dead. The dead are sprawled in every attitude. Their uniforms are dirty & torn, their faces are like yellow clay, and unshaven, brown, dried blood stains them."

He thought of poor Eleanor, too, as he wrote these letters: so loyal, so loving, so deeply invested in their lives together, reading his reports for too many years, ensconced now in her relatively new home on the old Roosevelt homestead at Orchard Bay; the place of her own and Ted's that they were just getting comfortable in when war interrupted the beginning of their sunset years.

"Just there a red-headed lieutenant . . . came in from patrol and in his soft southern drawl told me, 'Sah, when I got to the end of town there was a German smoking a pipe. I called to him to surrender but he was not quick enough so I tommy gunned him. I thought he was just one sniper so I turned around to get my patrol when four more came out of a house so I shot them.'"

Eleanor had to be conflicted, reading these endless reports of battle from Tunisia, Sicily, Italy, and now Normandy. Thankful when the letters arrived, not for the stories that Ted told of landing at Utah Beach, or fighting through the hedgerows of Normandy, or of boys tommy-gunning the enemy, not even for his proclamations of love, but for the fact that every time they were delivered, every time she saw his signature on the address, she knew at least one thing for sure: he was still alive.

"Yesterday evening when Stevie and I were coming back from launching another attack where battle was at its worst, we found a horse tangled in telephone wire, a big solemn black horse. We got out and unsnarled him and he started grazing. Somehow it made me feel that there would be an after the war and above all that the world intended to go on no matter what we did."[1]

Roosevelt and the 4th Division stalled about fifteen miles outside of Cherbourg, and Ted's command began to see mounting casualties as its units inched forward. By this time, E Company, the rifle unit with which he landed on Utah Beach, had suffered 80 percent casualties, and the division as a whole had lost five thousand men killed or wounded.

The hedgerows took their toll but the world intended to go on.

Cherbourg was finally surrendered by the Germans a full month after the D-Day landings, and only following a devastating bombardment by both the U.S. Navy and the U.S. Army Air Force. The Allied command quickly chose a military governor for the city, and it turned out to be Ted Roosevelt Jr.

It was a new and hectic assignment. Getting the port into shape for Allied use was the primary job, but Cherbourg was an utter mess, and Ted was exhausted by his duties. One comfort he found was a headquarters on wheels, a captured German truck that fell into his hands and was subsequently decked out for him by an aide and an ordnance unit. It was painted white on the interior and held a bed and headboard, an old French chair, a desk, and a place for his footlocker and bag, and it was illuminated by an electric bulb. It was the most luxurious battlefield headquarters Ted had ever had, and he relished it.[2]

The high command's plans for Roosevelt, however, were not confined to Cherbourg and the Cotentin Peninsula. The fighting in Normandy had revealed a number of problems in divisional leadership, and few generals had acted with the sort of decisiveness exhibited by Ted Roosevelt at Utah Beach. When the need to replace a divisional commander came up in discussions among Eisenhower, Beetle Smith, and Bradley, Ted's name was offered. They needed a fighting general now and weren't so concerned about finding a disciplinarian. Smith suggested that Ted be given the assignment, and Bradley agreed. Though he didn't yet know it, Roosevelt at long last was about to be promoted to his first divisional command, the 90th.

Ted had been feeling unwell for a few days, and his health was not improved by the constant rainy weather in Normandy or the strain of cleaning up Cherbourg. His clothes were perpetually wet and clammy, and despite his new headquarters, he was not getting much rest. A doctor visited and advised him that his troubles, as he wrote Eleanor, "were primarily from having put an inhuman strain on a machine that was not exactly new."[3]

Buoying Roosevelt's spirits was a visit from his son Quentin, who had survived the 1st Division's attack at Omaha Beach unscathed—news that Ted hadn't learned until a week after the invasion. The young Roosevelt's unit had had a tough fight on the beach, and later butted heads with a Panzer division in Normandy—facts that confirmed to Ted that he needed now to redouble his efforts at getting his boy out of the European theater and off to China. But there were other, less consequential things to chat about when Quentin arrived at his father's headquarters at seven thirty on the evening of July 12, 1944.

They talked of home, family, Quentin's future plans, the war. The two spent much of the evening together, enjoying the warmth of each other's presence. Ted confided to his son that he had suffered a series of chest pains that came and went, a fact he had hidden from others. The fatigue that had come over him in the past weeks was probably an offshoot of those attacks. Or vice versa. The bottom line was that he was not altogether well. When Quentin left the truck that night, he talked to Stevie and implored Ted's aide "to hold him down the next time he was sick. I told Pa, too," Quentin wrote to his mother, "but you know how much effect that had."[4]

About an hour after Quentin left, Ted suffered another attack. Coronary thrombosis was the ultimate medical definition of what struck the general. He lay in his quarters while attendants worked frantically to revive him. At eleven thirty that night, the 4th Division commander, Tubby Barton, came to see Ted, and found him barely alive. Later he wrote of the moment to Eleanor. "He was breathing but unconscious when I entered his truck. I sat helpless and saw the most gallant soldier and finest gentleman I have ever known expire. The show goes on. He would have it so and we shall make it so."[5]

Theodore Roosevelt Jr. was dead, just a couple of months shy of his fifty-seventh birthday. He was laid to rest on Bastille Day before a somber gathering of troops and a smattering of French civilians. For a few short hours, the war came to a halt as soldiers gathered to pay their respects to an American hero. Among the generals present to see off their fallen comrade were Omar Bradley, George Patton, Tubby Barton, and J. Lawton Collins. Ted's son was there, along with Marcus "Stevie" Stevenson, and Kurt Show, another frequent driver of the general's jeep. Hundreds of GIs and French Resistance leaders watched as Ted was buried with other U.S. soldiers who had lost their lives in the First, and now the Second, World War at the cemetery in Ste.-Mère-Église. Among rows of solemn white crosses, the 4th Division band played Chopin's Funeral

March as the body was laid to rest next to the grave of his brother Quentin. Three volleys sounded, and beyond the salute could be heard the
distant rattle of machine guns, while above, black patches of antiaircraft
fire floated in the breeze.

Patton, writing in his diary, remained typically sour: "The funeral,
which should have been impressive, was a flop. Instead of the regular
funeral service, two preachers of uncertain denomination made orations
which they concealed under the form of prayers. The guard of honor was
held far back and in column instead of line. Towards the end of the service,
our antiaircraft guns near Coutances opened on some German planes and
gave an appropriate requiem to the funeral of a really gallant man."[6]

Quentin had a different impression. To his mother he wrote of "how
terribly impressive it was, a warrior's funeral in every sense of the word—
the older great leaders paying homage, and his followers. Nothing else,
no matter where or when, could have fitted in so wonderfully, so perfectly
with what he was, what he wanted." Describing his last moments with his
father, Quentin reassured Eleanor, "Above all, remember that he was
happy, especially that last evening—with family and friends around
him . . . he was happy and had everything."[7]

At a memorial service back in New York, the tributes poured in.
Cousin Franklin sent a message that read in part, "Two members of the
family, General Theodore Roosevelt Jr. and Quentin Roosevelt, lie in the
sacred soil of France. The former died in this war shortly after the landing in Normandy which was the prelude to the liberation of France, while
his young brother gave his life in the cause of freedom in World War I. It
is fitting we commemorate these brave souls and all who have made the
supreme sacrifice that France might live."

Thomas Dewey, the candidate for whom Ted had campaigned in 1940,
wrote a heartfelt tribute: "Never was there a warmer friend, a stouter heart,
or a more public spirited American . . . I know that his family will be
comforted in their grief in the sure knowledge that everyone who knew
him loved and respected him as a great patriot who gave his life for his
country."

The *New York Times* was similarly affected. It wrote of his service, "In the present war, though well along in his fifties, he worked and fought as hard as if he were 20. He distinguished himself in several great theatres of operations. He was respected and loved by his officers and men. When he went about his division in England, no sooner would a band catch sight of him than it would strike up an American song called 'Old Soldiers Never Die.' This was his piece, he used to say. Nor is its title contradicted because that brave soldier hears its beat no more. He lives in the proud sorrow of those dearest to him, in the memory of countless friends and of all who love valor and kindness and self-sacrifice."[8]

Radio broadcasts across the country announced his death. "A news broadcaster has a painful job when he has to tell of the passing of a warm personal friend" is how old friend Lowell Thomas began his program. "Brigadier General Theodore Roosevelt is dead, in Normandy. He died as he would have wished, in the service of his country, a service always closest to his heart."[9]

A. J. Liebling of the *New Yorker*, who had written such a glowing portrait of Ted after El Guettar, probably hit the nail on the head when he compared Ted's legacy to his father's: "Old Teddy was a dilettante soldier and first-class politician; his son was a dilettante politician and a first-class soldier."[10]

Perhaps the eulogy that would have had the most meaning to Ted came from a private named Amos Buck, who had traveled to Utah Beach with the general on June 6 and later wrote a testimonial about that journey for his commander. "We had messages from all the Generals and from the President," he wrote of the evening before the invasion. "The best one to be remembered coming from Gen. 'Teddy' Roosevelt. It was an impromptu affair from the man's warm heart, and was short and to the point. He's been thru several landings, and knows whereof he speaks. Further than that the men all know he is a front line general, and respect and love him. We had the pleasure of meeting him several times. The man has a remarkable memory, too. Col., you have no idea how much good a man of that type does with a bunch of scared inexperienced G.I.'s. I later saw him on the beach—as far forward as the doughboys he led. Do you think they will ever forget seeing him in such a spot? I do not think so. A grand old guy—he takes everything the younger men do. Sure, it hurts, but he keeps going."[11]

On September 21, Eleanor appeared in a *New York Times* photo holding the Congressional Medal of Honor, presented to her by Secretary of War Henry Stimson for Ted's "gallantry and intrepidity at the risk of his life above and beyond the call of duty" in the invasion of France. "Although the enemy had the beach under constant direct fire, Brigadier General Roosevelt moved from one locality to another, rallying men around him, directed and personally led them against the enemy. Under his seasoned, precise, calm and unfaltering leadership, assault troops reduced beach strongpoints and rapidly moved inland with minimum casualties. He thus contributed substantially to the successful establishment of the beachhead in France."[12]

Decades later, Omar Bradley—the very man who had determined Ted unworthy to continue his role with the 1st Infantry Division—summed up Roosevelt's service in a line that represents an impressive reevaluation: "I have never known a braver man nor a more devoted soldier."

THE LAST ROUGH RIDER

In 1959, author Cornelius Ryan published an immensely popular history of D-Day called *The Longest Day*, which included an account of Ted Roosevelt's heroics at Utah Beach among a host of other vignettes and incidents of that storied day. Three years later, Hollywood produced a movie based on the book that was among the largest and most expensive films undertaken up to that time. The part of Ted Roosevelt Jr. was not only deemed one of the most heroic in a long list of brave and courageous characters, but due to Ted's age and background, his portrayal needed to represent heroism in a particularly mature way. Legendary actor Henry Fonda was cast in the role. Who better than a leading man who'd made a career of playing morally upright American figures such as Tom Joad, Wyatt Earp, Mr. Roberts, and Abraham Lincoln?

But those who had actually known Ted could be forgiven for blinking their eyes a few times when they spotted the handsome, rangy, laconic Fonda, with the nasally Midwestern twang in his voice, stomping around Utah Beach, cane in hand, doing his best to mimic Ted on the big screen. Seeing Ted Roosevelt as something other than a rather stumpy man with a deeply lined face, wide grin, bashed nose, and full willingness to express himself in a brash foghorn voice was jarring. Whatever he was, Ted Roosevelt was no classic Hollywood leading man.

In the years after his death, assessments of Ted's life came to focus and, finally, narrow on his actions on D-Day. His Medal of Honor, his cane and his age when he went ashore at Utah Beach, the inspiration he provided the troops hitting the beaches and moving inland—these became the shorthand images of his life. The fact that Ted led a full and terrifically eventful life beyond this tends to get lost in the telling. Sure, he was a World War I hero, there in the thick of America's first action of the war at Cantigny, there at Soissons, and there in America's last action; sure, he held a cabinet position and was involved in one of the great political scandals of the age; sure, his political career took him near to the governor's seat in New York, the stepping-stone to the White House at the time; sure, he climbed the Himalayas and was, along with brother Kermit, the first Westerner to see a giant panda in the wild; and sure, he was a fine diplomat, writer, editor, and publisher; sure, he was a leading figure in national politics for twenty years; and sure, he made some monumental missteps, such as pledging allegiance to the America First cause. Before his heroics at Utah Beach, he had one of the most brilliant records of a combat general in World War II, four amphibious assaults, there on the front lines at Oran, El Guettar, the Tine, the beaches of Sicily, Troina, and in the mountains of Italy. Not a general in the European command didn't heap praise on his courage; not a GI who saw him in the field failed to appreciate his presence.

But what did he do in comparison to his father? Or his fifth cousin? Or, for that matter, Franklin's wife, Eleanor? Even his half sister, the fascinating Alice, or his tragic brothers, Kermit and Quentin? Ted grew up in a very crowded and interesting house.

The big three Roosevelts—Theodore, Franklin, and Eleanor—have rightfully come to dominate the story of the Roosevelt family. As large figures in American history, they steered the nation and molded America's future. When Ted's name arises in the context of the others, it is usually to suggest his failings in comparison to his loftier relatives. He is viewed as a not very gifted politician and less-than-inspired political leader; his character takes a beating, too. Theodore's biographer Edmund Morris describes Ted at age fifteen as "[having] all of his father's purposeful force, but imagination and intellect were denied him." He was "Small, nervous, grim, plug-ugly."[1]

But in a historical sense, Ted's life was not only central to a description of the roiling party politics of the twenties and thirties; it also defined one of the deep fissures that characterized that era: the split between the Oyster Bay and Hyde Park Roosevelts. The fact that the Hyde Park Roosevelts won the political battle tended to obscure Ted's role in it. As the years slid by and the importance of the fight was surmounted by far more important struggles, the squabbles of one extended family seemed just that: squabbles.

Ted was given the solace of a hero's death. But he had largely moved out of the realm of someone who mattered. As time passed, his story became a footnote in the family saga. A closer look at Ted's life, however, reveals a man who doesn't quite fit the characterizations of failure that have often been thrust upon him. While he did have many personal disappointments, a simple look at Ted's brilliant grin in photographs suggests that he was not a man who spent his life moping. He made a wonderful marriage to a loving and devoted wife; they made a loving family and had a large and fascinating circle of literary, military, journalistic, and entertaining friends. He not only died a hero, but also died much as he had hoped he would as a young boy taking a stab at poetry back in his Groton days: "Would God I might die my sword in my hand; My gilded spur on my heel/with my crested helmet on my head/and my body closed in steel."

Indeed, it could be argued that there were few more successful Roosevelts. Ted was the rock of Oyster Bay, the son who willingly stayed most dedicated to the traditions and the moral firmament of one of the nation's most notable families. He remained loyal to the concept of Americanism, no matter how mushy and contradictory that concept had become by the time of his death. He was undeniably old-fashioned, undeniably true, undeniably the last of his father's Rough Riders.

His reward was a relatively peaceful death and burial in Normandy. In 2001 his father was posthumously awarded a Medal of Honor for his heroism in Cuba in 1898, making him and Ted one of only two sets of fathers and sons, along with Arthur and Douglas MacArthur, to ever receive the nation's highest military honor.

Acknowledgments

I'd like to thank my agent, Farley Chase, who has been a wonderful adviser and book whisperer for many years; my editor at Berkley, Brent Howard, who has been a terrific guide through the creation of *His Father's Son*; the librarians in the Manuscript Division of the Library of Congress; researcher Sarah Shoenfeld; my Friday lunchmates/writer friends/therapists/career counselors; and most especially my wife, Susan, and kids, Sam and Hannah.

Bibliography

COLLECTIONS

Eleanor Butler Scrapbooks (designated LOC scrapbooks), Library of Congress, Manuscript Division.
Theodore Roosevelt (1887–1944) Papers, Manuscript Division, Library of Congress (designated LOC papers).
Theodore Roosevelt (1859–1919) Papers at the Library of Congress. Accessed via Theodore Roosevelt Digital Library, Dickinson State University, www .theodore rooseveltcenter.org (designated TRDL Roosevelt Digital Library).

BOOKS

Allen, Grover. *The Mammals of China and Mongolia*. New York: Museum of Natural History, 1938.
Ambrose, Stephen E. *D-Day, June 6, 1944: The Climactic Battle of World War II*. New York: Simon & Schuster, 1994.
Astor, Gerald. *Terrible Terry Allen: Combat General of World War II—The Life of an American Soldier*. Novato, Calif.: Presidio Press, 2003.
Atkinson, Rick. *An Army at Dawn: The War in North Africa, 1942–1943*. New York: Henry Holt, 2002.
———. *Day of Battle: The War in Sicily and Italy, 1943–1944*. New York: Henry Holt, 2007.
———. *The Guns at Last Light: The War in Europe, 1944–1945*. New York: Henry Holt, 2013.
Babcock, Robert O. *War Stories: Utah Beach to Pleiku*. Marietta, Ga.: Deeds Publishing, 2001.
Balkoski, Joseph. *Utah Beach: The Amphibious Landings and Airborne Operations on D-Day, June 6, 1944*. Mechanicsburg, Pa.: Stackpole Books, 2005.
Blumenson, Martin, ed. *The Patton Papers, 1940–1945*. Boston: Da Capo Press, 1972.
Bradley, Omar. *A Soldier's Story*. New York: Henry Holt, 1951.
Butler, Major Allen S. *The Operations of the 1st Infantry Division at El Guettar, 20–30 March 1943, Tunisian Campaign, 1949–1950*. Washington, D.C.: U.S. Army.
Center of Military History. Kasserine Pass Battles, Readings, Vol. 1, Part 2. Washington, D.C.: U.S. Army, 1944.

——. *Utah Beach to Cherbourg* (6 June 1944–27 June 1944). Washington, D.C.: U.S. Army, 1990.

Collier, Peter, with David Horowitz. *The Roosevelts: An American Saga*. New York: Touchstone, 1994.

Coolidge, Harold J., and Theodore Roosevelt [Jr.]. *Three Kingdoms of Indo-China*. New York: Thomas Y. Crowell, 1933.

Cordery, Stacy. *Alice: Alice Roosevelt Longworth, from American Princess to Washington Power Broker*. New York: Viking/Penguin Group, 2007.

Croke, Victoria. *Lady and the Panda: The True Adventures of the First American Explorer to Bring Back China's Most Exotic Animal*. New York: Random House, 2006.

Curtis, Sandra R. *Alice and Eleanor: A Contrast in Style and Purpose*. Madison: University of Wisconsin Press, 1994.

Davenport, Matthew. *First Over There: The Attack on Cantigny, America's First Battle of World War I*. New York: St. Martin's Press, 2015.

Donn, Linda. *The Roosevelt Cousins, Growing Up Together, 1882–1924*. New York: Alfred A. Knopf, 2001.

Hagedorn, Hermann. *The Roosevelt Family of Sagamore Hill*. New York: Macmillan, 1956.

Hambucken, Dennis. *American Soldier of WWII: D-Day, a Visual Reference*. Woodstock, Vt.: Countryman Press, 2013.

Howe, George. *Northwest Africa: Seizing the Initiative in the West*. Washington, D.C.: U.S. Army, 1956.

Jeffers, Paul. *Theodore Roosevelt, Jr.: Life of a War Hero*. Novato, Calif.: Presidio Press, 2002.

Kahn, Chief Warrant Officer E. J. Jr. and Technical Sergeant Henry McLemore. "Fighting Division, the 26th." Dec. 1945 (1st Division history). Waltham, Mass.: National Archives.

Kerr, Joan Paterson. *A Bully Father: Theodore Roosevelt's Letters to His Children*. New York: Random House, 1995.

Larson, Erik. *Dead Wake: The Last Crossing of the* Lusitania. New York: Crown, 2015.

Longworth, Alice Roosevelt. *Crowded Hours: Reminiscences of Alice Roosevelt Longworth*. New York: Charles Scribner's Sons, 1933.

Marshall, George Catlett. *Papers of George Catlett Marshall: "The Right Man for the Job," Dec. 7, 1941–May 31, 1943*. Vol. 3. Baltimore: Johns Hopkins University Press, 1991.

McCullough, David. *Mornings on Horseback: The Story of an Extraordinary Family, a Vanished Way of Life, and the Unique Child Who Became Theodore Roosevelt*. New York: Simon & Schuster, 1981.

Mencken, H. L. *A Carnival of Buncombe: H. L. Mencken at His Best on Politics*. Edited by Malcolm Moos. Baltimore: Johns Hopkins University Press, 1956.

Millard, Candice. *The River of Doubt: Theodore Roosevelt's Darkest Journey*. New York: Broadway Books, 2005.

Morris, Edmund. *Colonel Roosevelt*. New York: Random House, 2011.

——. *The Rise of Theodore Roosevelt*. New York: Coward, McCann & Geoghegan, 1979.

——. *Theodore Rex*. New York: Random House, 2001.

Morris, Sylvia Jukes. *Edith Kermit Roosevelt, Portrait of a First Lady.* New York: Coward, McCann & Geoghegan, 1980.

"Operations of the 1st Battalion, 18th Infantry at El Guettar, Tunisia, 17–25 March 1943" (1st Division report). Waltham, Mass.: National Archives.

Persons, Benjamin S. *Relieved of Command.* Manhattan, Kan.: Sunflower University Press, 1996.

Pringle, Henry. *Big Frogs.* New York: Vanguard, 1928.

Pyle, Ernie. *Here Is Your War.* New York: Henry Holt, 1943.

Reid, Bill. *Big Time Football at Harvard, 1905: The Diary of Coach Bill Reid.* Edited by Ronald A. Smith. Champagne-Urbana: University of Illinois Press, 1994.

Renehan, Edward J. Jr. *Lion's Pride: Theodore Roosevelt and His Family in Peace and War.* New York: Oxford University Press, 1998.

Riis, Jacob. *Theodore Roosevelt, the Citizen.* New York: Macmillan, 1912.

Roosevelt, Eleanor Butler Alexander. *Day Before Yesterday: The Reminiscences of Mrs. Theodore Roosevelt, Jr.* Garden City, N.Y.: Doubleday, 1959.

Roosevelt, Hall. *Odyssey of an American Family: An Account of the Roosevelts and Their Kin as Travelers, from 1613 to 1938.* New York: Harper & Brothers, 1939.

Roosevelt, Kermit. *War in the Garden of Eden.* New York: Charles Scribner's Sons, 1919.

Roosevelt, Theodore. *The Rough Riders.* New York: Charles Scribner's Sons, 1919.

——. *Theodore Roosevelt: An Autobiography.* New York: Macmillan, 1913.

Roosevelt, Theodore [Jr.]. *All in the Family.* New York: G. P. Putnam's Sons, 1929.

——. *Average Americans.* New York: G. P. Putnam's Sons, 1920.

——. *Rank and File: True Stories of the Great War.* New York: Charles Scribner's Sons, 1928.

Roosevelt, Theodore [Jr.], and Kermit Roosevelt. *East of the Sun and West of the Moon.* New York: Charles Scribner's Sons, 1926.

——. *Trailing the Giant Panda.* New York: Charles Scribner's Sons, 1929.

Ryan, Cornelius. *The Longest Day.* New York: Simon & Schuster, 1959.

Samuels, Peggy, and Harold Samuels. *Teddy Roosevelt at San Juan: The Making of a President.* College Station: Texas A&M University Press, 1997.

Schaller, George. *The Last Panda.* Chicago: University of Chicago Press, 1993.

"Sicily: First Breach in the Axis Fortress of Europe." *S-1 Journal,* 26th Infantry Regimental Combat Team (1st Division report CD 1).

Slotkin, Richard. *Lost Battalions: The Great War and the Crisis of American Nationality.* New York: Henry Holt, 2005.

Smith, Maj. Edwin K. Jr., Staff Department, Infantry School. "Operation of the Anti-Tank Platoon 2nd BB, 26 INF, 1st Div, at El Ancor 8–11 November 1942, 1949–1950" (1st Division history), pp. 11–17. Waltham, Mass.: National Archives.

Walker, Dale. *The Boys of 98: Theodore Roosevelt and the Rough Riders.* New York: Tom Doherty Associates, 1998.

Walker, Robert. *The Namesake: The Biography of Theodore Roosevelt, Jr.* New York: Brick Tower Press, 2004.

Ward, Geoffrey. *A First Class Temperament: The Emergence of Franklin Delano Roosevelt.* New York: Harper & Row, 1989.

Wead, Doug. *All the President's Children: Triumph and Tragedy in the Lives of America's First Families.* New York: Atria Books, 2003.

Weingartner, Steven, ed. *Blue Spaders: The 26th Infantry Regiment, 1917–1967.* Wheaton, Ill.: Cantigny First Division Foundation, 1996.

Wheat, George Seay. *The Story of the American Legion.* New York: G. P. Putnam's Sons, 1919.

Zacks, Richard. *Island of Vice: Theodore Roosevelt's Doomed Quest to Clean Up Sin-Loving New York.* New York: Anchor Books, 2012.

JOURNALS, NEWSPAPERS, WEB SITES

Boy's Life, Aug. 1946, "Ted Roosevelt, Scouter Hero."
Brooklyn Sun, Apr. 11, 1919.
Chicago Tribune, Apr. 19, 1926.
Collier's, Oct.–Dec. 1905.
Discover Wildlife, Nov. 2011.
Firstdivisionmuseum.org.
HistoryNet, Alex Kershaw, "From D-Day to Paris," Apr. 4, 2012.
Ladies' Home Journal, Jacob Riis, Aug. 1902, p. 6.
Los Angeles Times, Aug. 1919.
——, Oct. 1940.
Natural History Magazine, Nov. 2011.
New Orleans Item, Apr. 14, 1919.
New Yorker, A. J. Liebling, May 1, 1943, p. 27.
——, July 29, 1944.
New York Evening Mail, May 11, 1919.
New York Sun, Apr. 11, 1919.
New York Times, Sept. 25, 1905.
——, Oct. 9, 1905.
——, Oct. 30, 1905.
——, Nov. 17, 1905.
——, Nov. 18, 1905.
——, Jan. 6, 1906.
——, Sept. 27, 1908.
——, July 17, 1918.
——, July 20, 1918.
——, Jan. 7, 1919.
——, Jan. 8, 1919.
——, Apr. 7, 1919.
——, Apr. 10, 1919.
——, Sept. 6, 1920.
——, May 24, 1922.
——, Mar. 15, 1924.
——, Sept. 23, 1924.
——, Sept. 24, 1924.

———, Sept. 25, 1924.

———, Nov. 2, 1924.

———, Feb. 22, 1939.

———, Nov. 11, 1939.

———, Jan. 29, 1940.

———, Apr. 21, 1941.

———, July 14, 1944.

———, Sept. 21, 1944.

Philadelphia Record, Apr. 10, 1919.

Science, May 1, 1925, p. 461.

The Smart Set: A Magazine of Cleverness 61, "Roosevelt and Others."

Time, Sept. 12, 1932.

Washington Post, Oct. 29, 1905.

———, Nov. 2, 1905.

———, Nov. 18, 1905.

Wilmington (Del.) Sunday Morning Star, May 2, 1926.

Notes

PROLOGUE: THE CROWDED HOUR

1 Hagedorn, *Roosevelt Family*, p. 50.
2 Ibid., p. 51.
3 Collier with Horowitz, *Roosevelts*, p. 77.
4 Sylvia Jukes Morris, *Edith Kermit Roosevelt*, p. 173.
5 The family doctor ultimately suggested these headaches might be due to stresses Theodore was placing on his son; the fact that his father was heading off to war could not have helped either.
6 Collier with Horowitz, *Roosevelts*, p. 94.
7 Samuels and Samuels, *Teddy Roosevelt at San Juan*, p. 203.
8 Theodore Roosevelt, *Rough Riders*, p. 116.
9 Ibid., p. 120.
10 Ibid., p. 122.
11 Ibid., p. 124.
12 Ibid., p. 126.
13 Ibid., p. 128.
14 Walker, *Boys of 98*, p. 214.
15 Samuels and Samuels, *Teddy Roosevelt*, p. 288.
16 Walker, *Boys of 98*, p. 214.
17 Samuels and Samuels, *Teddy Roosevelt*, p. 298.
18 Hagedorn, *Roosevelt Family*, pp. 63–64.

CHAPTER ONE: ALL IN THE FAMILY

1 Theodore Roosevelt [Jr.], *All in the Family*, p. 6.
2 Ibid.
3 Theodore Roosevelt [Jr.], *Average Americans*, p. 1.
4 Ibid., p. 3.
5 Theodore Roosevelt [Jr.], *All in the Family*, p. 172.
6 Renehan, *Lion's Pride*, p. 66.
7 Collier with Horowitz, *Roosevelts*, p. 22.
8 Ibid., p. 127.
9 Ibid.
10 Jacob Riis, *Ladies' Home Journal*, Aug. 1902, p. 6.
11 Eleanor Butler Alexander Roosevelt, *Day Before Yesterday*, p. 42.
12 Linda Donn, *Roosevelt Cousins*, p. 48.
13 Hagedorn, *Roosevelt Family*, p. 47.
14 Ibid., p. 46.
15 Ibid., p. 33.

16 Theodore Roosevelt (1887–1944) Papers, Theodore Roosevelt Jr. to Eleanor Roosevelt, Box 30, Sept. 10, 1924.

CHAPTER TWO: FIRST BOY

1 Hagedorn, *Roosevelt Family*, pp. 97–98.
2 Theodore Roosevelt (1859–1919) Papers at the Library of Congress, Theodore Roosevelt to Edward Martin, Nov. 1900.
3 Ibid., p. 98.
4 Ibid., p. 106.
5 Ibid.
6 Riis, *Ladies' Home Journal*, p. 6.
7 Library of Congress, scrapbooks documenting the families of Theodore Roosevelt Jr. and Eleanor Butler Alexander Roosevelt, online catalog, pp. 53–54.
8 LOC scrapbooks, pp. 54–55. Details of Ted's illness are collected in the Eleanor Roosevelt scrapbook, which features clippings from an assortment of newspapers.
9 Riis, *Ladies' Home Journal*, p. 7.
10 Ibid.
11 Ibid., p. 6.
12 LOC Box 7, Seth Bullock to TR, Oct. 23, 1903.
13 LOC Box 8, TR Jr. to TR, Sept. 1903.
14 LOC Box 7, TR to TR Jr., Oct. 4, 1903.
15 Ibid.
16 LOC Box 7, TR to TR Jr., Nov. 28, 1903.
17 LOC Box 7, TR to Coubertin, 1903.
18 LOC Box 7, TR to TR Jr., Jan. 11, 1904.
19 TRDL, TR to Kermit Roosevelt, Feb. 11, 1915.
20 Curtis, *Alice and Eleanor*, p. 64.

CHAPTER THREE: LEFT END

1 *New York Times*, Sept. 25, 1905.
2 Ibid., Nov. 17, 1905.
3 Ibid., Oct. 9, 1905.
4 *Washington Post*, Oct. 29, 1905.
5 *New York Times*, Oct. 30, 1905.
6 LOC Box 8, TR Jr. to TR, 1904.
7 LOC Box 7, TR to TR Jr., Oct. 2, 1905.
8 *Collier's*, Oct.–Dec. 1905.
9 *New York Times*, Oct. 9, 1905.
10 Ibid.
11 Ibid.
12 Ibid.
13 Reid, *Big Time Football*.
14 *New York Times*, Nov. 18, 1905.
15 *Washington Post*, Nov. 18, 1905.
16 *New York Times*, Nov. 18, 1905.
17 *Washington Post*, Nov. 18, 1905.
18 LOC Box 8, TR Jr. to Edith Roosevelt, Nov. 21, 1905.

CHAPTER FOUR: COMMENCEMENT

1 Curtis, *Alice and Eleanor*, pp. 66–74.
2 *Washington Post*, Nov. 2, 1905.

3 Ibid., Dec. 10, 1905.

4 *New York Times*, Jan. 6, 1906.

5 TRDL, TR to Kermit Roosevelt, Mar. 11, 1906.

6 TRDL, TR to KR, Apr. 18, 1906.

7 TRDL, TR to KR, Apr. 22, 1906.

8 TRDL, TR to KR, Apr. 18, 1906.

9 TRDL, TR to KR, Oct. 7, 1906.

10 Ibid.

11 LOC Box 8, TR Jr. to Greenway, 1907, Arizona Historical Society.

12 Jeffers, *Theodore Roosevelt, Jr.*, p. 62.

13 Ibid.

14 TRDL, TR to KR, Mar. 15, 1908.

15 Edmund Morris, *Theodore Rex*, p. 524.

16 *New York Times*, Sept. 27, 1908.

17 Eleanor Butler Alexander Roosevelt, *Day Before Yesterday*, p. 45.

18 Collier with Horowitz, *Roosevelts*, p. 161.

CHAPTER FIVE: LOVE AND MARRIAGE

1 Eleanor Butler Alexander Roosevelt, *Day Before Yesterday*, p. 11.

2 Ibid., p. 35.

3 Ibid., p. 36.

4 Ibid., p. 14.

5 LOC Box 8, TR Jr. to TR, 1910.

6 LOC scrapbooks, *Fort Worth Register*, Mar. 25, 1910.

7 Ibid.

8 Eleanor Butler Alexander Roosevelt, *Day Before Yesterday*, p. 50.

9 Ibid.

10 LOC. Details of the wedding come from unattributed clippings of pages of Eleanor's scrapbook.

11 Eleanor Butler Alexander Roosevelt, *Day Before Yesterday*, p. 52.

12 LOC Box 8, TR Jr. to TR, Oct. 1910.

13 Ibid.

14 LOC scrapbooks, *San Francisco Chronicle*, Mar. 1912.

15 Eleanor Butler Alexander Roosevelt, *Day Before Yesterday*, p. 60.

16 LOC scrapbooks, *San Francisco Examiner*, Mar. 22, 1912.

17 Sylvia Jukes Morris, *Edith Kermit Roosevelt*, pp. 386–87.

18 Eleanor Butler Alexander Roosevelt, *Day Before Yesterday*, pp. 61–62.

19 Collier with Horowitz, *Roosevelts*, p. 181.

20 LOC Box 7, TR to TR Jr., Sept. 22, 1911.

21 Collier with Horowitz, *Roosevelts*, p. 185.

22 TRDL, TR to KR, June 23, 1913.

23 Millard, *River of Doubt*, p. 337.

CHAPTER SIX: PLATTSBURGH

1 Larson, *Dead Wake*, p. 249.

2 Ibid., p. 302.

3 Renehan, *Lion's Pride*, p. 101; Edmund Morris, *Colonel Roosevelt*, p. 419.

4 LOC Box 8, TR Jr. to KR, May 29, 1915.

5 Slotkin, *Lost Battalions*, p. 26.

6 Theodore Roosevelt [Jr.], *Average Americans*, p. 6.

7 Eleanor Butler Alexander Roosevelt, *Day Before Yesterday*, p. 65.

8 Collier with Horowitz, *Roosevelts*, p. 184; TRDL, TR to KR, Nov. 10, 1916.

9 Ibid., p. 10.

10 LOC Box 8, TR Jr. to KR, July 21, 1915.

11 Ward, *First Class Temperament*, p. 346; Collier with Horowitz, *Roosevelts*, p. 194.

12 Kermit went off to Plattsburgh for training, hoping to catch up with Archie and Ted but subsequently accepted an offer from General Maude, commander of British forces in Mesopotamia, to serve in the Middle East. Already established as the Roosevelt boy with the greatest sense of wanderlust, the appointment in the Middle East seemed to suit his sense of adventure. Plans were made for his wife, Belle, whose father, Willard, was the U.S. ambassador to Spain, to spend the war there. To round out the Roosevelt family volunteers for duty, Dr. Richard Derby, husband of Ethel, signed up for service in the Medical Officers' Reserve Corps and would soon find himself in Europe with Ted and Archie. Nick Longworth was too old to be of service, to say nothing of his leadership role in the U.S. Congress.

13 Collier with Horowitz, *Roosevelts*, p. 203.

CHAPTER SEVEN: OVER THERE

1 LOC Box 8, TR Jr. to TR, July 20, 1917.

2 LOC Box 39, Charles Ridgeley testimonial, 1924.

3 TRDL, TR to Archibald Roosevelt, Aug. 8, 1917.

4 Weingartner, ed., *Blue Spaders*, p. 10.

5 Theodore Roosevelt [Jr.], *Average Americans*, p. 74.

6 Ibid., p. 76.

7 Weingartner, ed., *Blue Spaders*, p. 13.

8 *New York Tribune*, Jan. 2, 1918.

9 LOC, Ridgeley testimonial, 1924.

10 TRDL, TR to Anna Roosevelt Cowles, Dec. 31, 1917.

11 TRDL, TR to Archibald Roosevelt, Dec. 10, 1917.

12 Theodore Roosevelt [Jr.], *Average Americans*, p. 102.

13 TRDL, TR to Archibald Roosevelt, Jan. 10, 1918.

14 TRDL, TR to KR, Jan. 27, 1918.

15 TRDL, Quentin Roosevelt to TR, Jan. 1918.

16 Theodore Roosevelt [Jr.], *Average Americans*, p. 93.

17 Ibid., p. 109.

18 Davenport, *First Over There*, p. 72.

19 LOC Box 8, TR Jr. to TR, Mar. 1918.

CHAPTER EIGHT: CANTIGNY

1 Davenport, *First Over There*, pp. 79–80.

2 Theodore Roosevelt [Jr.], *Average Americans*, p. 126.

3 Ibid., p. 122.

4 Weingartner, ed., *Blue Spaders*, p. 22.

5 Davenport, *First Over There*, p. 140.

6 Theodore Roosevelt [Jr.], *Average Americans*, pp. 134–35.

7 LOC, Ridgeley testimonial, 1924.

CHAPTER NINE: QUENTIN

1 *New York Times*, June 24, 1918.

2 LOC Box 8, TR to TR Jr., June 1918.

3 McCullough, *Mornings on Horseback*, p. 15.

4 LOC Box 8, TR [Jr.] to TR, July 1918.

5 Weingartner, ed., *Blue Spaders*, p. 25.

6 Theodore Roosevelt Jr., *Average Americans*, pp. 149–50.

7 Weingartner, ed., *Blue Spaders*, pp. 27–28.

8 TRDL, Quentin Roosevelt to Flora Whitney, July 1918.

9 TRDL, TR to Quentin Roosevelt, July 11, 1918.

10 Edmund Morris, *Colonel Roosevelt*, p. 527.

11 *New York Times*, July 17, 1918.

12 Ibid., July 20, 1918.

13 Renehan, *Lion's Pride*, p. 7.

CHAPTER TEN: SOISSONS

1 Theodore Roosevelt [Jr.], *Average Americans*, pp. 163–64.

2 Ibid., p. 165.

3 Ibid., p. 170.

4 Ibid., p. 171.

5 Ibid., p. 172.

6 LOC, Ridgeley testimonial, 1924.

7 Ibid.

CHAPTER ELEVEN: THE COST OF WAR

1 Theodore Roosevelt [Jr.], *Average Americans*, p. 173.

2 Weingartner, ed., *Blue Spaders*, p. 44.

3 Ibid., p. 41.

4 Theodore Roosevelt [Jr.], *Average Americans*, p. 178; Weingartner, ed., *Blue Spaders*, p. 44.

5 Collier with Horowitz, *Roosevelts*, pp. 233–34.

6 Ibid., p. 236.

7 LOC Box 8, TR Jr. to TR, Aug. 9, 1918.

8 Weingartner, ed., *Blue Spaders*, p. 45.

9 Collier with Horowitz, *Roosevelts*, p. 234.

10 Ibid.

CHAPTER TWELVE: ARMISTICE

1 Renehan, *Lion's Pride*, pp. 210–11.

2 LOC Box 29, George Marshall to TR Jr., July 1920.

3 Theodore Roosevelt [Jr.], *Average Americans*, p. 205.

4 LOC, Ridgeley testimonial, 1924.

5 Theodore Roosevelt [Jr.], *Average Americans*, p. 207.

6 Ibid.

7 Ibid., p. 209.

8 Ibid., p. 213.

9 Ibid., pp. 213–15.

CHAPTER THIRTEEN: NEWS FROM SAGAMORE HILL

1 Edmund Morris, *Colonel Roosevelt*, p. 546.

2 Ibid., p. 548.

3 *Day Before Yesterday*, p. 118.

4 Theodore Roosevelt [Jr.], *Average Americans*, p. 221.

5 LOC Box 4, Edith Roosevelt to TR Jr., Jan. 12, 1919.

6 *New York Times*, Jan. 7, 1919.

7 Ibid., Jan. 8, 1919.

8 Ibid.

CHAPTER FOURTEEN: LEGIONS

1 LOC Box 36, Theodore Roosevelt Jr., "Founding of the American Legion," 1919.
2 Ibid.
3 *New York Times*, Apr. 7, 1919.
4 Ibid., Apr. 10, 1919.
5 Wheat, *Story of the American Legion*, p. 58.
6 *New York Evening Mail*, May 11, 1919.

CHAPTER FIFTEEN: AMERICANISM

1 *Los Angeles Times*, Aug. 1919.
2 Theodore Roosevelt [Jr.], *Average Americans*, pp. 234–52.
3 Eleanor Butler Alexander Roosevelt, *Day Before Yesterday*, p. 125.
4 Pringle, *Big Frogs*, p. 252.

CHAPTER SIXTEEN: RIVALS

1 Collier with Horowitz, *Roosevelts*, p. 270.
2 Ibid., p. 220.
3 Curtis, *Alice and Eleanor*, p. 163.
4 *New York Times*, Sept. 6, 1920; Collier with Horowitz, *Roosevelts*, p. 260.
5 Curtis, *Alice and Eleanor*, pp. 163–64; Collier with Horowitz, *Roosevelts*, p. 260.
6 Curtis, *Alice and Eleanor*, p. 163.

CHAPTER SEVENTEEN: WASHINGTON

1 Eleanor Butler Alexander Roosevelt, *Day Before Yesterday*, p. 131.
2 Collier with Horowitz, *Roosevelts*, p. 259.
3 LOC Boxes 1–2, TR Jr., Assistant Secretary of Navy diary, p. 16.
4 LOC Box 1, TR Jr. Department of Navy diary, p. 373.
5 Eleanor Butler Alexander Roosevelt, *Day Before Yesterday*, p. 147.
6 Collier with Horowitz, *Roosevelts*, p. 281.
7 *New York Times*, May 24, 1922.
8 Ibid.
9 Eleanor Butler Alexander Roosevelt, *Day Before Yesterday*, pp. 147–58; Eleanor covers the whole of the Teapot Dome scandal, pp. 147–58.
10 Curtis, *Alice and Eleanor*, p. 169.
11 LOC Boxes 1–2, TR Jr. diary, Aug. 3, 1923.
12 Ibid., Sept. 24, 1923.
13 Eleanor Butler Alexander Roosevelt, *Day Before Yesterday*, p. 154.
14 Ibid.
15 *New York Times*, Mar. 15, 1924.
16 Eleanor Butler Alexander Roosevelt, *Day Before Yesterday*, p. 186.
17 Ibid., p. 157.
18 Ibid., p. 158.
19 Collier with Horowitz, *Roosevelts*, p. 290.
20 Pringle, *Big Frogs*, p. 243.
21 LOC Boxes 1–2, TR Jr. diary, summary of 1924 Republican National Convention.
22 LOC Boxes 1–2, TR Jr. diary, Aug. 27, 1924.

CHAPTER EIGHTEEN: WHO TOLD ME THAT?

1 LOC Boxes 1–2, TR Jr. diary, Aug. 28, 1924.
2 Pringle, *Big Frogs*, p. 244.

3 *New York Times*, Sept. 23 and 24, 1924.
4 Pringle, *Big Frogs*, p. 240.
5 *New York Times*, Sept. 25, 1924.
6 Pringle, *Big Frogs*, p. 245.
7 Eleanor Butler Alexander Roosevelt, *Day Before Yesterday*, p. 163.
8 Collier with Horowitz, *Roosevelts*, p. 298.
9 Pringle, *Big Frogs*, p. 247.
10 *New York Times*, Nov. 2, 1924.
11 LOC Box 37, George Marshall to TR Jr., Nov. 10, 1924; TR Jr. to Marshall, Jan. 2, 1925.

CHAPTER NINETEEN: POLITICAL ANIMALS

1 Eleanor Butler Alexander Roosevelt, *Day Before Yesterday*, p. 167.
2 Cutting would achieve fame in his own right as the first Westerner to enter the forbidden city of Lhasa in Tibet, in 1937.
3 *Science*, May 1, 1925, p. 461.
4 Theodore Roosevelt [Jr.] and Kermit Roosevelt, *East of the Sun*, p. 11.
5 Ibid., p. 14.
6 Ibid., p. 53.
7 Ibid., p. 56.
8 Ibid., p. 62.
9 Ibid., p. 111.
10 Ibid., p. 144.
11 Ibid., p. 222.
12 Ibid., p. 228.
13 Ibid., p. 243.
14 LOC Box 50, Eleanor Roosevelt, "We Go Hunting in Kashmir," 1926.
15 Ibid.
16 W. P. Montague Jr., *Wilmington (Del.) Sunday Morning Star*, May 2, 1926.
17 *Chicago Tribune*, Apr. 19, 1926.
18 Eleanor Butler Alexander Roosevelt, *Day Before Yesterday*, p. 206.

CHAPTER TWENTY: OFF THE MAP

1 Pringle, *Big Frogs*, p. 240.
2 Ibid., p. 241.
3 Collier with Horowitz, *Roosevelts*, p. 308.
4 Ibid., p. 323.
5 Theodore Roosevelt [Jr.] and Kermit Roosevelt, *Trailing the Giant Panda*, pp. 1–2.
6 Ibid., p. 2.
7 Grover Allen, *Mammals of China and Mongolia*, p. 323.
8 Henry Nicholls, *Discover Wildlife*, Nov. 2011.
9 George Schaller, *Last Panda*, p. 47; Schaller says that the Roosevelts were the first Westerners to see the gaint panda in the wild, in 1929.

CHAPTER TWENTY-ONE: GIANT PANDAS

1 Theodore Roosevelt [Jr.] and Kermit Roosevelt, *Trailing the Giant Panda*, p. 32.
2 Ibid., p. 54.
3 Ibid., p. 57.
4 Ibid., p. 91.
5 Ibid., p. 103.
6 Ibid., p. 176.
7 Ibid., p. 185.

8 Eleanor Butler Alexander Roosevelt, *Day Before Yesterday* (according to Eleanor, this advice came from the famed explorer Roy Chapman Andrews), p. 218.

9 Theodore Roosevelt [Jr.] and Kermit Roosevelt, *East of the Sun* (the reference is to the pine trees in the Tian Shan Mountains), p. 219.

10 Karl Malcolm, *Natural History*, Nov. 2011.

11 Theodore Roosevelt [Jr.] and Kermit Roosevelt, *East of the Sun*, p. 221.

12 Victoria Croke, *Lady and the Panda*, p. 171.

CHAPTER TWENTY-TWO: THE WRONG ROOSEVELT

1 Collier with Horowitz, *Roosevelts*, p. 325.

2 Ibid., p. 332.

3 Eleanor Butler Alexander Roosevelt, *Day Before Yesterday*, p. 239.

4 *New York Times, Macon Telegraph*, quoted in *Day Before Yesterday*, pp. 248–49.

5 Collier with Horowitz, *Roosevelts*, p. 331.

6 Ibid.

7 Eleanor Butler Alexander Roosevelt, *Day Before Yesterday*, p. 278.

8 Ibid.

9 Collier with Horowitz, *Roosevelts*, p. 333.

10 *Time*, Sept. 12, 1932.

11 Ibid.

12 Ibid.

13 Collier with Horowitz, *Roosevelts*, p. 334.

14 Ibid., p. 335.

15 Eleanor Butler Alexander Roosevelt, *Day Before Yesterday*, p. 302.

CHAPTER TWENTY-THREE: FIFTH COUSIN TO THE PRESIDENT

1 Eleanor Butler Alexander Roosevelt, *Day Before Yesterday*, p. 367.

2 Ibid., p. 368.

3 Ibid., p. 369.

4 LOC Box 28, Felix Frankfurter to TR Jr., Nov. 26, 1938.

5 LOC Box 28, Harpo Marx to TR Jr., Nov. 4, 1940.

6 LOC Box 36, Baseball Team, June 9, 1938.

7 LOC Box 30, TR Jr. to George Herman Ruth, June 1, 1938.

8 LOC Box 30, Lowell Thomas to TR Jr., Aug. 1938.

9 *New York Times*, Feb. 22, 1939.

10 Eleanor Butler Alexander Roosevelt, *Day Before Yesterday*, p. 423.

CHAPTER TWENTY-FOUR: AMERICA FIRST

1 "Meddling Abroad Hit by Col. T. Roosevelt," *New York Times*, Nov. 11, 1939.

2 *New York Times*, Jan. 29, 1940.

3 *Los Angeles Times*, Oct. 1940.

4 Renehan, *Lion's Pride*, p. 230.

5 LOC Box 3, TR Jr. to Cornelius Roosevelt, Jan. 29, 1941.

6 Ibid.

7 Ibid., Mar. 14, 1941.

8 LOC Box 3, TR Jr. to Archie Roosevelt, Apr. 9, 1941.

9 LOC Box 5, Eleanor Roosevelt to Cornelius Roosevelt, Apr. 1941.

10 *New York Times*, Apr. 21, 1941.

CHAPTER TWENTY-FIVE: OUR COUNTRY, OUR CAUSE, OUR PRESIDENT

1 Kahn and McLemore, "Fighting Division, the 26th," pp. 33–35.
2 Eleanor Butler Alexander Roosevelt, *Day Before Yesterday*, p. 420.
3 LOC Box 4, TR Jr. to Edith Roosevelt, Dec. 1941.
4 Ibid.
5 LOC Box 29, Marshall to TR Jr., Dec. 22, 1941.
6 LOC Box 30, FDR to TR Jr., May 20, 1939.
7 International News Service, Dec. 22, 1941.
8 Marshall, *Papers of George Catlett Marshall*, vol. 3; to Brigadier General Terry de la M. Allen from George C. Marshall, June 5, 1942.
9 LOC Box 9, TR Jr. to Eleanor Butler Alexander Roosevelt [ER], multipart letter, July 16, 1942.
10 Ibid.
11 Gerald Astor, *Terrible Terry Allen*, p. 102.

CHAPTER TWENTY-SIX: TORCH

1 LOC Box 9, TR Jr. to ER, Oct. 26, 1942.
2 Ibid.
3 Atkinson, *An Army at Dawn*, pp. 79–80.
4 LOC Box 9, TR Jr. to ER, Nov. 5, 1942.
5 Atkinson, *Army at Dawn*, pp. 74–78.
6 Smith, "Operation of the Anti-Tank Platoon," pp. 11–17.
7 LOC Box 9, TR Jr. to ER, Nov. 5, 1942.
8 Atkinson, *Army at Dawn*, p. 86.
9 Howe, *Northwest Africa*, p. 217.
10 LOC Box 9, TR Jr. to ER, Nov. 5, 1942.
11 Howe, *Northwest Africa*, p. 227.

CHAPTER TWENTY-SEVEN: DESERT

1 LOC Box 9, TR Jr. to ER, Nov. 1942.
2 Pyle, *Here Is Your War*, p. 46.
3 LOC Box 9, TR Jr. to ER, Nov. 18, 1942.
4 Ibid., Nov. 27, 1942.
5 Atkinson, *Army at Dawn*, pp. 259–60.
6 LOC Box 10, TR Jr. to ER, Nov. 26, 1942; see also memo attached to Maxwell Hamilton article in *Human Events*, LOC TR Jr. papers.
7 A copy of this memorandum was kept at Oyster Bay for many years after, as proof that it existed.
8 LOC Box 10, TR Jr. to ER, Jan. 4, 1943.
9 LOC Box 39, TR Jr. World War II record, Terry Allen to Dwight D. Eisenhower, Feb. 9, 1943.
10 LOC Box 10, TR Jr. to ER, Feb. 1943.
11 Ibid., Jan. 1943.
12 Ibid., Feb. 13, 1943.
13 Ibid., Feb. 24, 1943.
14 Ibid.
15 Bradley, *Soldier's Story*, p. 43.
16 Astor, *Terrible Terry Allen*, pp. 162–63.
17 LOC Box 10, TR Jr. to ER, Mar. 6, 1943.
18 Ibid., Mar. 2, 1943.

19 Ibid., Mar. 3, 1943.
20 Liebling, *New Yorker*, May 1, 1943, p. 27.
21 Bradley, *Soldier's Story*, pp. 110–11.

CHAPTER TWENTY-EIGHT: A BATTLE PLAYED AT MY FEET

1 "Operations of 1st Battalion, 18th Infantry, report CD 1."
2 LOC Box 10, TR Jr. to ER, Mar. 25, 1943.
3 Ibid., Apr. 11, 1943.
4 Ibid., Mar. 25, 1943.
5 Atkinson, *Army at Dawn*, p. 440.
6 LOC Box 10, TR Jr. to ER, Apr. 11, 1943.
7 Liebling, *New Yorker*, May 1, 1943, p. 27.
8 LOC Box 10, TR Jr. to ER, Oct. 25, 1943.
9 Ibid., Apr. 11, 1943.
10 Ibid.
11 LOC Box 39, TR Jr. World War II papers, Apr. 12, 1943, headquarters, 1st U.S. Infantry Division.
12 Liebling, *New Yorker*, May 1, 1943, p. 28.
13 LOC Box 10, TR Jr. to ER, Mar. 25, 1943.

CHAPTER TWENTY-NINE: THE TINE

1 "Operations of the 1st Infantry Division at Mateur, Tunisia, Apr. 23–May 3, 1943," p. 7 (CD 1).
2 LOC Box 10, TR Jr. to Edith Roosevelt, Apr. 19, 1943.
3 LOC Box 10, TR Jr. to ER, Apr. 21, 1943.
4 Ibid., Apr. 27, 1943.
5 The reference is to an Oliver Wendell Holmes poem about an old one-horse shay built to last by a deacon "so it wouldn't break down." In fact the shay does last a hundred years, only to fall completely apart in the middle of an earthquake.
6 Astor, *Terrible Terry Allen*, p. 177.
7 Ibid., p. 176.
8 Astor, *Terrible Terry Allen*, p. 184 (author sources Merle Miller, writing for *Yank*).
9 Bradley, *Soldier's Story*, p. 111.

CHAPTER THIRTY: KERMIT

1 LOC Box 10, TR Jr. to ER, July 2, 1943.
2 Ibid., May 26, 1943.
3 Renehan, *Lion's Pride*, pp. 229–32.

CHAPTER THIRTY-ONE: SICILY

1 LOC Box 10, TR Jr. to ER, July 7, 1943.
2 "Sicily: First Breach in the Axis Fortress of Europe," *S-1 Journal*, 26th Infantry Regimental Combat Team (1st Division Report CD 1), p. 7.
3 Ibid., p. 19.
4 Ibid.
5 Ibid.
6 Bradley, *Soldier's Story*, p. 130.
7 "Sicily: First Breach," p. 30.
8 LOC Box 10, TR Jr. to ER, July 17, 1943.
9 Ibid.
10 Bradley, *Soldier's Story*, p. 154.
11 Ibid., p. 155.

12 Ibid.
13 Blumenson, ed., *Patton Papers*, pp. 303, 309.
14 "Sicily: First Breach," p. 97.
15 Ibid., pp. 97–98.

CHAPTER THIRTY-TWO: EXILE

1 Blumenson, ed., *Patton Papers*, p. 313.
2 LOC Box 10, TR Jr. to ER, Aug. 6, 1943.
3 Ibid., Aug. 19, 1943.
4 Ibid., Sept. 6, 1943.
5 Ibid., Jan. 1944.
6 LOC Box 10, TR Jr. to Omar Bradley, Jan. 1944.
7 LOC Box 10, Bradley to TR Jr., Feb. 1944.
8 LOC Box 10, TR Jr. to ER, Feb. 1944.
9 Eleanor Butler Alexander Roosevelt, *Day Before Yesterday*, p. 450.
10 LOC Box 10, TR Jr. to ER, Feb. 28, 1944.
11 Ibid.

CHAPTER THIRTY-THREE: NOWHERE ELSE TO BE

1 LOC Box 10, TR Jr. to ER, Mar. 27, 1944.
2 Ibid., Mar. 31, 1944.
3 Eleanor Butler Alexander Roosevelt, *Day Before Yesterday*, p. 452.
4 LOC Box 10, TR Jr. to ER, May 13, 1944.
5 Balkoski, *Utah Beach*, pp. 81–83.
6 LOC Box 10, TR Jr. to ER, Apr. 28, 1944.
7 Ibid., May 30, 1944.

CHAPTER THIRTY-FOUR: THE DELECTABLE MOUNTAINS

1 Balkoski, *Utah Beach*, p. 91.
2 Ibid., p. 92.
3 Ambrose, *D-Day*, p. 168.
4 LOC Box 10, TR Jr. to ER, June 3, 1944.
5 Ibid.
6 Balkoski, *Utah Beach*, p. 202.
7 LOC Box 10, TR Jr. to ER, June 3–5, 1944.

CHAPTER THIRTY-FIVE: "SEE YOU ON THE BEACH"

1 Ambrose, *D-Day*, p. 258.
2 LOC Box 10, TR Jr. to ER, June 3–6, 1944.
3 Balkoski, *Utah Beach*, p. 204.
4 Babcock, *War Stories*, p. 97.
5 Atkinson, *Guns at Last Light*, p. 59; Babcock, *War Stories*, p. 97.
6 Ryan, *Longest Day*, p. 133.
7 Balkoski, *Utah Beach*, p. 110.
8 LOC Box 10, TR Jr. to ER, June 11, 1944.
9 Ibid.
10 Ibid.
11 Ibid.
12 Ambrose, *D-Day*, p. 279.
13 Balkoski, *Utah Beach*, p. 211.

14 Babcock, *War Stories*, pp. 96–103.

15 Ibid., p. 54.

16 Ibid., p. 83.

17 Ibid., p. 68.

18 Ibid., p. 88.

19 Balkoski, *Utah Beach*, p. 242.

20 Ibid., p. 246.

21 Ryan, *Longest Day*, p. 261.

22 LOC Box 10, TR Jr. to ER, June 11, 1944.

CHAPTER THIRTY-SIX: OLD SOLDIERS NEVER DIE

1 LOC Box 10, TR Jr. to ER, June 11, 1944.

2 Eleanor Butler Alexander Roosevelt, *Day Before Yesterday*, p. 456.

3 LOC Box 10, TR Jr. to ER, July 10, 1944.

4 Eleanor Butler Alexander Roosevelt, *Day Before Yesterday*, p. 458.

5 Atkinson, *Guns at Last Light*, p. 127.

6 Blumenson, ed., *Patton Papers*, p. 481.

7 Eleanor Butler Alexander Roosevelt, *Day Before Yesterday*, pp. 458–59.

8 *New York Times*, July 14, 1944.

9 LOC Box 32, TR Jr. condolences, July 13, 1944.

10 Liebling, *New Yorker*, July 29, 1944.

11 LOC Box 39, TR Jr. World War II record, W. A. Buck to Colonel Collins, June 27, 1944.

12 *New York Times*, Sept. 21, 1944; Medal of Honor citation.

EPILOGUE: THE LAST ROUGH RIDER

1 Edmund Morris, *Theodore Rex*, p. 252.

Index